Alcott in Her Own Time

WRITERS IN THEIR OWN TIME

Joel Myerson, *series editor*

ALCOTT

in Her Own Time

A BIOGRAPHICAL

CHRONICLE OF HER LIFE,

DRAWN FROM RECOLLECTIONS,

INTERVIEWS, AND

MEMOIRS BY FAMILY,

FRIENDS, AND

ASSOCIATES

EDITED BY

Daniel Shealy

University
of Iowa Press
Iowa City

University of Iowa Press, Iowa City 52242
Printed in the United States of America
http://www.uiowa.edu/uiowapress

[Louisa May Alcott in the Early 1860s], [A Visit to the Alcotts in 1864], and [A Visit with Anna Alcott Pratt] are taken from Joel Myerson and Daniel Shealy, "Three Contemporary Accounts of Louisa May Alcott, with Glimpses of Other Concord Notables," *New England Quarterly* 59 (March 1986), copyright © 1986 by *New England Quarterly*.

[Memories of the Alcott Family] (1922) is taken from Julian Hawthorne, "The Woman Who Wrote *Little Women*," *Ladies Home Journal* 39 (1922), copyright © 1922 by *Ladies Home Journal*.

[Memories of the Alcott Family] (1932) is taken from Julian Hawthorne, "By One Who Knew Her," *New York Times Magazine* (27 November 1932), copyright © 1932 by *New York Times*.

"Louisa May Alcott: By the Original 'Goldilocks,'" is taken from Maude Appleton McDowell, "Louisa May Alcott: By the Original 'Goldilocks,'" *St. Nicholas* 64 (November 1936), copyright © 1936 by Scribners.

"Glimpses of the Real Louisa May Alcott" is taken from Marion Talbot, "Glimpses of the Real Louisa May Alcott," *New England Quarterly* 11 (December 1938), copyright © 1938 by *New England Quarterly*.

Letter from Lydia Maria Child to Sarah Shaw is from p. 535 of *Lydia Maria Child: Selected Letters, 1817–1880*, ed. Milton Meltzer, Patricia G. Holland, and Francine Krasno, copyright © 1982, by University of Massachusetts Press. All rights reserved. Reproduced with permission.

"Miss Clara and Her Friend, Louisa" is taken from Nina Ames Fry, "Miss Clara and Her Friend, Louisa," *Yankee* 24 (December 1960), copyright © 1960 *Yankee Publishing*.

Printed on acid-free paper

Library of Congress Cataloging-in-Publication Data
Alcott in her own time: a biographical chronicle of her life, drawn from recollections, interviews, and memoirs by family, friends, and associates / edited by Daniel Shealy.
    p.   cm.—(Writers in their own time)
  Includes bibliographical references (p.   ) and index.
  ISBN 0-87745-937-1 (cloth), ISBN 0-87745-938-x (pbk.)
1. Alcott, Louisa May, 1832–1888. 2. Authors, American—19th century—Biography. I. Shealy, Daniel. II. Writers in their own time (University of Iowa Press).
PS1018.A53 2005
813'.4—dc22
[B]   2004058859

05 06 07 08 09 C 5 4 3 2 1
06 07 08 09 P 5 4 3

Contents

Introduction

LATE IN HER LIFE, only months before her death in March 1888, Louisa May Alcott wrote her own recollections of her childhood. These were happy memories. Hard times appeared glossed over: no mention of the Fruitlands failure that almost broke up the family, only a passing nod to the Temple School episode that effectively ended her father's teaching career. Now in her mid-fifties, these days were only memories to the prolific author. Her mother, Abigail, and her two younger sisters, Elizabeth and May, were dead; her father, Bronson, had suffered a paralytic stroke five years earlier, leaving him partially paralyzed. She herself was plagued with various illnesses that kept her from writing as much as she desired. Since December 1886, Alcott had lived primarily at Dr. Rhoda Lawrence's convalescent home in Roxbury, Massachusetts, at Dunreath Place. But still she was able to pass time with her older sister, Anna, and her two nephews at the large home on Main Street in Concord that she had helped purchase. Other days were spent at the fashionable Beacon Hill home in Louisburg Square with her niece, Lulu, the daughter of her late sister May. Surely there existed reminders of those difficult times in the 1840s and 1850s, but her own literary success was able to ease them more gently into the recesses of memory. But at least one indication of the former hard times was evident in her recollections. It was a small incident, but a significant one. In November 1848, the Alcotts decided to move from Concord to Boston, where Bronson would hold conversations and classes, Abigail would work in an employment office for the poor, and Anna and Louisa would teach. Leaving the family discussing the move, Louisa ran alone over the hill, in search of her "favorite retreat"—an old cart wheel partially covered in the tall grass. Wrapped in her red shawl and looking up at the gray November sky and bare-branched trees, Louisa "shook [her] fist at fate." Defiantly, she vowed: "I will do something by-and-by. Don't care what, teach, sew, act, write, anything to help the family; I'll be rich and famous and happy before I die, see if I won't" (Alcott, *Recollections,* 3). Was Louisa, in this recollection, recounting some apocryphal episode of her life, illustrating her own American rags-to-riches story—a determined young girl defies the odds and wins? Was she consciously beginning to shape her own biography, the way she wished young readers to remember her? Her journal for 1848 holds no clues to her real inner thoughts that fateful day. It has been destroyed.

Louisa May Alcott was, even by the 1870s, keenly aware of her own reputation, the image that the public had constructed of her. She took a real interest in what people said and wrote about her, even which photograph of her appeared in print. For example, she concealed the large quantity of sensational stories she had written for Frank Leslie and others, more than thirty tales in all. As she told LaSalle Corbell Pickett: "I indulge in gorgeous fancies and wish that I dared inscribe them upon my pages and set them before the public." She could not, she confessed, create the works she longed to: "And my favorite characters! Suppose they went to cavorting at their own sweet will, to the infinite horror of dear Mr. Emerson, who never imagined a Concord person as walking off a plumb line stretched between two pearly clouds in the empyrean. To have had Mr. Emerson for an intellectual god all one's life is to be invested with a chain armor of propriety. . . . And what would my own good father think of me . . . if I set folks to doing the things that I have a longing to see my people do? No, my dear, I shall always be a wretched victim to the respectable traditions of Concord" (Pickett, 107–8).

Even in 1877, when she did "indulge in gorgeous fancies" with the writing of *A Modern Mephistopheles,* she published it anonymously as part of Roberts Brothers' No Name series. The revelation of true authorship could then be easily explained as all part of a contest, a game. Secluding herself for weeks at the Bellevue Hotel on Beacon Street in Boston, she revisited the genre of the blood-and-thunder tale she had mastered as a young writer: "It has been simmering ever since I read *Faust* last year. Enjoyed doing it, being tired of providing moral pap for the young" (*Journals,* 204). Influenced by both Goethe and Hawthorne's *The Scarlet Letter,* Alcott returned to the world of a devilish villain, a young heiress, sexual conflict, and even hashish use. It is no surprise that Alcott would record the following in her journal in April: "M. M. appears and causes much guessing. It is praised and criticized, and I enjoy the fun, especially when friends say, 'I know you did n't write it, for you can't hide your peculiar style'" (*Journals,* 204).

By August, with her "gorgeous fancies" a few months behind her, Alcott was hard at work on *Under the Lilacs,* another juvenile story, part of what is now called "The Little Women Series." Only in 1887 was she ready for Roberts Brothers to release *A Modern Mephistopheles* under her own name, in an edition that was uniform in size and style with her other books. Included with it was "A Whisper in the Dark," a thriller written in 1863 for *Frank Leslie's Illustrated Newspaper.* When agreeing to the publication, Alcott wrote Thomas Niles, her editor at Roberts Brothers: "'A Whisper' is rather a lurid tale, but might do if I add a few lines to the preface . . . saying that this is put in to fill the volume, or to give a sample of Jo March's necessity stories, which many girls have asked for" (*Selected Letters,* 310). Her concept of Jo March's "necessity stories" had already appeared in the preface to *Proverb Stories* (1882): "As many girls have asked to see what sort of tales Jo March wrote at the beginning of her career, I have added . . . a sample of the romantic rubbish which paid so well once upon a time. If it shows them what not to write, it will not have been rescued from oblivion in vain" (1). By the time decisions were finalized and the book was published, Alcott would be dead, and the work acknowledged under her own name would appear posthumously. But it would be almost sixty years before the extent of her "gorgeous fancies" would be made public.

With the success of *Little Women, Part One* (1868) and *Little Women, Part Two* (1869), Alcott found the fame and fortune she had long sought. She also discovered that fame brought with it a price. The anonymity she had possessed during the first fifteen years of her writing career was now at an end. In April 1869, she confided in her journal: "People begin to come stare at the Alcotts. Reporters haunt the place to look at the authoress, who dodges into the woods a la Hawthorne, and won't be even a very small lion" (*Journals,* 171). A month later she submitted a letter to the Springfield *Republican,* mocking the autograph seekers and "lion hunters" who arrived in Concord to search for the famous—herself now included. She declared: "Telescopes will be provided for the gifted eyes which desire to see the Oversoul, when visible, and lassoes with which the expert may catch untamed hermits, or poets on the wing." Supplied for free would be "photographs of the faces divine which have conferred immortality upon one of the dullest little towns in Massachusetts." Giving readers some idea of the ridiculousness of strangers wanting some word or touch, some glimmer of fame, she confessed:

No spot is safe, no hour is sacred, and fame is beginning to be considered an expensive luxury by the Concordians. Their plaints are pathetic, though many of the performances behind the scenes are decidedly comic; for, following the examples of the Great Tormented, some of these haunted ones step out of the back window when the hunter enters the front door; others take refuge in the garret, while the more timid flee into the wilderness and do not emerge until a bell is rung to inform them that the peril is past. It is whispered that one irascible spinster, driven to frenzy by twenty-eight visitors in a week, proposed to get a garden engine and "play away" whenever a suspicious stranger was seen entering her gates. (*Selected Letters*, 127–28)

One can easily imagine the "irascible spinster," Louisa May Alcott, aiming a garden hose full force on approaching curiosity seekers.

Alcott was never one to turn away her old acquaintances, but that did not mean that they should feel free to bring onlookers with them to the house of Alcott. By 1875, she would write to a friend:

I don't believe any one knows how we are bored by company, over a hundred a month, most of them strangers. A whole school came without warning last week & Concord people bring all their company to see us. This may seem pleasant, but when kept up a whole season is a great affliction. Mother says we have no home now & no chance to see our own friends. . . . It is only fair that I take the scoldings as I have been, quite innocently, the cause of much of this discomfort. I am sure you will understand this, & see that it is easier for you to say to your friends that the Alcotts are not on exhibition in any way, than for me to shut the door upon them & seem very rude. . . . Sometime when you are alone we shall be glad to see you. (*Selected Letters,* 193)

One wonders if Louisa's father felt the same burdens of such fame. That same year, he would issue a poster advertising one of his conversations under the large heading "ALCOTT." Beneath, in somewhat smaller type: "Dr. Brunson [*sic*] Alcott, The Concord Sage and Gifted Sire of LOUISA M. ALCOTT."[1] Certainly Louisa May's fame proved to be a strong draw for his conversations now. Audiences wanting to hear of the real "Little Women" competed with those inspired by the Oversoul.

By 1883, when Louise Chandler Moulton was preparing a biographical sketch of her, Louisa May Alcott reminded Moulton: "Dont forget to mention that L. M. A. does n't like lion hunters, does n't send autographs, photographs & autobiographical sketches to hundreds of boys and girls who ask them, & that she heartily endorses Dr Holmes Atlantic article on the subject"

(*Selected Letters,* 267). Oliver Wendell Holmes had recently addressed the subject in the January 1883 *Atlantic Monthly,* suggesting that no author was "under any obligation" to respond to a request for an autograph. He added rules for the autograph seeker: Do not ask for more than one autograph; do not ask the author to copy out lines from his or her works; do not ask for a photograph. He added: Do send a blank sheet for the autograph and include a stamped, self-addressed envelope. Of course, he reminded readers, the stamp "does not constitute a claim on the author for an answer." The author was free to keep the stamp for private use or free to offer it to "some appropriate charity, as, for instance, the Asylum for Idiots and Feeble-Minded Persons" (Holmes, 73). Two years later, Alcott would admit to a teacher: "I dislike to receive strangers who come out of mere curiosity, as some hundreds do, forgetting that an author has any right to privacy. Autograph letters I do not answer, nor half the requests for money and advice upon every subject from 'Who shall I marry' to 'Ought I to wear a bustle?' Mss. I have no time to read and 'gush' is very distasteful to me." She added one last bit of advice: "If you can teach your five hundred pupils to love books but to let authors rest in peace, you will give them a useful lesson and earn the gratitude of the long suffering craft, whose lives are made a burden to them by the modern lion hunter and autograph fiend" (*Selected Letters,* 296).

By 1886, Alcott had put into print her dislike of "the lion hunter and autograph fiend." *Jo's Boys,* the final book in the March family trilogy, was published by Roberts Brothers in October of that year. One of the chapters, "Jo's Last Scrape," details Jo March's disdain for strangers, including children, who bother authors, wanting information, autographs, or even their time. When reviewing the novel, the *Boston Daily Advertiser* believed that this chapter contained "too much personal gossip" ("Books and Authors," 4). But Alcott wrote to Thomas Niles on 3 October 1886 defending her use of her own real life in the chapter and arguing for its inclusion: "Another reason is that in no other way can the rising generation of young autograph fiends be reached so well & pleasantly, & by a little good natured ridicule be taught not to harass the authors whom they honor with thier regard" (*Selected Letters,* 300).

Alcott also found that fame brought with it the public's desire to know even more about her. Editors and reporters wanted to publish biographical sketches of the bestselling author. The first one of any real substance would be written by Frank Sanborn, who had been introduced to the Alcott family in 1852 by Ednah Dow Cheney and who became good friends with Bronson

Alcott. Appearing in the 16 July 1870 issue of *Hearth and Home* magazine, the unsigned article, entitled "The Author of 'Little Women,'" presented an overview of Alcott's literary career, beginning with *Flower Fables* in 1854. No mention was made, of course, of her numerous blood-and-thunder tales. Sanborn ended with her "American" heritage: the May family's connection to the Sewalls and Quincys and a more recent discovery that she was, in fact, distantly related to the poet Henry Wadsworth Longfellow. The front-page article contained a large woodprint of Alcott, made from a photograph by E. L. Allen of Boston taken just before she journeyed abroad in 1870. Although Alcott had, on the whole, liked Sanborn's piece and even recommended it to people in the future, she disliked the woodcut, writing across the top of her copy: "Not a good likeness—Too dark, & the nose all wrong" (*Selected Letters*, 161).

Even abroad on a grand European tour in hopes of obtaining a much-needed rest, Louisa May could not escape the fame. Informing her family of the adventures of her "Highness Princess Louisa," she declared: "She is such a public character now-a-days that even her bones are not her own" (*Selected Letters*, 137). In September 1871, Louisa May Alcott returned from a year and a half abroad and was met by her father and Thomas Niles in Boston "With a great red placard of 'Little Men' pinned up in the carriage" (*Journals*, 178). Written in Rome during the last year, *Little Men*, dedicated to her brother-in-law, John Bridge Pratt, who had died unexpectedly a few months earlier, told the story of Jo March and Plumfield, as well as the lives of Meg and Amy. By the end of the year, 44,000 copies of the continuation of the March family saga would be printed, along with 51,000 copies of her other books (*Journals*, 181). Alcott found her reputation growing and the public demanding more information about the author. That same month, John Seely Hart wrote Alcott of his plan to include her in a forthcoming book on American writers. She responded: "I send you an account of myself & books done by my friend Sanborn which is better than any thing I could do myself on so uninteresting a subject." She ended her short letter with figures of the sales of her last three books and thanked Hart for the honor. But she then included a postscript: "Over a hundred letters from boys & girls, & many from teachers & parents assure me that my little books are read & valued in a way I never dreamed of seeing them. This success is more agreeable to me than money or reputation" (*Selected Letters*, 161). Hart's sketch of Alcott appeared in his book *A Manual of American Literature* (Philadelphia: Eldredge and Brother, 1873), using facts and phrases from Alcott's own letter.

Frank Sanborn published another sketch of Alcott in December 1877 for *St. Nicholas* magazine. Edited by Mary Mapes Dodge, author of *Hans Brinker; or, the Silver Skates* (1865), and published by Scribners, *St. Nicholas*, begun in 1873, had already printed a number of Alcott's stories and serialized two of her books. It became the bestselling children's magazine of the nineteenth century and certainly helped to build Alcott's reading audience and to canonize her as the "children's friend." Sanborn's sketch, in fact, was entitled "The Friend of Little Women and Little Men," and he began by asking readers if they would like to know more about "this kind friend . . . who has been giving them so much pleasure by her stories, and never writes so well as when she writes for boys and girls?" After reminding readers that she teaches them to be good, kind, generous, "to love others and not always be caring and working for yourselves," he points out that Alcott can do this well "by first being noble and unselfish herself" (Sanborn, 129). He then tells the story of Bronson Alcott and his family and ends by painting a portrait of "Duty's child": "In the last summer, as for years before, the citizen or the visitor who walked the Concord streets might have seen this admired woman doing errands for her father, mother, sister, or nephews, and as attentive to the comfort of her family as if she were only their housekeeper. In the sick-room she has been their nurse, in the excursion their guide, in the evening amusements their companion and entertainer. Her good fortune has been theirs, and she has denied herself other pleasures for the satisfaction of giving comfort and pleasure to them" (131).

Alcott herself liked Sanborn's piece, recommending it to Louise Chandler Moulton in 1883, as she was preparing a chapter on Alcott for *Our Famous Women* (Hartford, CT: A. D. Worthington, 1885). Alcott also encouraged her to speak with Thomas Niles and to examine several of her semiautobiographical works (*Selected Letters,* 267). She later sent her two rather lengthy letters in which she provided material about herself and her family, which Moulton borrowed generously from for her final sketch.[2] Thus, by supplying information to editors, Alcott was helping to construct her own biography for the public.

These biographical sketches, of course, provided readers with details of Alcott's current life, telling about her family and her hometown. The publicity these short biographical pieces brought—coupled with the number of copies of books sold, the reviews written, and the stories printed in magazines and newspapers — only added to Alcott's rising popularity. Under the imprint of Roberts Brothers, Alcott earned approximately $103,375 on her book publications alone during the years 1868 to 1886. This amount did not even include royalties from European sales (Myerson and Shealy, 67). By comparison, during the same eighteen-year period, the prolific author Henry James would earn royalties from book sales, both in the United States and Europe, amounting to just $58,503 (Anesko, 176). Herman Melville would earn only $10,444.33 from total book sales during his lifetime (Tanselle, 199). Alcott was, indeed, by 1888, one of the most popular and successful writers America had yet produced. But she would always be chiefly remembered as the author of *Little Women.*

Alcott's career will always be divided by the year 1868 — the pre-*Little Women* years, where she experimented with numerous genres for low wages, and the post-*Little Women* years, where she focused on domestic novels and short stories for juveniles. In fact, had Alcott published only *Little Women,* she would have contributed an enduring classic to the literature of American childhood. Not only was *Little Women* a novel that touched universal hearts and minds, but it was one primarily constructed of Alcott's own life experiences. By imitating the style she had created in *Little Women* and by constructing similar characters (and even continuing the story of the Marches in two other novels), Alcott ensured the continuation of her success — as well as the problems it brought. People who had read and loved the novel believed they too could experience the March family by knowing more about Alcott herself. Her fictionalized account of growing up in Concord with her sisters was so entertaining and inspiring that surely meeting the real Louisa May Alcott would be even more so. Visitors came often, and some wrote of their brief time with the author who had so touched their lives. Others, who had known Louisa May in Concord, would later recount the childhoods spent with the "Little Women."

While most of the printed recollections in this volume appeared after the fame of *Little Women,* many focus upon Alcott's own teenage years when she was living the role of Jo March that she would later recreate for a reading public. For instance, Anna Alcott Pratt, Frank Preston Stearns, Edward Emerson, Alfred Whitman, Anne Brown Adams, Annie Clark, Frank B. Sanborn, Clara Gowing, Lydia Hosmer Wood, Frederick Llewellyn Willis, and Julian

Hawthorne all show us Alcott before she became a household name. They give us private glimpses into the life of the Alcott family. One conclusion stands out after reading all of these accounts of Alcott's early life: the family was happy, fun, and entertaining. While many note the Alcotts' impoverished life and the difficulty growing up in a poet-philosopher's home, the overall impression is one of a family's love and support. They appear, indeed, very much like the fictional Marches.

A number of other recollections give us a view of an older Louisa May Alcott, one who is at ease with her fame and with the luxuries her wealth has provided. Yet they seem to show a woman little changed by either money or celebrity status. Bessie Holyoke, Alexander Ireland, Mary Bartol, Frances Bellows Sanborn, Maria S. Porter, John S. P. Alcott, LaSalle Corbell Pickett, Russell Conwell, Mary Hosmer Brown, Maude Appleton McDowell, and Marion Talbot all write of Louisa May Alcott, author of *Little Women,* a woman known to thousands as a masterful storyteller. All show a writer who is kind and generous of her time—despite all of her admonishments to the public about her dislike of interruptions into her personal life.

Two pieces, those by Lurabel Harlow and Ednah Dow Cheney, focus on either a personal description of the writer or a depiction of her character— the manner in which she carried herself. These important details are rarely mentioned in the other recollections, and yet they go a long way in completing the portrait of the artist.

Many of the recollections in this volume also feature the Alcott family. Family was vital to Alcott's life, just as it was to her fiction. The lives of her mother, Abigail, and her father, Bronson, along with those of her sisters, Anna, Elizabeth, and May—and later, those of her nephews, Fred and John, and her niece, Lulu—are so intertwined with Alcott's own life that it is difficult to separate them. Many of the people who visited the author were also intensely interested in meeting the other members of the family who figure so dramatically in *Little Women.* Friends and neighbors, such as Edward Emerson and Julian Hawthorne, knew how influential family members were to Louisa May, and they show the integral part that her parents and sisters played in her life. Since Bronson Alcott was an important figure in the Transcendentalist movement, he, of course, often figures disproportionately in these recollections. To show all of this remarkable family is crucial in understanding Louisa May Alcott as an author, a daughter, and a sister; therefore, these recollections often venture from the limited view of Alcott herself to include the wider focus of her family.

The Alcott family was also protective of Louisa May. They showed patience with the constant interruptions in their lives by curious strangers who wanted to meet her, often entertaining them when Louisa was too tired to talk or was not at home. As the letter from Anna Alcott Pratt in this volume demonstrates, she also answered Louisa May's letters from readers wanting to know more about the "Little Women." The family knew too that Louisa wanted to remain as private as possible. Several times in her life, most noticeably after her mother's death in 1877, she even destroyed personal correspondence. In 1885, Louisa May wrote: "Sorted old letters & burned many. Not wise to keep for curious eyes to read, & gossip-lovers to print by & by" (*Journals,* 262). She was obviously concerned with the future, with how she would be viewed. After her death, her sole surviving sister, Anna, continued to help shape the biography of Louisa May Alcott. When Ednah Dow Cheney published *Louisa May Alcott: Her Life, Letters and Journals* a year after Alcott's death, Anna provided access to her sister's manuscript journals and letters. Cheney had been a family friend; she understood the Alcotts. But Anna also played the role of editor, perhaps even having the final say as to what could be used. For example, Cheney wrote to Thomas Niles after the biography was published and mentioned "'the many who revised the book'" (quoted in *Journals,* 33). Manuscript journals, which Cheney clearly had access to and published excerpts from, have vanished, most likely destroyed by Anna or her two sons. Interestingly, her existing manuscript journals now begin in 1863, the year of her first real success—the publication of *Hospital Sketches.* Those journals recounting the decades of the 1840s and 1850s, troubling times for the family, are gone forever. Even after her death, the presentation of Louisa May's life was being tightly controlled by the Alcott family.

But biographies of Alcott would hardly have been possible without many of the recollections found in this volume. In many ways these recollections form another story of her life—from the twelve-year-old Louisa arriving in Concord in 1840 to the literary lion revolving for the Sorosis Club in 1875, from Alcott in her early twenties serving lemonade to a Union regiment marching by her home during the Civil War to Alcott in her fifties caring for her aged father. These reminiscences show how Alcott was viewed, both by her close friends who grew up with her and by curious strangers who stopped at her home for an hour's visit.

The last recollection in this volume was published in 1960. Here, Nina Ames Frey remembers her great-aunt's stories about living in Concord with Louisa May Alcott. By then, accounts of Alcott's life were secondhand. Almost everyone who had known her was deceased. Of Alcott's immediate family, only Louisa May "Lulu" Nieriker Rasim, May's daughter, was still alive in 1960. Almost fifteen years later, living in Switzerland, she died at the age of ninety-five. With her disappeared the last of the living links to the Alcotts, those who were there to witness the remarkable lives of a remarkable family.

The texts used in this volume are from the first printed version. In preparing these works for publication, I have made emendations only where the text was obviously in error or unclear without them. For example, I have silently corrected some of the obvious spelling and typographical errors, inserted words and punctuation marks for clarity, and provided missing single or double quotation marks. I have let stand nineteenth-century spellings, misspellings Alcott consistently made (such as "thier" for "their"), and inconsistencies in capitalization, hyphenation, and commas in series. While my goal was to give present-day readers a straightforward text, I have in general modernized or "corrected" these texts as little as possible. The names of authors and the titles of essays and other works have been enclosed in brackets when they have been supplied by the editor. In the headnotes, I have consistently used shortened forms of the titles for *The Selected Letters of Louisa May Alcott* (ed. Joel Myerson, Daniel Shealy, Madeleine B. Stern [Athens: University of Georgia Press, 1995]) and *The Journals of Louisa May Alcott* (ed. Joel Myerson, Daniel Shealy, Madeleine B. Stern [Athens: University of Georgia Press, 1997]). The complete bibliographic information for each entry is given in an unnumbered footnote following the text.

I would like to acknowledge my research assistant, Mary Frances Jiménez, for her help during the preparation of this volume. This work was supported in part by funds from the Foundation of the University of North Carolina at Charlotte and from the State of North Carolina. A Reassignment of Duties Leave provided me time to research material for this volume. I also acknowledge the support of Schley R. Lyons, dean of the College of Arts and Sciences, and Cy Knoblauch, chair of the Department of English at UNC–Charlotte. Jan Turnquist, executive director of Orchard House — Home of the Alcotts, provided her usual generosity by allowing the use of archival photographs from the Louisa May Alcott Memorial Association collection (for more information about Orchard House and the Alcotts, please visit their website at www.louisamayalcott.org). Leslie Wilson, head of Special Collections at the Concord Free Public Library, shared her knowledge of Concord history and families. Ronald A. Bosco provided his good counsel in textual editing matters. I would also like to thank Joel Myerson for his help and encouragement in seeing the volume through press. I am also grateful to Holly Carver for the opportunity to publish this book. Finally, I offer my thanks to Luke and Hannah, whose love makes all the work worthwhile.

Notes

1. See figure 32.

2. In two letters, both undated, located in the Houghton Library, Harvard University, Alcott provided Moulton with biographical information about her mother and herself.

Works Cited

Alcott, Louisa May. *The Journals of Louisa May Alcott.* Ed. Joel Myerson, Daniel Shealy, and Madeleine B. Stern. Athens: University of Georgia Press, 1997.

———. Preface. *Proverbs Stories.* Boston: Roberts Brothers, 1882, 1.

———. "Recollections of My Childhood." *Lulu's Library.* Vol. 3, *Recollections.* Boston: Roberts Brothers, 1889.

———. *The Selected Letters of Louisa May Alcott.* Ed. Joel Myerson, Daniel Shealy, and Madeleine B. Stern. Athens: University of Georgia Press, 1995.

Anesko, Michael. *"Friction with the Market": Henry James and the Profession of Authorship.* New York: Oxford University Press, 1986.

"Books and Authors." *Boston Daily Advertiser,* 2 October 1886, p. 4.

Holmes, Oliver Wendell. "An After Breakfast Talk." *Atlantic Monthly* 51 (January 1883): 73.

Myerson, Joel, and Daniel Shealy. "The Sales of Louisa May Alcott's Books." *Harvard Library Bulletin New Series* 1 (Spring 1990): 47–86.

Pickett, LaSalle Corbell. *Across My Path: Memories of People I Have Known.* New York: Brentano's, 1916.

S[anborn], F. B. "Miss Alcott, The Friend of Little Women and Little Men." *St. Nicholas* 5 (December 1877): 129–31.

Tanselle, Thomas G. "The Sales of Melville's Books." *Harvard Library Bulletin* 18 (April 1986): 197–215.

Chronology

1799
29 November   Bronson Alcott is born

1800
8 October   Abigail May is born

1830
23 May   Bronson Alcott and Abby May are married in Boston

1831
16 March   Anna Bronson Alcott is born in Philadelphia

1832
29 November   LMA is born in Germantown, Pennsylvania

1834
September   The Alcotts move to Boston; Bronson begins his Temple
School

1835
24 June   Elizabeth Sewall Alcott is born in Boston

1839
23 March   The Temple School closes

1840
26 July   Abby May Alcott is born in Concord

1841
8 May   Bronson sails for England

1842
20 October   Bronson returns to America with Charles Lane and
Henry Wright

1843

20 May   Lane buys the Wyman Farm at Prospect Hill in Harvard, Massachusetts

1 June   The Alcotts, Lane, and Wright move to Fruitlands

1844

14 January   Lane leaves Fruitlands; the Alcotts stay with the Lovejoys in Still River

12 November   The Alcotts board with the Hosmers in Concord

1845

January   The Alcotts buy the Cogswell House (Hillside) on Lexington Road in Concord

1 April   The Alcotts move into Hillside

Winter   LMA attends John Hosmer's school in Concord

1846

March   LMA gets her own room for the first time

1848

Winter   LMA writes "The Rival Painters: A Tale of Rome," her first story

17 November   The Alcotts move to Dedham Street, Boston

1849   LMA writes *The Inheritance,* her first novel; unpublished until 1997

Summer   The Alcotts move in with Samuel Joseph May, Atkinson Street

19 July   "The Olive Leaf," a family newspaper, is "published"; later renamed "The Pickwick"

1850

January   The Alcotts move to Groton Street; Anna opens a school

Summer   The Alcotts contract smallpox

1851

September   LMA's poem "Sunlight," by "Flora Fairfield," is published in *Peterson's Magazine*

Winter   The Alcotts move to 50 High Street; LMA goes out to service in Dedham and earns four dollars for seven weeks, which her family returns

1852

8 May	"The Rival Painters" is published in the *Olive Branch*
Fall	Hawthorne purchases Hillside and renames it Wayside; the Alcotts move to 20 Pinckney Street, Boston, where LMA and Anna open a school in the parlor
December	LMA hears Theodore Parker preach at the Music Hall

1853

January–May	LMA keeps a school
Fall	Anna takes a teaching position in Syracuse
October	Bronson begins his first midwestern lecture tour

1854

February	Bronson returns from lecturing with a dollar profit
Spring	James T. Fields rejects LMA's story about her going out to service
Summer	LMA keeps a school
11 November	"The Rival Prima Donnas" is published in the *Saturday Evening Gazette*
December	*Flower Fables* is published

1855

June	LMA moves to Walpole, New Hampshire, where she organizes plays by the Walpole Amateur Dramatic Company
July	LMA's family joins her in Walpole
Fall	Anna returns to Syracuse to work in Dr. Wilbur's asylum
November–December	LMA keeps a school in Boston, staying with cousins Samuel E. Sewall in Melrose or Thomas Sewall in Boston

1856

Summer	LMA moves to Walpole; Abby and Lizzie contract scarlet fever
October	LMA boards with Mrs. David Reed, 34 Chauncy Street, Boston
December	LMA tutors Alice Lovering, living with the family

1857

| Summer | LMA goes to Walpole |

September	The Alcotts purchase the John Moore house in Concord (Orchard House)
October	The Alcotts move to Concord
Fall	LMA regularly visits Frank B. Sanborn's school; she begins the Concord Dramatic Union

1858

14 March	Lizzie Alcott dies
March	The Alcotts move into Wayside while Hawthorne is abroad and repairs are being made to Orchard House
7 April	Anna and John Bridge Pratt announce their engagement
July	The Alcotts move into the refurbished Orchard House (called Apple Slump by LMA)
October	LMA moves to Thomas Sewall's house, 98 Chestnut Street, Boston, again tutoring Alice Lovering

1859

April	Bronson is appointed Concord's superintendent of schools; Abby returns to Concord

1860

March	"Love and Self-love" appears in the *Atlantic Monthly*
23 May	Anna and John Pratt are married in Concord
August	LMA writes *Moods* in four weeks
December	Abby goes to work at Dr. Wilbur's asylum in Syracuse

1861

early January	LMA begins writing *Success* (later called *Work*)
February	LMA revises *Moods*
July	LMA goes to Gorham, New Hampshire
August	Abby returns to teach in Sanborn's school

1862

January	LMA boards with James T. Fields in Boston; begins a kindergarten at the Warren Street Chapel
April	LMA gives up her school, returning to Concord while commuting to Boston
6 May	Thoreau dies
June	LMA writes "Pauline's Passion and Punishment" for a hundred-dollar prize offered by *Frank Leslie's Illustrated Newspaper*

November	LMA applies for a nursing position in a Washington hospital
11 December	LMA is accepted by the Union Hotel Hospital
13 December	LMA arrives in Georgetown
late December	LMA learns that "Pauline's Passion" has won the prize

1863
3 January	"Pauline's Passion" begins serialization (ends 10 January)
7 January	LMA is struck by a serious illness
16 January	Bronson arrives in Georgetown
24 January	LMA and Bronson return to Concord
22 March	LMA is finally able to leave her room
28 March	Anna gives birth to Frederick Alcott Pratt
April	Sanborn asks for "Hospital Sketches"
22 May	"Hospital Sketches" begins serialization in the *Boston Commonwealth* (ends 26 June)
August	*Hospital Sketches* is published
October	Abby announces that she wants to be called May
December	*The Rose Family* and *On Picket Duty and Other Tales* are published
14 December	LMA's dramatization of *Scenes from Dickens* opens in Boston

1864
February	LMA finishes revision of *Moods*
August	LMA goes to Gloucester with May
December	*Moods* is published

1865
1 February	"V. V.; or, Plots and Counterplots" begins serialization in *The Flag of Our Union* (ends 25 February)
24 June	Anna gives birth to John Sewall Pratt
19 July	LMA leaves for Europe with Anna Weld
November	LMA meets Ladislas Wisniewski in Vevey, Switzerland

1866
19 July	LMA returns home to Boston
August	*Moods* is published in England
3 October	"Behind a Mask; or, A Woman's Power" begins serialization in *The Flag of Our Union* (ends in November)

1867

5 January	"The Abbot's Ghost; or, Maurice Treherne's Temptation" begins serialization in *The Flag of Our Union* (ends 26 January)
August	LMA goes to Clarks Island, Massachusetts
September	Thomas Niles asks LMA to write a girl's book; Horace Fuller asks her to edit *Merry's Museum*.
October	LMA agrees to edit *Merry's Museum* for five hundred dollars a year
28 October	LMA moves to 6 Hayward Place, Boston

1868

January	The first number of *Merry's Museum* under LMA's editorship appears
1 January	*Morning Glories, and Other Stories* is published
March–May	LMA moves to Concord
May	LMA begins *Little Women*
15 July	LMA finishes *Little Women, Part 1*
1 October	*Little Women, Part 1*, is published
26 October	LMA moves to Brookline Street, Boston
1 November	LMA begins *Little Women, Part 2*
December	LMA closes Orchard House for the winter, she and May engage rooms at the Bellevue Hotel, Beacon Street, Boston
December	*Little Women, Part 1*, is published in England

1869

1 January	LMA finishes *Little Women, Part 2*
March	LMA moves to Concord
14 April	*Little Women, Part 2*, is published in America
15 May	*Little Women, Part 2*, is published in England
July	LMA visits the Frothinghams at Rivière du Loup, Quebec, on the St. Lawrence
July	*An Old-Fashioned Girl* begins serialization in *Merry's Museum* (ends December)
August	LMA and May go to Mount Desert, Maine
16 August	*Hospital Sketches and Camp and Fireside Stories* is published

October	LMA moves to 14 Pinckney Street, Boston
1870	
April	*An Old-Fashioned Girl* is published in America and England
2 April	LMA leaves for Europe with May and Alice Bartlett
27 November	John Bridge Pratt dies
1871	
January	LMA begins *Little Men*
15 May	*Little Men* is published in England
June	*Little Men* is published in America
6 June	LMA returns to Boston
October	LMA moves to a boardinghouse at 23 Beacon Street, Boston
19 November	May returns to America
1872	
1 January	*Aunt Jo's Scrap-Bag: My Boys* is published
October	LMA moves to Pamela May's boardinghouse, 7 Allston Street, Boston
November	LMA revises *Success* as *Work*
28 November	*Aunt Jo's Scrap-Bag: Shawl-Straps* is published
18 December	*Work* begins serialization in the *Christian Union* (ends 18 June 1873)
1873	
26 April	May returns to London
2 June	*Work* is published in England
10 June	*Work* is published in America
August– October	LMA is in Concord
November	LMA closes Orchard House for the winter and moves to a boardinghouse at 26 East Brookline Street, Boston
December	*Aunt Jo's Scrap-Bag: Cupid and Chow-Chow* is published in America and England
1874	
March	May returns from London on a visit
May	LMA moves to Joy Street, Boston

Summer	LMA visits Conway, New Hampshire, with Anna and her children
October	LMA moves with May to the Bellevue Hotel, Boston
5 December	*Eight Cousins* begins serialization in *Good Things* (ends 27 November 1875)

1875

January	*Eight Cousins* begins serialization in *St. Nicholas* (ends October)
February	LMA finishes *Silver Pitchers*
22 February	LMA attends Vassar's tenth anniversary and goes to New York afterward
March	LMA goes to Concord
25 September	*Eight Cousins* is published in America and England
October	LMA moves to Dr. Eli Peck Miller's Bath Hotel, 39 West Twenty-sixth Street, New York

1876

early January	LMA goes to Philadelphia
February	LMA goes to Boston
June	*Silver Pitchers* is published in America and England
July	LMA starts *Rose in Bloom*
September	LMA finishes *Rose in Bloom*
4 September	May returns to Europe
November	*Rose in Bloom* is published in America and England

1877

January	LMA moves to the Bellevue Hotel, Boston, and writes *A Modern Mephistopheles*
28 April	*A Modern Mephistopheles* is published
May	Anna and LMA purchase the Thoreau House for $4,500 (LMA supplies $2,500)
July	The Alcotts begin moving into the Thoreau House
August	LMA begins *Under the Lilacs*
7 September	Mrs. Alcott's final illness begins
14 November	Orchard House is closed and the Thoreau House is opened
25 November	Mrs. Alcott dies

December	*Under the Lilacs* begins serialization in *St. Nicholas* (ends October 1878)
1 December	*Aunt Jo's Scrap-Bag: My Girls* is published
1878	
February	May's engagement to Ernest Nieriker, a Swiss business-man, is announced
22 March	May is married in London
June	LMA and Bronson read Mrs. Alcott's letters and diaries
15 October	*Under the Lilacs* is published in America
November	*Under the Lilacs* is published in England
1879	
January	LMA moves to the Bellevue Hotel, Boston
Spring	LMA moves to Concord
14 July	The Concord School of Philosophy opens
August	LMA goes to Magnolia, Massachusetts
September	LMA goes to Concord
18 October	*Aunt Jo's Scrap-Bag: Jimmy's Cruise in a Pinafore* is published
8 November	May gives birth to Louisa May "Lulu" Nieriker in Paris
December	*Jack and Jill* begins serialization in *St. Nicholas* (ends October 1880)
29 December	May dies in Paris
1880	
April	LMA moves to the Bellevue Hotel, Boston
June	LMA goes to Concord
July–August	LMA goes to New York with Fred and John
August	LMA moves to Concord
19 September	Lulu Nieriker arrives in Boston
9 October	*Jack and Jill* is published
Winter	LMA moves to Elizabeth Sewall Willis Wells's house, 81 Pinckney Street, Boston, on Louisburg Square
1881	
Spring	LMA moves to Concord
July	LMA and Lulu go to Nonquitt, Massachusetts

1882

27 April	Emerson dies
Summer	LMA goes to Nonquitt
Fall	LMA moves to the Bellevue Hotel, Boston, with John; she begins *Jo's Boys*
14 October	*Aunt Jo's Scrap-Bag: An Old-Fashioned Thanksgiving* is published
24 October	Bronson suffers a stroke

1883

March	LMA moves to the Bellevue Hotel, Boston, with Lulu
April	LMA goes to Concord
July	LMA and Lulu go to Nonquitt
10 August	LMA moves to Concord
27 November	LMA moves to Boylston Street, Boston, with Lulu

1884

June	LMA sells Orchard House to W. T. Harris and buys a cottage at Nonquitt
24 June	LMA goes to Nonquitt with Lulu and John
7 August	LMA moves to Concord
October	LMA moves to the Bellevue Hotel, Boston, with John
November	LMA moves to 31 Chestnut Street, Boston, with John and Fred
8 November	*Spinning-Wheel Stories* is published
December	LMA works to exhaustion on *Jo's Boys* and is forbidden to write for six months

1885

February	LMA undergoes mind-cure treatments
Summer	LMA goes to Nonquitt and begins *Lulu's Library*
8 August	LMA moves to Concord
1 October	LMA moves to 10 Louisburg Square, Boston, with Lulu, Anna, John, and Fred
20 November	*Lulu's Library,* vol. 1, *A Christmas Dream,* is published

1886

January	LMA begins treatments with Dr. Rhoda Lawrence and continues work on *Jo's Boys*
September	LMA moves to Boston

18 September	*Jo's Boys* is published in England
9 October	*Jo's Boys* is published in America
December	LMA moves to Dr. Lawrence's, Dunreath Place, Roxbury, Massachusetts

1887

June	LMA and the family move to Melrose, Massachusetts, and she works on *A Garland for Girls*
July–August	LMA goes to Princeton
10 July	LMA makes and signs her will
1 September	LMA moves to Roxbury
25 October	*Lulu's Library,* vol. 2, *The Frost King,* is published
November	*A Garland for Girls* is published

1888

8 February	Fred Pratt marries Jessica L. Cate
1 March	LMA visits Bronson at Louisburg Square
4 March	Bronson dies
6 March	LMA dies

1889

| 5 October | *Lulu's Library,* vol. 3, *Recollections,* and Ednah Dow Cheney's *Louisa May Alcott: Her Life, Letters and Journals* are published |

1893

| 17 July | Anna Pratt dies |
| October | *Comic Tragedies* is published |

Alcott in Her Own Time

[Reminiscences of a Childhood in Concord in the 1840s]

[ANNIE SAWYER DOWNS]

Annie Sawyer Downs's recollections of the town of Concord and its famous literary men and women were written in late 1891, almost fifty years after the fact. These childhood memories are thus filtered through the eyes of an adult who had long lost contact with the personages of whom she writes. Despite the years, however, Downs's stories provide little-known facts about these Concordians and often paint a concise picture of how the village of Concord reacted to its literary lions.

Born in Manchester, New Hampshire, in 1836, Annie Sawyer moved with her family in the early 1840s to Concord, where her father became an established physician for almost a decade. Her father's position allowed her the opportunity to meet and know many Concordians. She moved with her family to Haverhill, Massachusetts, in 1852 and completed her education at Bradford Female Academy. After marrying S. M. Downs, a music teacher at Abbot Academy, she lived the rest of her life in Andover, Massachusetts, where she died in 1901. While her memories of Louisa May are few (she was closest to Elizabeth and especially May), her comments on Abigail and Bronson present us with one of the most honest reflections on how the town viewed the family. As she elevates Abigail to an "almost saintly reputation," she remembers Bronson as "largely responsible for a great number of the whimsical schemes and paradoxical theories which sometimes made Concord appear ridiculous."

Therefore to those acquainted with the circumstances, it does not appear surprising that so many remarkable persons were attracted to Concord, Massachusetts, between 1830 and 1880. The name of the town is itself significant of the character and aim of its founders. What appears to have been the most important factor in the fashioning of Concord character was the presence in the settlement from a very early period of an unusual number of books. The fact that there were many books is probably due to the liberal education and

[1]

easy circumstances of the founders, and the wide and constant use of the books themselves, to the sheltered situation of the town, and that it never offered any inducements to trade or manufacturers. Mr. Hawthorne used to say Concord character was like the Concord river,—so slow that even Henry Thoreau never was quite certain it had any current!

However that may be, it is undoubtedly true that there never has been in Concord any sympathy with the hurry, distraction, and never-ending whirl characterizing adjacent towns and cities. On the contrary, circumstances have always favored plain living, honest speech, and a singular quality of condition which may have existed in Utopia, but I know not where else.

And what more could be desired to render a beautiful village fit residence for poets, orators, and genius generally than a library . . . proximity to Boston and Harvard College, an appreciative constituency, a history of two hundred years, and numerous woods, fields, and thickets wherein to roam at will? . . .

Of Miss Louisa Alcott I had no knowledge as a child excepting as I remember her and Ellen Emerson bringing to school in manuscript a book of fairy stories Miss Alcott had written for her. I knew slightly the sister whom all the world afterwards knew and loved as "Beth" in *Little Women,* but Miss May Alcott, the Amy of the same story, was a frequent companion.

Mrs. Alcott, whose pleasant voice and tender smile won the heart of every child, bore an almost saintly reputation in Concord, and whatever wild pranks or reckless speeches might be reported of her ever conspicuous daughters, there never was the slightest doubt of their unusual cleverness and brilliant future. The ups and downs of the Alcott family in Concord would make as lively a novel as Miss Alcott herself could have written, and whenever I hear her incidents pronounced impossible and her conversations forced and unnatural, I long to say, "My dear sir, or Madam, you do not know; you simply did not live in Concord." This, while really detracting from Miss Alcott's literary art, undoubtedly adds to the human interest of her books. Sometimes the Alcotts would be so poor rumor would declare the family must be scattered among relatives, then somebody would leave Mrs. Alcott a little money and friends would breathe easier. The next tidings would be that she had been persuaded to let her husband have it to put into the Fruitlands or some other scheme and it was all gone!

A pathetic anecdote was frequently repeated that when the whole family was setting out for Fruitlands, which was situated in the town of Harvard, not far from Concord, a friend met them and noticing that they were on foot and heavily laden said, "I hear you have done away with beasts of burden." "O, no," returned Mrs. Alcott, "they have me." Looking back on this period I think Mr. Alcott was largely responsible for a great number of the whimsical schemes and paradoxical theories which sometimes made Concord appear ridiculous. I recall vividly the amusement produced in one of his conversations by the following occurrence. The great drawing room of the biggest house in the town was crowded. Mr. Alcott divided man into the "Knower, Thinker and Doer." Then he paused to allow any who either approved or disapproved of his not very original classification an opportunity to speak. Instantly a worthy sister who had strayed somewhat late in life into the transcendental fold eagerly asked if that was the same Noah who came out of the ark.

Mr. Emerson's endorsement of Mr. Alcott, which puzzled many other sensible people besides Thomas Carlyle, undoubtedly procured him many hearers but at that time he was not regarded so highly in Concord as he was out of it, and I confess I was very much pleased to hear Mr. Emerson say in later years that he deplored the uncertainty of Mr. Alcott's inspiration in public conversation, and that the man he knew and prized could not be found in any of his writings.

In his venerable age, when he was supported and surrounded with luxury by his devoted and successful daughter, he was a picturesque and charming figure, but if he had not so early and so persistently attached himself to Mr. Emerson I am convinced he would have been regarded as a merely interesting person of marked intellectual endowments, but in whom discrimination was so entirely lacking that he never seemed able to comprehend how unpoetical many of his poems and how unphilosophical much of his philosophy.

Miss May Alcott, the youngest of the family and the Amy of *Little Women,* was Miss Louisa Alcott's pet and darling for whom nothing was too good and whose beauty deserved all praise. Some such fascination as Mr. Alcott exercised over Mr. Emerson, May must have exercised over Louisa. May was tall, possessed abundant light hair, and a turned up nose, and was an artist or at least possessed ambition to be one. But the grace and vivacity of the charming Amy were largely in the eyes of her partial sister and I think many friends who loved them both often felt a heart-ache when Miss Alcott pinched that May might spend, going year after year in the most inexpensive attire that May might ruffle it with the best.

The last time I had any conversation with Miss Alcott was on the day of Mr. Emerson's burial, April 30, 1882. She had arranged a harp of yellow jonquils which against a background of green hemlock she fastened to the front of the pulpit in the church where Mr. Emerson rested. She spoke with feeling of Mr. Emerson's kindness to her and to her family and added that she brought the jonquils because they were the ancient Greek emblem not only of death, but of immortality. I had never associated them in that manner and questioned their right to so much of sentiment and antiquity, but she was as satisfied in her belief as if she had been able to adduce the reason which to my mind was totally lacking. Every newspaper reporter described the harp of yellow jonquils given by Miss Alcott and went out of his way to mention they were the flowers of death and immortality.

Often now when I visit Sleepy Hollow Cemetery where lie so many of the Alcotts, I turn a little aside to look at Louisa's grave, and in spite of my incredulity in regard to the jonquils, it gives me pleasure to see as I sometimes do a great bunch of them at her head.

Annie Sawyer Downs, "Mr. Hawthorne, Mr. Thoreau, Miss Alcott, Mr. Emerson, and Me," ed. Walter Harding, *American Heritage* 30 (December 1978): 95, 101–2.

[Louisa May Alcott in 1860]

Augusta Bowers French

Born in Concord in 1846, Augusta Bowers French grew up there for the first eighteen years of her life. Her recollections of her childhood in the town, written when she was eighty years old, were composed for her own grandchildren and not intended for publication. Louisa May occasionally wrote poems for the school festivals when Bronson, for the annual salary of one hundred dollars, was superintendent of schools in Concord from April 1859 to 1865. The verses French fairly accurately recalls here are from Alcott's "The Children's Song," which was composed for the March 1860 festival. The poem, sung to the tune of "Wait for the Wagon," contains brief descriptions of her Concord neighbors, including Thoreau as "the Hermit of blue Walden" and Emerson as "the Poet of the Pines." Louisa recorded her memory of the event also: "Wrote a song for the school festival, and heard it sung by four hundred happy children. Father got up the affair, and such a pretty affair was never seen in Concord before. He said, 'We spend much on our cattle and flower shows; let us each spring have a show of our children, and begrudge nothing for their culture.' All liked it but the old fogies who want things as they were in the ark" (*Journals*, 98).

Many of our literary townspeople were interested in our schools—Louisa Alcott often wrote verses for the High School when there was to be a public entertainment—I recall one verse of a little poem—

> "And one there comes among us
> With counsels wise and mild,
> With snow upon his forehead,
> But at heart a very child."

Miss Alcott had reference to her father—I can see Miss Alcott now, breezy and snappy and using a lot of slang—I also see Henry Thoreau with bowed head, on his way to Walden pond—Mr. Hawthorne also with head down, speaking to no one and seeing no one—Mr. Emerson, with bowed head, but seeing everything and missing no one—and Mr. Alcott, head bowed, but always raised to greet a friend—

"Reminiscences of Augusta Bowers French," *Thoreau Society Bulletin* 130 (Winter 1975): 5–7.

[Louisa May Alcott in the Early 1860s]

ANNE BROWN ADAMS

Anne Brown, born in 1843, was the daughter of the abolitionist John Brown and his second wife, Mary Ann Day. After the death of her father, she had enrolled, along with her sister, Sarah, in Frank Sanborn's academy in Concord, while her mother remained on the family's farm in North Elba, New York. Sanborn, long a supporter of John Brown, had helped the abolitionist meet people and raise money when Brown first visited Concord in 1857. In 1869, Anne married Samuel Adams, a blacksmith from Ohio, and they moved to Rohnerville, California, where Brown's widow and several of his children had settled in the mid-1860s.

Adams wrote her recollections of her Concord days late in life, but they show Louisa May as the budding writer prior to her fame. Not only does Adams report on Concord's illustrious literati but she also writes of town events during the Civil War years. She captures Alcott in the afterglow of her first real literary success—the publication of her story "Love and Self-Love" in the March 1860 *Atlantic Monthly*. The editor, James Russell Lowell, had paid her fifty dollars for the tale after reading it in November 1859. Alcott confided in her journal: "Hurrah! My story was accepted. . . . I felt much set up, and my fifty dollars will be very happy money. People seem to think it a great thing to get into the 'Atlantic,' but I've not been pegging away all these years in vain, and may yet have books and publishers and a fortune of my own. Success has gone to my head, and I wander a little. Twenty-seven years old and very happy." For her next entry—just a month later—she would note the hanging of John Brown in December 1859: "The execution of Saint John the Just took place on the second. A meeting at the hall, and all Concord was there" (*Journals*, 95).

I first met Louisa M. Alcott, at a party given for my sister and myself, by Mrs. and Miss Thoreau, mother and sister of the late Henry D. Thoreau, in the early spring of 1860. A short story of hers had just been published in the Atlantic Monthly, and people had just "found her out," and were congratulating her. I am sorry I have forgotten the name of the story. It was a fancy sketch of "a quarrel and make up" between a young wife and her husband.

She told me afterwards, that she wrote the story to amuse her sister May, during a short illness, and a cousin of theirs came there on a visit at the time, and some member of the family showed him the story. He asked her why she did not send it to the Atlantic Monthly. She replied that they would not publish any of her writings, as she had tried them several times. He took the manuscript and told her laughingly that he would bet her as much as they paid for it, against a new hat, that he could get them to publish it. A short time after she was surprised by receiving a check for the full amount. As the family were then in very straitened circumstances, it proved an agreeable surprise. This was the real beginning of her literary career. Her chief ambition was to make money to supply her mother's wants. She used to talk to me a great deal about it. I afterwards boarded with them a while. They took a few boarders to help "make ends meet" in the household expenses, she and her mother doing all the work themselves, except the washing. They were the first persons I ever knew who advocated folding clothes and giving them "a brush and a promise" instead of spending so much useless time at the ironing board. I used to think that if Mr. Alcott's philosophy had made him wear a few less clean shirts, that his wife might have rested instead of toiling and sweating over the ironing board so long to pamper his fastidious notions.

Mrs. Alcott was very fond of gathering the young people about her in the evening and playing games with them. She had a theory, and she practiced it too, that it is the duty of every mother in the land to invite a few young men to spend their evenings at their home, and so fill them with quiet rational amusements that it would draw the young men away from bad places. The Hawthornes lived next door. They lived a very secluded English life. Mrs. Alcott tried hard to get the children to spend some of their evenings with her. She only succeeded once while I was there. When they went home Miss Louisa, my sister and I escorted them. I remember on our way back, Miss Louisa would run a few steps then whirl around and squat down on the side walk and "make a cheese," with her wide full skirts.[1]

One day Miss Louisa came bounding in, whirled around and clapped her hands above her head, exclaiming "I came, I saw, I've conquered." When she saw me looking at her in astonishment, she burst into a laugh and told me she was not quite crazy, but that she had for a long time been trying to get Hawthorne to ask her up into his tower, which he used as a study, that she had racked her brains for subjects to ask questions of him, and on that day he told her he was too busy to look in a certain volume in his library and invited

[8]

her to come up and look it out herself. She was perfectly happy over her success in getting into Hawthorne's den, where he created his stories. . . .

Mrs. Alcott told me that on the morning of the day that her daughter Anna (Meg in Little Women) married John Pratt, while they were arranging the rooms for the wedding, she found Louisa putting a small wreath of wood violets around a picture of Lizzie (Beth) that hung in the parlor. When she approached her, she looked up with tears in her eyes and said "I am trying to keep Lizzie's memory inviolate (in violet)."

Mrs. Alcott was very patriotic and so much interested in the early war news, that one day I remember, she sat down in an easy chair in the parlor, where I was studying, to wait for some expected news, instead of going to her room to take her accustomed afternoon nap, and dropped off to sleep. I heard her draw a deep sigh, then she moved her head slightly and said, "I've enlisted," very earnestly, in her sleep. This was before Louisa went as hospital nurse. One evening a little, old, white haired woman called. Her name was Mrs. Cook, and she lived alone in a little old wood colored house, some distance down the street. She had a large roll carefully wrapped in her hand, which she "unfurled, and threw a (homemade) American flag to the breeze." The poor, little, old soul with a big heart brim full of patriotism had bought the material and made the flag herself, which she wanted to display on a flag staff in her yard, but she had no staff, so she had come to good motherly Mrs. Alcott for advice. Mrs. Alcott called Mr. Alcott in and he told Mrs. Cook that she should have a flag staff, that he would ask Mr. Moore who owned a large wood lot back of the Alcott place to contribute a tree for the purpose. Mrs. Alcott noticed some small round spots of red cloth sewed on in the lower corners of the blue field, and asked Mrs. Cook what they were for. She replied in her shrill voice, which amounted to a screech, "they are to represent the blood dont you know spilt for our country dont you know." Miss Louisa pretended to not understand and so got her to repeat it. I think the little old woman was Scotch by the peculiar way she pronounced the words blood and country. We all gathered around her to examine the singular blood, and she told us that she had the little scraps left and did not like to waste them, when the happy thought suggested itself to utilize them in that way, thus mixing her economy and patriotism.

Mr. Alcott called on Mr. Moore that evening, and he sent his men to cut a nice tall tree, which they peeled and placed in Mrs. Cook's front yard. The next forenoon, Mr. Alcott gathered quite a crowd including a lame, old

[9]

soldier of 1812 and Mexican war notoriety, who sawed wood around town, and a company of boy soldiers, and went and helped make appropriate speeches for the occasion and raised the flag. Miss Bull, sister of the Concord Horticulturalist by that name and also sister of Capt. John Bull formerly of Arcata, Humboldt Co., Cal., and lighthouse keeper at Point Arenas, and aunt of two of the boy soldiers, carried a large basket of luncheon, which Mr. Alcott, the old soldier, and the boy soldiers, staid and enjoyed with Mrs. Cook, after the rest of us came away. Little Mary Bull could not keep from laughing as she was so much amused at the happy expression on the little old woman's face, so Miss Louisa would keep saying in a low tone, "girls don't laugh now, when we get home we will lie down and roll, to relieve ourselves," and Mary Bull would stuff her handkerchief in her mouth while the tears rolled down her cheeks. Of all the great flag raisings on this continent, I doubt if any other, ever gave so much happiness as that one. One morning the boy soldiers were marching by and Mr. Alcott was in the yard, and he heard them wishing they had an opportunity to shoot the enemy. He stopped them while he went into the wood shed and carried out an armfull of pumpkins which were so soft that they were not a hard enemy to fight and set them up and told the boys to relieve their feelings, by charging into them, and then gave them a short lecture on the wickedness of such warlike feelings. Mr. Alcott was so much of a peace man that he would not kill a mosquito. Miss Louisa used to laughingly tell him that she believed that a mosquito bite did not poison and annoy him like it does most people, or he would sometime forget his peace principles and kill one.

Mrs. Alcott was one of the best cooks I ever knew. She used spices and extracts to flavor, instead of the foundation of, dishes, like the modern cooks do. I have read a great many absurd stories of Mr. Alcott's starved appearance, on account of the vegetarian diet. His wife was fat, and ate the same food he did. They used tea, coffee, chocolate, good milk, cream, butter, eggs, fruit and the endless variety of breadstuffs in abundance with their well cooked and nicely seasoned vegetables. Meat was always served for visitors and boarders, who wished it, and cooked in excellent style too.

Miss May Alcott was absent, teaching, while I boarded there, but for the benefit of the vast army of home decorators, I will describe some fire boards she made. She had a carpenter make a smooth board to fit into the front of the fireplace. I think plain unvarnished oak was the wood she used. First she traced an outline head of some goddess, or a pretty child, then she went over the tracings with a red hot poker, burning an etching on the board. This done, the fire board was complete.

The walls, windowcasings, doors and doorcasings of her room were completely covered with sketches, which lack of means to buy drawing paper, had compelled her to use.

Mr. Alcott and Miss Louisa used to spend their evenings in their rooms and Mrs. Alcott played nine men's Morris, alternate games with my sister and myself, then a game of cribbage with my sister, next a game of chess with me, and then Miss Louisa would come down and we all would play Casino (perhaps I have not spelled that right,) with cards, until tired of it, ending by playing "Old Maid," chatting pleasantly and going to bed.

I one time asked Miss Louisa why she did not marry a man who was quite attentive to her. "Ah he is too blue (*blew) and too prudent (*prewdent) for me, I should shock him constantly," she replied. *(Pronounce those two words with a Yankee nasal drawl like she did.)

One day Miss Louisa and I, called at the home of two noted women, who have for years been connected with all sorts of educational improvements. After we entered the yard Miss Louisa said, "Now draw a long breath and take in fresh air enough to last while we stay here, for you will not get any more until we come out again. These people never ventilate their house. When the door opens I always fancy I can smell all the dinners they have had cooked for a month. I often wonder of what use is so much education if they have not learned to breathe fresh, pure air, and to ventilate their rooms."

1. To "make a cheese" means to make a "low curtsy — so called on account of the cheese form assumed by a woman's dress when she stoops extending the skirts by a rapid gyration." (*Webster's Revised Unabridged Dictionary* [Springfield, MA: G. and C. Merrian Co., 1913], p. 245.)

"Three Contemporary Accounts of Louisa May Alcott, with Glimpses of Other Concord Notables," ed. Joel Myerson and Daniel Shealy, *New England Quarterly* 59 (March 1986): 116–22.

[A Visit to the Alcotts in 1864]

Elizabeth B. Greene

Elizabeth B. Greene (1837–1915) was a Massachusetts artist and illustrator, and her 1864 letter offers a contemporaneous picture of Louisa Alcott soon after the publication of *Hospital Sketches*. Such accounts are rare. Most of the recollections about the young Alcott, like those written by Edward Emerson or Julian Hawthorne, were composed long after the events happened—often presented by an adult looking back on childhood. Instead, Greene, accompanied by Elizabeth "Lizzy" Bartol, the daughter of Rev. Cyrus Bartol, captures the young, informal Louisa May. Alcott's comment, upon first meeting Greene, sounds just like the words of Jo March, a character who would not emerge for another four years: "Excuse me if I appear to flop!" A different, secondhand version of the visit is presented in Mary Bartol's article, published in 1888. Alcott recorded the visit in her own journal: "Miss [Elizabeth] Bartol and Miss Green the artist passed a pleasant day with us" (*Journals,* 130). Greene would go on to illustrate Alcott's *Morning-Glories, and Other Stories,* published in January 1868. However, by 1874, Alcott had begun to show some displeasure with Greene's work and she would sarcastically confess to Mary Mapes Dodge, the editor of *St. Nicholas* magazine: "I love E. B. G. & dont mind her infants dropsical heads very much" (*Selected Letters,* 117).

I dont know when or how to begin my journal! Such a crowd & whirl of good time, & great events was never crammed into three days before! Three days! It seems a fortnight.

I was last heard from I believe in the Concord cars, on the way to Miss Alcott at 7 in the morning. We got there at 8½, & found Miss May Alcott & Edith Emerson at the depot, & had a few words with Mr. R. W. E. who was just coming into Boston. Then Miss Emerson drove us in her little wagon to the Alcotts, & we began the day. First we were introduced to Pa & Ma— Mrs. A. was the kindest motherliest old lady, & Mr. A. Bronson Alcott ever so amiable. *Lu* or *Louie,* the Authoress, then appeared, a comic, bright, talented extravaganza of a girl—and we went out on the grass & played Croquet, a nice little game with balls and mallets. Then we took a walk through pine woods, full of ladies slippers, violets & all kind of flowers, right back of the house—by that time it was 11 o'c, & we went in to lunch, & then upstairs to see Miss May's little studio. Such a pretty room full of pictures & things of her own making. Then we all sat down in Louey's chamber, & she marched in & tumbled onto the bed, remarking "Excuse me if I appear to flop!" & proceded to keep us in fits of laughter for two hours with the jolliest kind of talk. Then it came out that we were to dine at the Emerson's, so May marched us over there, where we found Mrs. Emerson expecting us, & a real good dinner, & more nice & pretty & rare things than I can possibly write here. About three, we, (that is, Lizzy, Miss May Alcott & I) went down to the river, by the old Monument where "Louey" met us with a big basket of provisions, & we embarked in a heavy Dory, or row boat, for a sail. We rowed & laughed & had a real good time all the way for quite a distance on the lovely river—a really beautiful country it is, flat but so luxuriant & fresh. Then clouds threatened, so we turned back, but they blew over, and we disembarked, & went into a nice little summer house on the banks, & had a hearty tea, & certainly I never laughed so much in all my life as I did at those Alcott absurdities—& we all "carried on" to the very last extent. Well—finally it came time to go to the depot—& there we went, & said bye to the Alcotts. Now comes the great wonder of our journey. —we waited & waited, & then came up a magnificent thundershower in the meanwhile—but *no cars* for Boston. After an hour's waiting we found the engine had broken beyond, & mightn't come on at all—& just as we were getting ready to call a carriage & go back to the Alcotts, in came Mr. Emerson in the train from Boston. He spied us at once, & came up full of paternal benevolence, fun, & decision— "What!" he said "you two children! Why I shall put you both in my pocket & take you home with me! Alcotts! no such thing—you're coming with me!" So, like an irresistible whirl wind he stowed us into his carry all, which was waiting for him, & to his house we went! We had a cosey tea (another one!) with him—& then he sat down & talked to us & read to us all the long evening in the most fascinating way—just as if we were the most distinguished & intellectual people! You would have supposed we were *folks* sure enough if you had been there!

Then we went to bed, slept beautifully under his hospitable roof—& came home safe & sound. . . .

"Three Contemporary Accounts of Louisa May Alcott, with Glimpses of Other Concord Notables," ed. Joel Myerson and Daniel Shealy, *New England Quarterly* 59 (March 1986): 111–12. In the *New England Quarterly*, Greene's letter is incorrectly dated 1859.

[A Letter about Louisa May Alcott in London] (1866)

MOSES COIT TYLER

Moses Coit Tyler, often called the father of American studies, was born in Griswold, Connecticut, in 1835. He graduated from Yale College in 1857, studied at Yale Theological Seminary, and became a minister of the Congregationalist Church. Despite his Calvinist background, Tyler was active in temperance reform, abolitionism, and women's rights. He suffered a physical and mental breakdown in 1862 and resigned the Congregational Church. Soon afterward, he met Dr. Dio Lewis, a reformer in the field of physical and health education and the inventor of what was called "musical gymnastics," a series of exercises with dumbbells accompanied by music (Lewis had visited Concord in 1860, turning everyone into "a preambulating windmill" [*Selected Letters*, 60]). Tyler credited his revitalization to Lewis's regimen, teaching and lecturing about it in Boston. He worked in England from 1863 to 1866, promoting Lewis's ideas.

After returning to America, he became a professor of rhetoric and literature at the University of Michigan and in 1881 was appointed the first chair of American history at Cornell. Tyler became an extraordinary scholar and a champion of the study of American literature. His two groundbreaking masterpieces, still considered classics in the field, are his two-volume *History of American Literature during the Colonial Time* (1878) and his two-volume *Literary History of the American Revolution* (1897). He died in Ithaca, New York, in 1900.

At the time of the following letter, Tyler was in London promoting Lewis when he served as a guide for Louisa May, especially to those locales associated with Charles Dickens. Alcott wrote to Tyler the following day, thanking him for the "lark" and calling him "my prince of guides" for taking about "an irrepressable spinster on the rampage" (*Selected Letters*, 114). Her account of the tour with Tyler was published as "A Dickens Day" in the 26 December 1867 *Independent*.

Moses Coit Tyler to His Wife, 15 September 1866

I have also been piloting Miss Alcott of Concord, author of *Moods* and *Hospital Sketches*. She is a jolly Yankee girl, full of the old Nick and thoroughly posted on English literature so that it is great fun to take her about, as she appreciates all the literary associations. We have had some most ludicrous adventures in the old haunts of London. She had resolved to see the street in which "Sairy Gamp" lived if she saw nothing else. So I took her to Kingsgate street, and after we had gawked through it and had fixed upon a house we thought most likely to have been Sairy's, the idea entered my head that it would be rare fun to inquire at the shop for Mrs. Gamp, as if she were a real person. Well, the conversation I had at the shop door, with the people who thought it all earnest was killing. Miss Alcott had continually to turn her back to hide her laughing and finally ran away to the end of the street to let off. You know she is of the Emerson and Hawthorne set. . . .

Moses Coit Tyler: 1835–1900. Selections from His Letters and Diaries, ed. Jessica Tyler Austin (Garden City, New York: Doubleday, Page, 1911), pp. 30–31.

"A Letter from Miss Alcott's Sister about 'Little Women'" (1871)

ANNA ALCOTT PRATT

> Born in 1830, Anna was the oldest of the four Alcott sisters. She had been ed-
> ucated primarily at home, though she did attend Bronson's Temple School for
> a time in the late 1830s. She herself opened a small school with about twenty
> pupils in Boston in 1850. Later, in 1853, she accepted a teaching position in
> Syracuse, New York. In the spring of 1858, the Alcotts announced the engage-
> ment of Anna to John Bridge Pratt, son of Minot Pratt, a former participant at
> Brook Farm. The two were married in the Orchard House in Concord in
> May 1860. They had two sons, Frederick Alcott Pratt (1863–1910) and John Se-
> wall Pratt (1865–1923). Unfortunately, John Bridge Pratt died unexpectedly in
> late 1870, while both Louisa and May were together on their grand European
> tour. After his death, Louisa did much to help her older sister, especially finan-
> cially, as evidenced by the purchase of the large "Thoreau" house on Main
> Street in Concord, where Anna lived until her death in 1893. In turn, Anna pro-
> vided Louisa with a loving family and often protected her sister from intrusions
> by admirers wishing to meet the author of *Little Women*. In this letter, Anna an-
> swers, less than two months after her husband's death, what must have been
> a common fan letter while Louisa was abroad. As many writers in this volume
> attest, Alcott, although she disliked intrusions into her private life, always
> seemed to have time for her child admirers.

Concord, January 20, 1871

Dear Julia and Alice: From your note to Miss Alcott I infer that you are not
aware that she is at present in Italy, having gone abroad in April last, with the
intention of remaining a year or more, trying to get well. But knowing how
pleased she would be with your friendly note, I think perhaps a word from
sister "Meg" will be better than leaving it unanswered, and far better than that
any "little woman" should feel that "Jo" was unkind or ungrateful.

Of course you know that neither "Meg" nor "Jo" are young and pretty girls now, but sober old women, nearly forty years of age, full of cares and troubles like other people; and that although nearly every event in the book is true, of course things did not happen exactly as they are there set down.

You ask if "Amy" is not May Alcott, and I can truly say she is her very self, and she is the only one of the "Little Women" who would, I think, realize your ideal drawn from the story. She is, indeed, "Lady Amy," and a fair and noble woman, full of graces and accomplishments, and, what is better far, a pure and generous heart. "Jo," "Beth," and "Amy" are all drawn from life, and are entirely truthful pictures of the three dear sisters who played and worked, loved and sorrowed together so many years ago. Dear "Beth"— or Lizzie, as we called her — died, after long suffering, twelve years since. She was a sweet and gentle creature, and her death was so great a sorrow to poor "Jo" that she has never been quite happy since her "conscience" was laid away under the pines of Sleepy Hollow. "Meg" was never the pretty vain little maiden, who coquetted and made herself so charming. But "Jo" always admired poor, plain " Meg," and when she came to put her into the story, she beautified her to suit the occasion, saying, "Dear me, girls, we must have one beauty in the book!"

So "Meg," with her big mouth and homely nose, shines forth quite a darling, and no doubt all the "little women" who read of her admire her just as loving old "Jo" does, and think her quite splendid. But, for all that, she is nothing but homely, busy, and, I hope, useful "Annie" who writes this letter to you.

As for dear old "Jo" herself, she was just the romping, naughty, topsy-turvy tomboy that all you little girls have learned to love; and even now, when care and sickness have made her early old, she is at heart the same loving, generous girl. In "Little Women" she has given a very truthful story of her haps and mishaps, her literary struggles and successes, and she is now enjoying her well-earned honors and regaining her health in travel with her sister Amy. They are spending the winter in Rome, in a delightful circle of artists, receiving attentions and honors that make proud the heart of the sister left behind. "Amy" is in the studio of a well-known painter, working hard to perfect herself in her chosen art, while "Jo" is resting and gaining strength and courage for her promised "Little Men," of which I imagine "Meg's" boys, Freddie and Johnnie, are to be the heroes.

You inquire about "Laurie." The character was drawn partly from imagination, but more perhaps from a very nice boy Louisa once knew, whose good looks and "wheedlesome" ways first suggested to her the idea of putting him into a book. She has therefore put upon him the love-making and behavior of various adorers of her youthful days.

Dear little friends, if I have told you all you wish to know, and shown that you need have no fear of being thought "intrusive," perhaps sometime you will honor "Meg" herself with a letter.

Be assured she will be glad to hear from any of the "little women." Sincerely yours, ANNIE ALCOTT PRATT.

St. Nicholas 30 (May 1903): 631.

[Louisa May Alcott Visits the Sorosis Club in 1875]

ANONYMOUS

The account of Louisa May Alcott's visit to the Sorosis Club, where she was presented as "the most successful woman author in America" is typical of the lionizing that she was now experiencing. The year 1875 had been a profitable one, with Roberts Brothers printing sixteen thousand copies of her newest novel, *Eight Cousins,* which had already been serialized (January to October) in *St. Nicholas,* and eleven thousand copies of her other books. Eight short stories also appeared that year, most in *The Youth's Companion.* She earned $7,264—not a bad sum for one who had been told almost a dozen years earlier by James T. Fields: "Stick to your teaching, Miss Alcott. You can't write."

The Sorosis Club in New York City had been founded by Jane Croly, editor of *Demorest's Magazine,* in 1868 to promote women's interest in art, science, and literature. Reporting on her February 1875 trip to Vassar College, Alcott wrote: "talk with four hundred girls, write in stacks of albums and schoolbooks, and kiss every one who asks me" (*Journals,* 196). Her extended visit to New York during the late fall and winter of 1875 saw her hailed as a celebrity, and she attended dinners, receptions, galleries, and theaters, including the fashionable Sorosis Club. She noted: "See many people, and am very gay for a country-mouse. Society unlike either London or Boston" (*Journals,* 197).

Louisa M. Alcott may be credited with inventing a substitute for a speech. She visited the Sorosis the other day, and was formally presented to the Club by the president as the "most successful woman author in America," and being on her feet told a little story. She said at Vassar College the girls, as usual, asked for a speech; and when she, also as usual, told them she never had and never intended to make one, they requested that she would place herself in a prominent position, and turn around slowly. This she consented to do; and, if revolving would satisfy or gratify Sorosis, she was willing to "revolve."

"Personalities," *New York Graphic* (18 December 1875): 374.

[A Letter about the Alcotts and Orchard House]
(1876)

Lydia Maria Child

A fervent abolitionist, Lydia Maria Child was a friend of the Alcott family, especially Abigail. Born in 1802, she established herself early as one of the first American women of literature with her debut novel, *Hobomok* (1824), a tale of the Puritans and Indians. She edited the first magazine for children in the United States, *The Juvenile Miscellany*, to which she herself contributed greatly. Books aimed at women, such as *The Frugal Housewife* (1830) and *The Mother's Book* (1831), offered practical advice and sold well. After meeting William Lloyd Garrison in 1833, Child turned her pen to the abolitionist cause with *An Appeal in Favor of That Class of Americans Called Africans*, a move that branded her as a radical by many and saw her lose much popular appeal. She moved to New York City in 1841 to edit *The National Anti-Slavery Standard* for two years. Throughout the rest of her life, until her death in 1880, she continued to write both fiction and nonfiction and to espouse the causes of women, blacks, and Native Americans.

Abigail Alcott had met Child, who was also good friends with her brother Samuel J. May, before her marriage to Bronson, and in 1838 the two were neighbors in Boston. According to Ednah Dow Cheney, the Alcott girls made a dramatic version of Child's *Philothea* (1836), which they acted under the trees of Fruitlands, with Louisa taking the role of Aspasia (Cheney, 41). Child's brief description of the Alcotts here shows why their friendship lasted: they both disliked "conventional *fetters*."

Lydia Maria Child to Sarah Shaw, 18 June 1876

I have been gadding unusually for me. I went to the meeting of the Free Religious Association, where I was sorely tempted to speak; because the only woman who did speak was so flippant and conceited, that I was ashamed of her. In the same excursion, I spent a day and night at Concord, with the Alcotts. Mrs. Alcott was a friend of my youth, and the sister of my dear friend

S[amuel] J. May. We had a charming time talking over the dear old eventful times. I like Louisa and her artist-sister, May, very much. Some people complain that they are brusque; but it is merely because they are very straightforward and sincere. They have a Christian hatred of lionizing; and the Leo Hunters are a very numerous and impertinent family. Moreover, they don't like conventional *fetters* any better than I do. There have been many attempts to saddle and bridle me, and teach me to keep step in respectable processions; but they have never got the lasso over my neck *yet;* and "old hoss" as I am now, if I see the lasso in the air, I snort and gallop off, determined to be a free horse to the last, and put up with the consequent lack of grooming and stabling.

The house of the Alcotts took my fancy greatly. When they bought the place, the house was so very old, that it was thrown into the bargain, with the supposition that it was fit for nothing but fire-wood. But Mr. Alcott has an architectural taste, more intelligible than his Orphic Sayings. He let every old rafter and beam stay in its place; changed old ovens and ash-holes into Saxon-arched alcoves; and added a wash-woman's old shanty to the rear. The result is a house full of queer nooks and corners, and all manner of juttings in and out. It seems as if the Spirit of some old architect had brought it from the Middle-Ages and dropped it down in Concord, preserving much better resemblance to the place whence it was brought, than does the Virgin Mary's house, which the Angel carried from Bethlehem to Loretto. The capable Alcott-daughters painted and papered the interior themselves. And gradually the artist-daughter filled up all the nooks and corners with panels on which she had painted birds, or flowers; and over the open fire-places she painted mottoes in ancient English characters. Owls blink at you, and faces peep from the most unexpected places. The whole leaves a general impression of harmony, of a medieval sort, though different parts of the house seem to have stopped in a dance that became confused, because some of the party did not keep time. The walls are covered with choice engravings, and paintings by the artist-daughter. She really *is* an artist. If you wanted a copy of some of Turner's pictures, I think hers would please you. She is an enthusiast for Turner. Those two girls are the stay and staff of the family; pecuniarily, and otherwise. I am *so* glad that Mrs. Alcott has such gifted daughters to lean upon, after all the toil and struggle of her self-sacrificing life! . . .

Lydia Maria Child: Selected Letters, 1817–1880, ed. Milton Meltzer, Patricia G. Holland, and Francine Krasno (Amherst: University of Massachusetts Press, 1982), p. 535.

[A Visit with Anna Alcott Pratt] (1878)

BESSIE HOLYOKE

Bessie Holyoke provides a private look at a visit to the home of the "Little Women," thus illustrating the type of "interruptions" fame made into the lives of the Alcotts. Here, the daughter of an old friend drops in unexpectedly on Anna Alcott Pratt for a glimpse of the famous family. Anna had known the young girl's father, Augustus Holyoke, when she had resided in Syracuse, New York, teaching the children of Charles Sedgwick during the last six months of 1854. While there, Anna, who always loved theatricals, had acted in *Scenes from Dickens* in December of that year. Anna also returned to Syracuse in 1855 to teach for several years in Dr. Harvey B. Wilbur's asylum. Orchard House had been closed in November 1877, when Louisa May helped Anna purchase the large home at 26 Main Street from Sophia Thoreau, sister of Henry David. Abigail Alcott had died eleven days after moving into the "Yellow House," as it was called by the Thoreau family. Holyoke was fortunate indeed to have seen, however briefly, the famous author of *Little Women* watering the plants with a hose. In order to obtain the privacy and the quietness she needed to work, Louisa May often escaped from the "lion hunters" and the noise that Anna's two boys brought to a household. By the winter of 1877, she had begun to live, for at least part of every year, in Boston, moving frequently until she bought the 10 Louisburg Square home in the Beacon Hill area.

Syracuse, Aug. 8th, 1878

MY DEAR UNA,

I was very much pleased at receiving such a nice letter from you while I was in Medford, but thought I would not answer it till I had made my call on Mrs. Pratt and could tell you something about the "Little Women.". . . .

Found Mrs. Pratt's house without any difficulty, as it is very near the depot and the ticket-agent pointed it out for me from the doorway. She lives in a very pretty, cosey home, which she has recently bought and which once belonged to Thoreau. Her Father and sister Louisa live with her and the old Alcott home is closed, as it has been ever since the Mother's death last No-

[23]

vember. When I reached the house I saw a lady, whom I recognized as Miss *Louise Alcott,* in the front yard, watering plants with a hose, so I walked in and asked if Mrs. Pratt lived there. She said she did and that she would call her if I would step into the house. The front door stood invitingly open so I did step in and after a few minutes Mrs. Pratt appeared, evidently just from the dinner table where she had been feasting on huckleberries in some form. She was a stout middleaged lady with gray hair and a plain, but very pleasant face. I told her my name merely and after looking at me for a few seconds she said "I know you, you are Augustus Holyoke's daughter." Then she sat down by me on a sofa and we had a long and delightful talk. She was very much pleased to think I had taken the pains to go and see her. Said she supposed she was forgotten long ago by our family and was delighted to have such an assurance that she was not.

She told me that my Father was one of the kindest and dearest friends that she ever had and that she always liked my Brother very much indeed. She had a great many questions to ask about us all and told me of the pleasant visits she used to have in Syracuse and of the theatricals in which she used to take part. She said she was "stage struck" at that time and my Father also. She said your Mother used to act with them sometimes and inquired particularly about her. So I told her of the three little daughters and how the oldest who was with my Mother this summer, had written and asked me to find out all I could about "Little Women" if I had an opportunity. She seemed very willing to tell me and began in this way: "Well you can tell her that you saw Meg and that she is a stout, old woman, with gray hair, not at all good-looking and that her lips and teeth were blackened with the huckleberry pie she had just been eating."

She said it was necessary to have one of the sisters *pretty,* in the *story,* so she was the one so described, but not from life. She showed me a picture of "Marmee" and one of John Brooke, really John Pratt, her husband, a fine looking man with a very sweet mild face. Then she showed me pictures of her two boys, John & Fred, or Daisy & Demi. The elder is now fifteen, both of them bright-looking and one quite girlish in his appearance, more so a few years ago than now, and for that reason called "Daisy" then.

The history of "Beth" or Lizzie is really true. She died from the effects of scarlet fever, which she caught from two little children whom she nursed. She had a long illness of two years and was only twenty two when she died. The description of Jo, she told me, was a real portrait of her sister Louise "who was a dreadful girl, always full of wild pranks." In the parlor where we sat there hung above the mantel a large picture of May Alcott. She wore a pale blue dress with a broad white ruffle at the throat and had on her head a little blue hat of a fancy shape. She had no special beauty excepting her hair which was golden and hung in great, natural curls on her neck. Mrs. Pratt said that she did not have a pretty face but had a fine figure, small, well shaped hands and feet and was altogether a very attractive woman. She has been married recently to a Swiss gentleman whom she met in London last year and is now living in Paris where her husband is a banker. The family have never seen him as they were married abroad. Mrs. Pratt showed me a picture of him and called my attention to his nose which was a very handsome one. Her sister's on the contrary is very homely and has always been a trial to her, as the story says; so it is a great gratification to her that her husband's nose is beyond criticism. "May was always a very charming girl" her sister says "and people were constantly falling in love with her whether she asked them to do so or not. Laurie was never Jo's lover but Amy's and Amy did not marry him." I asked who Laurie really was and Mrs. Pratt said it was hard to tell, that they knew a number of charming boys when they were young and he was like several different ones. But she herself thought he was really Julian Hawthorne, the writer, of whom you may have heard. It seems his father lived next to the Alcott family and Julian was a constant playfellow of theirs and a lover of May's who was always "flirty." Miss Louise thinks however that Laurie is a young Polish boy called "Laddie" who was very kind to her abroad. Isn't it funny that the two disagree? And doesn't it seem to you that Miss Alcott should know best. The account of Amy's party and the one girl in the omnibus is true. Also that of the fair and the difficulty about the tables. Also the history of the currant preserves only the currants were tomatoes. "I suppose," Mrs. Pratt said, after telling me all this, "that your little cousin wished you to take a look at and have a little talk with the writer of the book didn't she?" So she went to call her but found her taking a nap and did not wish to disturb her so I did not have the pleasure of being introduced to her, but it was quite a satisfaction to have seen and spoken to her at the gate.

I staid at Mrs. Pratt's about an hour and a half and she urged me to spend the whole afternoon but I could not do so very conveniently and was afraid of taxing her hospitality as I was a stranger and unexpected. She took my

Mother's address and said she should write to her and that she wished she might hear from her also now that she knew Mother remembered her so well. She spoke of her beautiful voice and asked if she ever sang now. . . .

"Three Contemporary Accounts of Louisa May Alcott, with Glimpses of Other Concord Notables," ed. Joel Myerson and Daniel Shealy, *New England Quarterly* 59 (March 1986): 113–16.

"Miss Alcott's Birthplace" (1891)

ANONYMOUS

> The following anonymous letter reprinted from the Germantown *Telegraph*
> contains a recollection not found in any other source—a reaction to Bronson
> Alcott's brief teaching career in Germantown, just outside of Philadelphia, and
> a description, albeit brief, of Louisa May Alcott's birthplace. The author of *Little
> Women* is so often associated with Concord and Boston that few remember
> the important role the Germantown teaching experience played in the life of
> the Alcotts.

Louisa May Alcott, authoress of "Little Women," and other stories, was born
Nov. 29, 1832, in a house somewhat retired from the main street, and known
as "The Pinery," or "Pine Place," owing to its being surrounded by pine
trees and situated where the Post Office now stands, a few doors northwest
of St. Luke's Church. Here her father taught school, composed of children of
tender age. Mr. Alcott had original notions on the subject of education, and
part of his system was to fortify his pupils against surprises and to prepare
them for all emergencies. One of his means of achieving this end was to walk
stealthily behind them when absorbed in study, and, without warning, suddenly kick the chair from under them. Whether this heroic practice answered
the end desired or not I am unable to say, but I am able to say that it was far
too advanced a method for the latitude of Germantown, where but one house
had been built in forty years, and the risk of breaking the children's heads too
great to commend it to their parents. So, after experimenting for a year or
two, Mr. A., in despair, shook the dust of the stagnant old town from his feet,
and didn't draw rein until he had reached Boston, in whose intellectual atmosphere his "advanced thought" probably met with greater sympathy. . . .

The Critic 18 (10 January 1891): 22.

"Mr. Alcott and His Daughters" (1882)

ANONYMOUS

By the mid-1870s, newspapers and magazines around the United States had printed stories of literary Concord and reports of the Alcott family. The following anonymous account was published by Alexander Ireland in his *Ralph Waldo Emerson: His Life, Genius, and Writings* (1882). Editor of the British Manchester *Examiner and Times,* Ireland was friends with Thomas Carlyle and managed Emerson's lecture tour of England in 1847. Author of numerous works, Ireland also amassed a collection of some twenty thousand volumes in his personal library, including extensive reviews and clippings of Emerson's work in Great Britian. The piece below was reprinted from "Literati at Concord," published in a New York paper, *Home Journal,* in November 1874.

The following account of the venerable Mr. A. Bronson Alcott, Emerson's life-long friend, still living, in his eighty-third year, will be read with interest. His name is inseparably associated with that of his distinguished fellow-townsman. It is from a paper in the New York "Home Journal," entitled "Literati at Concord," November, 1874:—

"Not far from Mr. Emerson's hemlock grove—writes a pilgrim of the Inter-Ocean—is the picturesque home of the Alcotts. It is the queerest little cottage in the world. It stands at the foot of the hill which the British soldiers crossed the morning, nearly a hundred years ago, when they marched up from Lexington. The house is a dull brown colour, with peaked roof and many a gable end, in one of which, hooded by the jutting roof and festooned by some airy sprays of woodbine, is the window whence 'Aunt Jo' looks out on the sunny meadows. On each side of the front walk there is a huge elm with rustic seat built around its roots, and among the branches tame squirrels hold high revelry. Yonder a hammock swings under some apple trees, and around the whole runs a rustic fence, built by Mr. Alcott himself. It is made entirely of pine boughs, knotted, gnarled, and twisted into every conceivable shape. No two pieces are alike; the gates are wonderful, and they alone would make credible the story that he spent years collecting the branches.

"Mr. Alcott, the 'Orphic Alcott,' as Curtis calls him, is one of the Concord philosophers, and has his 'ism,' of course. Vegetables and conversation are his *forte*, and he reared his family on a diet of both, apparently with great success, judging from appearances. He ate weeds and talked and built summerhouses, whose chief use was to be targets for George William Curtis' wit. Once he kept a young ladies' school in Boston, where books were discarded and teaching done entirely by conversation. He was also a member of those extraordinary assemblages, practicable in Boston alone, over which Margaret Fuller presided, and it must have been a rare sight to see how these two inexhaustible talkers managed to tolerate each other. For it is said that Mr. Alcott's conversations are very much like the Irishman's treaty — the reciprocity is all on one side; or, as a Western host described him once in his invitations to some friends, 'Come up this evening. I have a philosopher on tap.'

"It is all well enough to joke about Mr. Alcott till you see him. Then to come face to face with this white-haired, benign, gracious old man, makes levity seem irreverent. He is over six feet tall, but a good deal stooped. His long, grey hair falls scantily around a face beautified by the placidity and dignity of old age; he is a perfect counterpart of the pictures of venerable *curés* one sees in French storybooks. His manners are very simple and unaffected, and it is his great delight to gather some of his daughters' young friends in his cosy, crimson-lined study and chat with them. Mr. Emerson esteems him highly, but his books seem to be less appreciated by his own people than they are abroad, a fate common to prophets if not philosophers. His most valuable work is a journal faithfully kept for fifty years, carefully bound, indexed, and with letters and other valuable papers ranged on his library shelves. This taste for minute detail, his orderly arrangement, his distinguished associates, and the number of years covered by the record will make these volumes priceless to historians or biographers. If in Emerson's study perpetual twilight reigns, in Alcott's it is always noon. The sun shines in it all day long, the great fireplace roars, and the warm crimson hangings temper the sunlight and reflect the firelight. Quaint mottoes and pictures hang on the walls. The most noticeable picture is a photograph of Carlyle. It is what is called a 'Cameron photograph.' An English woman of rank takes these photographs of distinguished men just for her own amusement. The camera is set out of focus, the heads nearly life-size, and the general effect is singular—interesting, if nothing else. All you can see against a black background is the indistinct outlines of a shaggy white head and beard and sharp features. With all deference to Mr. Carlyle, we must say that he looks like an old beggar.

"Miss May Alcott, a fine-looking, stylish woman, is an artist whom the critic of critics, Ruskin, has declared to be the only successful copyist of Turner. She surely has one attribute not usually allied to her profession—the most generous interest in other artists—not only by word of mouth, but with substantial endeavour. She brought home with her several English water colours, for whose artists she is trying to find American patrons. She herself paints in oil and water colours, and sketches in crayons, charcoal, sepia, ink, and pencil, and is one of the most popular Boston teachers. Her studio at home, a most cobwebby, disorderly, fascinating little den, is frescoed with profiles of her acquaintances—that is the toll cheerfully paid by her visitors—they must be drawn on the wall. She is known to the general reading public through her illustrations of 'Little Women,' in which she fell far short of her usual ability. She and Louisa planned subsequently a charming little book called 'Concord Sketches,' which it is a great pity was never made public. Beside painting, Miss May models in clay sometimes. A head of Mercury and all sorts of pretty little sketches from her hands adorn her home, which is made a still sunnier remembrance to all visitors by her brightness and cordiality.

"Louisa Alcott, the elder of the two, the darling of all American nurseries, is something of an invalid. She is amiable and interesting, and, like her sister, sociable, unless you unluckily approach her in her character of author, and then the porcupine bristles. There is no favour to be curried with her or Gail Hamilton by talking 'shop.' 'Little Women' is drawn chiefly from Miss Alcott's own home life. Amy the golden-haired, is May, Hemmie and Demmie are her two little nephews, Mr. and Mrs. March her father and mother; she herself is Jo, of course. When the book was first published, children used to come by the dozen from all parts of the country to see 'Jo.' To the calls of these little pilgrims she always presented herself cheerfully, though she used to be infinitely amused at the unmistakable disappointment of her young admirers when they saw this delicate, practical-looking lady, slightly stooped, for their rollicking, romping, nimble Jo. Miss Alcott struck a rich vein of popularity and more substantial reward in her juvenile books, though she herself considers 'Hospital Sketches' the best of her writings.

"Some four or five years ago she went into a Boston book-store to leave an order, which the clerk told her could not be attended to, 'because,' said he, not knowing to whom he spoke, 'we shall be busy all day packing books for a Western firm. Two weeks ago we sent ten thousand copies of "Little Women" out there, and to-day comes an order for twenty thousand more.' As soon as they got out of the store her companion turned to her with some congratulatory expression.

"'Ah!' said Miss Alcott, drawing a long breath, 'I have waited fifteen years for this day.'

"Mrs. Alcott is a beautiful old lady, herself something of a writer, or, as one of her daughters lovingly says, 'the brightest one of the family.'"

From *Ralph Waldo Emerson: His Life, Genius, and Writings, A Biographical Sketch, to Which Are Added Personal Recollections of His Visits to England, Extracts from Unpublished Letters, and Miscellaneous Characteristic Records* (London: Simpkin, Marshall, 1882), pp. 273–78.

"Recollections of My Childhood" (1888)

Louisa May Alcott

Although Alcott makes no reference to writing her recollections, she must have composed them sometime during her last year of life. The article would not be published until two months after her death, first appearing in *The Youth's Companion* on 24 May 1888 and reprinted two days later in *The Woman's Journal*. The work would also be the first piece in *Lulu's Library, Volume Three, Recollections* (1889).

Alcott had published a number of thinly veiled "autobiographical" works, such as *Hospital Sketches* (1863), *Shawl-Straps* (1872), "Transcendental Wild Oats" (1873), and "How I Went Out to Service" (1874). They adhered mostly to the facts—often being culled from her own letters or journals. But "Recollections" was different from any autobiographical work in her canon. Here, as a woman who feels she is nearing the end of life, Alcott looks back on her unique and remarkable childhood: her earliest memories in Boston, her reading and literary influences, her amateur plays with her sisters, her idyllic pastoral days in Concord, her struggling, late-teenage years with her family in Boston. Her reminiscences end before her twentieth birthday—before her Civil War nursing experience, before her fame and fortune as a writer. Several sketches of Alcott's life had already appeared, most notably F. B. Sanborn's article in the December 1877 *St. Nicholas* and a sketch by Louise Chandler Moulton, a popular poet, in *Our Famous Women* (1885), for which Alcott herself provided biographical material set forth in two lengthy letters. She had written Moulton in January 1883, as she was contemplating the piece: "I have not the least objection to the writing of a sketch of L. M. A. by any one, & should feel quite comfortable in your hands." She obviously refused Moulton access to her journals and diaries, however, as she told her: "I have very little material to offer for my journals were all burnt long ago in terror of gossip when I depart & on unwise use of my very frank records of people & events" (*Selected Letters*, 267). Clearly, Alcott was interested in how she would be remembered, how her life would be portrayed. Published posthumously, "Recollections" almost appears as though Alcott wanted the final say.

One of my earliest memories is of playing with books in my father's study. Building towers and bridges of the big dictionaries, looking at pictures, pretending to read, and scribbling on blank pages whenever pen or pencil could be found. Many of these first attempts at authorship still exist, and I often wonder if these childish plays did not influence my after life, since books have been my greatest comfort, castle-building a never-failing delight, and scribbling a very profitable amusement.

Another very vivid recollection is of the day when running after my hoop I fell into the Frog Pond and was rescued by a black boy, becoming a friend to the colored race then and there, though my mother always declared that I was an abolitionist at the age of three.

During the Garrison riot in Boston the portrait of George Thompson was hidden under a bed in our house for safe-keeping, and I am told that I used to go and comfort "the good man who helped poor slaves" in his captivity. However that may be, the conversion was genuine, and my greatest pride is in the fact that I have lived to know the brave men and women who did so much for the cause, and that I had a very small share in the war which put an end to a great wrong.

Being born on the birthday of Columbus I seem to have something of my patron saint's spirit of adventure, and running away was one of the delights of my childhood. Many a social lunch have I shared with hospitable Irish beggar children, as we ate our crusts, cold potatoes and salt fish on voyages of discovery among the ash heaps of the waste land that then lay where the Albany station now stands.

Many an impromptu picnic have I had on the dear old Common, with strange boys, pretty babies and friendly dogs, who always seemed to feel that this reckless young person needed looking after.

On one occasion the town-crier found me fast asleep at nine o'clock at night, on a door-step in Bedford Street, with my head pillowed on the curly breast of a big Newfoundland, who was with difficulty persuaded to release the weary little wanderer who had sobbed herself to sleep there.

I often smile as I pass that door, and never forget to give a grateful pat to every big dog I meet, for never have I slept more soundly than on that dusty step, nor found a better friend than the noble animal who watched over the lost baby so faithfully.

My father's school was the only one I ever went to, and when this was broken up because he introduced methods now all the fashion, our lessons went on at home, for he was always sure of four little pupils who firmly believed in their teacher, though they have not done him all the credit he deserved.

I never liked arithmetic or grammar, and dodged these branches on all occasions; but reading, composition, history and geography I enjoyed, as well as the stories read to us with a skill which made the dullest charming and useful.

"Pilgrim's Progress," Krummacher's "Parables," Miss Edgeworth, and the best of the dear old fairy tales made that hour the pleasantest of our day. On Sundays we had a simple service of Bible stories, hymns, and conversation about the state of our little consciences and the conduct of our childish lives which never will be forgotten.

Walks each morning round the Common while in the city, and long tramps over hill and dale when our home was in the country, were a part of our education, as well as every sort of housework, for which I have always been very grateful, since such knowledge makes one independent in these days of domestic tribulation with the help who are too often only hindrances.

Needle-work began early, and at ten my skilful sister made a linen shirt beautifully, while at twelve I set up as a doll's dress-maker, with my sign out, and wonderful models in my window. All the children employed me, and my turbans were the rage at one time to the great dismay of the neighbors' hens, who were hotly hunted down, that I might tweak out their downiest feathers to adorn the dolls' head-gear.

Active exercise was my delight from the time when a child of six I drove my hoop round the Common without stopping, to the days when I did my twenty miles in five hours and went to a party in the evening.

I always thought I must have been a deer or a horse in some former state, because it was such a joy to run. No boy could be my friend till I had beaten him in a race, and no girl if she refused to climb trees, leap fences and be a tomboy.

My wise mother, anxious to give me a strong body to support a lively brain, turned me loose in the country and let me run wild, learning of nature what no books can teach, and being led, as those who truly love her seldom fail to be, "Through nature up to nature's God."

I remember running over the hills just at dawn one summer morning, and pausing to rest in the silent woods saw, through an arch of trees, the sun rise over river, hill and wide green meadows as I never saw it before.

Something born of the lovely hour, a happy mood, and the unfolding aspirations of a child's soul seemed to bring me very near to God, and in the hush of that morning hour I always felt that I "got religion" as the phrase goes. A new and vital sense of His presence, tender and sustaining as a father's arms, came to me then, never to change through forty years of life's vicissitudes, but to grow stronger for the sharp discipline of poverty and pain, sorrow and success.

Those Concord days were the happiest of my life, for we had charming playmates in the little Emersons, Channings, Hawthornes and Goodwins, with the illustrious parents and their friends to enjoy our pranks and share our excursions.

Plays in the barn were a favorite amusement, and we dramatized the fairy tales in great style. Our giant came tumbling off a loft when Jack cut down the squash vine running up a ladder to represent the immortal bean. Cinderella rolled away in a vast pumpkin, and a long, black pudding was lowered by invisible hands to fasten itself on the nose of the woman who wasted her three wishes.

Little pilgrims journeyed over the hills with scrip and staff and cockleshells in their hats; elves held their pretty revels among the pines, and "Peter Wilkins'" flying ladies came swinging down on the birch tree-tops.[1] Lords and ladies haunted the garden, and mermaids splashed in the bath-house of woven willows over the brook.

People wondered at our frolics, but enjoyed them, and droll stories are still told of the adventures of those days. Mr. Emerson and Margaret Fuller were visiting my parents one afternoon, and the conversation having turned to the ever interesting subject of education, Miss Fuller said:

"Well, Mr. Alcott, you have been able to carry out your methods in your own family, and I should like to see your model children."

She did in a few moments, for as the guests stood on the door steps a wild uproar approached, and round the corner of the house came a wheelbarrow holding baby May arrayed as a queen; I was the horse, bitted and bridled and driven by my elder sister Anna, while Lizzie played dog and barked as loud as her gentle voice permitted.

All were shouting and wild with fun which, however, came to a sudden end as we espied the stately group before us, for my foot tripped, and down we all went in a laughing heap, while my mother put a climax to the joke by saying with a dramatic wave of the hand:

"Here are the model children, Miss Fuller."

My sentimental period began at fifteen when I fell to writing romances, poems, a "heart journal," and dreaming dreams of a splendid future.

Browsing over Mr. Emerson's library I found "Goethe's Correspondence
with a Child," and was at once fired with the desire to be a second Bettine,
making my father's friend my Goethe. So I wrote letters to him, but was wise
enough never to send them, left wild flowers on the doorsteps of my "Master," sung Mignon's song in very bad German under his window, and was
fond of wandering by moonlight, or sitting in a cherry-tree at midnight till the
owls scared me to bed.

The girlish folly did not last long, and the letters were burnt years ago, but
Goethe is still my favorite author, and Emerson remained my beloved "Master" while he lived, doing more for me, as for many another young soul, than
he ever knew, by the simple beauty of his life, the truth and wisdom of his
books, the example of a good, great man untempted and unspoiled by the
world which he made nobler while in it, and left the richer when he went.

The trials of life began about this time, and my happy childhood ended.
Money is never plentiful in a philosopher's house, and even the maternal pel-
ican could not supply all our wants on the small income which was freely
shared with every needy soul who asked for help.

Fugitive slaves were sheltered under our roof, and my first pupil was a very
black George Washington whom I taught to write on the hearth with charcoal, his big fingers finding pen and pencil unmanageable.

Motherless girls seeking protection were guarded among us; hungry trav-
ellers sent on to our door to be fed and warmed, and if the philosopher happened to own two coats the best went to a needy brother, for these were practical Christians who had the most perfect faith in Providence, and never
found it betrayed.

In those days the prophets were not honored in their own land, and
Concord had not yet discovered her great men. It was a sort of refuge for re-
formers of all sorts whom the good natives regarded as lunatics, harmless but
amusing.

My father went away to hold his classes and conversations, and we women
folk began to feel that we also might do something. So one gloomy November day we decided to move to Boston and try our fate again after some years
in the wilderness.

My father's prospect was as promising as a philosopher's ever is in a money-making world, my mother's friends offered her a good salary as their missionary to the poor, and my sister and I hoped to teach. It was an anxious council; and always preferring action to discussion, I took a brisk run over the hill and then settled down for "a good think" in my favorite retreat.

It was an old cart-wheel, half hidden in grass under the locusts where I used to sit to wrestle with my sums, and usually forget them scribbling verses or fairy tales on my slate instead. Perched on the hub I surveyed the prospect and found it rather gloomy, with leafless trees, sere grass, leaden sky and frosty air, but the hopeful heart of fifteen beat warmly under the old red shawl, visions of success gave the gray clouds a silver lining, and I said defiantly, as I shook my fist at fate embodied in a crow cawing dismally on the fence near by,—

"I *will* do something by-and-by. Don't care what, teach, sew, act, write, anything to help the family; and I'll be rich and famous and happy before I die, see if I won't!"

Startled by this audacious outburst the crow flew away, but the old wheel creaked as if it began to turn at that moment, stirred by the intense desire of an ambitious girl to work for those she loved and find some reward when the duty was done.

I did not mind the omen then, and returned to the house cold but resolute. I think I began to shoulder my burden then and there, for when the free country life ended the wild colt soon learned to tug in harness, only breaking loose now and then for a taste of beloved liberty.

My sisters and I had cherished fine dreams of a home in the city, but when we found ourselves in a small house at the South End with not a tree in sight, only a back yard to play in, and no money to buy any of the splendors before us, we all rebelled and longed for the country again.

Anna soon found little pupils, and trudged away each morning to her daily task, pausing at the corner to wave her hand to me in answer to my salute with the duster. My father went to his classes at his room down town, mother to her all-absorbing poor, the little girls to school, and I was left to keep house, feeling like a caged sea-gull as I washed dishes and cooked in the basement kitchen where my prospect was limited to a procession of muddy boots.

Good drill, but very hard, and my only consolation was the evening re-union when all met with such varied reports of the day's adventures, we could not fail to find both amusement and instruction.

Father brought news from the upper world, and the wise, good people who adorned it; mother, usually much dilapidated because she *would* give away her clothes, with sad tales of suffering and sin from the darker side of life; gentle Anna a modest account of her success as teacher, for even at seventeen her sweet nature won all who knew her, and her patience quelled the most rebellious pupil.

My reports were usually a mixture of the tragic and the comic, and the children poured their small joys and woes into the family bosom where comfort and sympathy were always to be found.

Then we youngsters adjourned to the kitchen for our fun, which usually consisted of writing, dressing and acting a series of remarkable plays. In one I remember I took five parts and Anna four, with lightning changes of costume, and characters varying from a Greek prince in silver armor to a murderer in chains.

It was good training for memory and fingers, for we recited pages without a fault, and made every sort of property from a harp to a fairy's spangled wings. Later we acted Shakespeare, and Hamlet was my favorite hero, played with a gloomy glare and a tragic stalk which I have never seen surpassed.

But we were now beginning to play our parts on a real stage, and to know something of the pathetic side of life with its hard facts, irksome duties, many temptations and the daily sacrifice of self. Fortunately we had the truest, tenderest of guides and guards, and so learned the sweet uses of adversity, the value of honest work, the beautiful law of compensation which gives more than it takes, and the real significance of life.

At sixteen I began to teach twenty pupils, and for ten years learned to know and love children. The story writing went on all the while with the usual trials of beginners. Fairy tales told the Emersons made the first printed book, and "Hospital Sketches" the first successful one.

Every experience went into the chauldron to come out as froth, or evaporate in smoke, till time and suffering strengthened and clarified the mixture of truth and fancy, and a wholesome draught for children began to flow pleasantly and profitably.

So the omen proved a true one, and the wheel of fortune turned slowly, till the girl of fifteen found herself a woman of fifty with her prophetic dream beautifully realized, her duty done, her reward far greater than she deserved.

1. *The Life and Adventures of Peter Wilkins* (1750) by Robert Taltock is often described as a cross between *Robinson Crusoe* and *Gulliver's Travels*. In one of his many adventures, the main character, after being deserted on a small island, encounters a beautiful girl who can fly.

The Youth's Companion 61 (24 May 1888): 261.

From *Louisa May Alcott: A Souvenir* (1888)

LURABEL HARLOW

Harlow's privately printed *Louisa May Alcott: A Souvenir* was issued to commemorate Alcott's death in March 1888. Although Harlow never identifies her connection to the author, one can assume from the following passage that she did indeed meet her—perhaps more than once. Harlow presents what many writers of recollections about Alcott often omit—a physical description and the manner of her speech. The twenty-eight-page volume, with illustrations, also testifies to how affected much of Alcott's reading public was by the news of her sudden death.

Miss Alcott was a much more beautiful woman, before her illness, than one would perhaps judge from any portrait of her. These have not been notable successes, and once caused her to remark, "When I don't look like the tragic muse, I look like a smoky relic of the great Boston fire."

Her face, with its strong, firm forehead, crowned with a wealth of beautiful chestnut hair, the hazel eyes, merry and keen, and cheeks glowing with the flush that amusement or vexation brought to them, was a most pleasing one to look upon. Her conversation was just as we might imagine it from her books,—racy, pungent, and quaint. She was quick to feel, and keen to criticise, but never in a scathing way; and it need hardly be said that she never descended to invidious comparisons or petty fault-finding. On the contrary, her enthusiasm over the good works of any new author was delightful to witness, so full was it of interest and good-will. Her sympathy was always given wholly and unreservedly to every cause of philanthropy, and all that tended to the higher education and greater development of women could be sure of the ready enlistment of her tongue and pen. Her character was noble, her disposition sweet; and we learn from reminiscences of her, and also from the lips of one who was a personal friend, that the principle of right-doing she so strongly advocated found no truer adherent than herself, and, as one has said, "She lived a life sweeter, nobler, wholesomer, and more inspiring, than the best chapters of her best books."

From *Louisa May Alcott: A Souvenir* (Boston: Samuel E. Cassino, 1888), pp. 26–27.

"The Author of 'Little Women'" (1888)

Mary Bartol

Published just two months after Louisa Alcott's death in March 1888, Mary Bartol's recollections provide an assessment of Alcott's life and especially her character. A number of pieces were published that year, most of which helped to establish the view of the author of *Little Women* as selfless and hardworking, a view that would last well into the next century. Bartol (1823?–1902), originally from Freeport, Maine, was the sister of Rev. Cyrus A. Bartol, Unitarian minister of the West Church in Boston between 1836 and 1889. He was briefly a member of the Transcendental Club, though he disagreed with many of Emerson's ideas. He was also a member of the later Radical Club, which often met at his home. Cyrus Bartol was an admirer of Bronson Alcott, speaking several times in the early 1880s at Alcott's School of Philosophy and delivering a sermon in 1888 entitled "Amos Bronson Alcott: His Character." By 1860, Mary Bartol was living in Portland, Maine. Her recollections here start with a visit that her niece, Elizabeth, the daughter of Cyrus Bartol, made to the Alcott home in May 1864, providing a rare look at Louisa recovering from the prolonged illness she suffered after contracting typhoid fever as a Civil War nurse at the Union Hotel Hospital in Georgetown. She is also the first observer to comment on Alcott's use of her hands to illustrate words when talking. Demonstrating how time can often blur details, Bartol, who wrote about her niece's Concord visit twenty-four years after the event, is incorrect about the publication of *Hospital Sketches*. Alcott's book was published in August 1863. Elizabeth Greene's letter about the visit offers another view of the same meeting, one recollected only days after the fact. By 1880, Mary had been living in Boston with her brother, Cyrus, on Chestnut Street in Beacon Hill not far from Louisa's home on Louisburg Square. Thus, she completes the account with a few recollections of her own and offers a view of a much older Alcott, ending with an observation on her funeral—one at which Cyrus Bartol gave a eulogy.

In the year 186[4] two young women, sojourning a few days in Concord, sought out Miss Alcott, their old acquaintance and friend. The description of this meeting comes to memory with peculiar freshness, whenever I recall it, for the account of a congregation of three served as my introduction to the dear resident of the river town. The visitors found her easily and received a cordial welcome. She had returned from her post of nurse in hospital wards, during the war of Secession, returned through compulsion, for her own strength had been sapped in watching over the pillows of wounded men.

By the side of her patients she stayed, struggling with their maladies and her own increasing disability, till she was reported "off duty." Then, and only then, did she yield to the burning grasp of fever, which held the fortress of life, and burnt its supplies to the margin. On this day of their visit she entered the room, where the guests waited and gave them greeting—then adding humorously "Excuse me if I seem to"—she uttered a quaint word, and sank on a couch, as if erect posture could no longer be thought of. She could not say "rest" or "lie down." These words would have expressed an abnegation against which she rebelled. After this preamble, came what may be called talk, rather than conversation, for the speaker was one—the listeners were two.

Though suffering from a drain of physical forces through anxiety and care for others, though weary at the middle hour of the day, she kept mental poise and magnetic power. If eloquence be "fluent speech," then was Miss Alcott eloquent. With this gift did she hold the couple near. I know not the time that passed, while two pairs of ears drank in "words, words, words," tinkling to constant laughter. There are witty people, who weary their admirers, there are comic tongues that grow foolish, but this speaker could not do the first, neither did any meaningless phrases fall from her lips. Thus went the minutes, and many of them, till an outing suggested itself.

The three left the house and walked towards the banks of the river. Here in a chosen spot had Mr. Alcott raised an arbor, in which he could pay vows of fealty to his beloved mistress, Nature. He had twisted it into form with tree branches, which, dispossessed of foliage, kept supple shape, tokens of the forest and never ending growth. To this arbor did Miss Alcott lead her friends, who soon turned again to eager listeners. No watery current could flow and flash more brilliantly than did the stream of speech, and Concord girl and Concord river told tales that day never to be forgotten by those who heard them.

Not long afterwards appeared "Hospital Sketches" filled with recitals which many a mind would have made altogether sombre, yet "Nurse Periwinkle" spins so truly that every gray thread dropping from her fingers holds here and there a golden sparkle. What woes are here recounted, and miti-gated by the buoyant pleasantries of her speech! Only a nature like Miss Al-cott's could have pulled out the thorns from those wounded soldiers' beds.

Wit is defined as "quickness of fancy and invention." She owned both in one and humor, too, wit's twin sister. To alert thought she joined a dra-matic sense, which held her friends captive. Not only did she use the seeing faculty, but transferred it to representation, putting her own irresistible ideas into visible form. I have heard that Miss Alcott was specially endowed with this same gift, and that if she asked for so slight a thing as an oval dish, she would unconsciously make the figure of an oval in the air, to emphasize her meaning.

This and great courage the mother transmitted to the daughter. Even while in the hands of an operating oculist did the former relieve pain and te-dium by anecdote and repartee.

It is now more than two years ago that Miss Alcott became disabled by a lameness in her right wrist, known as writer's cramp.

I saw her occasionally as a Boston neighbor (for she was spending the win-ter in town,) and respected her patience, and hopefulness.

Though foiled in her dearest pursuits, though afflicted with poor days and wakeful nights, I heard no words of dejection from her lips. I recall an eve-ning spent with her at that season, when she lifted what might easily have been dull hours into an atmosphere of her own.

Her conversation held the distinct charm of unconsciousness. Images ap-peared in her brain, as within the tiny circle of a kaleidoscope, but the motive power sprang from her perceptions, which turned and changed at the sug-gestion or response of a listener. In our familiar circle, Miss Alcott's recital of passages in her early and later life had the fresh and spicy flavor of an Isabella grape. When resting from composition, she led a rural life in her native town. She was the country girl, who would push a wheelbarrow of apples, if they needed pushing, without waiting for a hand, which might offer two minutes later. Healthy realism pervades her stories. She talks to girls and boys on their own plane of life, colored with the robustness of sports and strength, and while she grasps their hands, she holds before them a lofty ideal. It is no wonder that they flocked into her presence, whenever they had the opportu-nity; it is no wonder that Mr. Alcott, returning from a Western tour, reported that his best welcome there had been from the children, when they knew him to be Miss Alcott's father. While insisting that young people can attain to a

lofty standard, she unconsciously accents her counsel, for to this did she as-
pire throughout her life. "Little Women" had been published a year, before I
knew it—absence from New England had kept the book from my view. An
acquaintance with it began on shipboard. The day was blue and breezy, the
steamer ploughed steadily on her way and several passengers, heretofore
confined below by that tyrant *mal de mer*, had emerged from the obscurity of
state-rooms into sunlight on deck. One among them held a small volume in
her hand, by Louisa M. Alcott, from which she proceeded to read extracts.

How funny these were! Not many minutes passed before lugubrious faces
had brightened, half-closed eyes had opened, drooping mouths had curled
themselves into smiles and finally into stretches of laughter. O, the adventures of little women, who lived on the banks of the Concord river! How they
dared and lost and won! What boatings, what spills, what strandings, what
escapes were theirs! As the passenger continued to read to the circle round
her sea-chair, all who could listen, listened. In fifteen minutes, and less, life
had changed from a sea-trough to steady terra firma and middle-aged folks
were living their childhood over. To cheer was Miss Alcott's mission. In the
early part of her literary life, she met with some disappointments; yet she did
not lose courage for that. Strong in the conviction of power, which would be
ultimately recognized, she persevered with her pen and won success.

A modern French novelist gives this advice: "*Continuez et vous ar-
riverez*"—and this is what Miss Alcott did. After some more rejections of her
manuscript from publishers, one appeared—in the columns of a newspaper.

This she took to the bedside of a sister (then ill), and holding the sheet before her own face, to conceal any consciousness, which her features might be-
tray, she read the tale aloud.

As she finished, her auditor exclaimed "That is a very good story." "It is
mine" responded the author. In this way began the popularity of sketches,
the lovers of which cannot to-day be counted. I remember an afternoon hour
in her own house in town, when she was enduring, Spartan-like, the affliction of her father's illness and her own pain. No casual observer would have
suspected the last.

She talked brightly, while looking at photographs and describing their
originals. "That one is extremely graceful" she said; "this is my mother, and
here," she exclaimed archly, "is brother——!"

It has been remarked by friends that Miss Alcott was more distinctly the
child of her mother than of her father, yet in some respects she resembled the

latter. I recall a few days during which I enjoyed the companionship of this individual man. On Saturday, Sunday and a portion of Monday I had the opportunity of hearing words of wisdom from a nature "without guile." A class of scholars had assembled the second day for their Sabbath lesson, but the usual instruction gave place to the influence of a new and benign teacher. With a book of favorite German sketches in hand, as basis for his words, Mr. Alcott talked of the good will, which he illustrated in his daily life. So simple, so innocent his ways, that I found myself asking if he were not as pure as the children to whom he spoke.

Miss Alcott blessed those within her home and those without. She remembered the trials of the poor, she recognized the perils of prosperity. Honesty formed an integral part of her character—and character, as well as mind, was her possession. Directly at the truth did she aim her arrows, and they hit the centre—but no sting lurked in her shafts. Clean they cleaved the air and often to the ring of humorous echoes. She laughed away clouds, she laughed away care, she laughed away praise, and held fast to purposes of serious action. Ingenuous, as well as imaginative, she had in her being a vein of simplicity, which did not allow her to remember self.

As I listened to the tributes paid her memory over the casket holding the garment of flesh cast off by her spirit, my heart said "Amen." They were not eulogies, but truth from lips of those who loved her.

The Cottage Hearth 14 (May 1888): 139–40.

"The Alcotts" (1888)

Frances Bellows Sanborn

Frances Bellows Sanborn's piece was typical of those published soon after Louisa May's and Bronson's deaths in March 1888. Part recollection and part biographical overview, Sanborn highlights both figures, telling a brief story of how Bronson's philosophical ideals influenced his career as a teacher and helped shape the lives of his children. The dates of the Alcotts' time in Walpole, New Hampshire, seem confused by the author, as it had been more than thirty years earlier—not twenty-five, as she mentioned. Louisa May moved to Walpole in June 1855 and the rest of the family joined her in July. They remained there about two years, until settling into Orchard House in Concord in October 1857. Louisa helped form the Walpole Amateur Dramatic Company while there and continued her writing; however, she did have extended stays in Boston during those years, teaching school and tutoring. Benjamin Willis, whose deceased first wife was Abigail Alcott's sister, resided in Walpole and allowed the Alcotts to live rent-free in one of his homes. Louisa wrote: "No better plan offered, and we are all tired of the city. Here Father can have a garden; Mother can rest and be near her good neice; the children have freedom and fine air" (*Journals*, 75).

Twenty-five years ago, it was my fortune to spend nearly a year in the beautiful little village of Walpole, New Hampshire.

Opposite my uncle's house was a large and hospitable-looking mansion, in which dwelt a family widely known in that neighborhood for their generosity, as well as for their wealth.

In this house I first met Louisa M. Alcott and the three sisters whom she describes in her well-known stories. Here I saw the good, motherly, though over-worked woman whom Miss Alcott has immortalized in the dear "Marmee" with whom we are all so familiar. Here, too, I first saw Mr. Alcott,—a tall, pale, spiritual-looking man, who even then seemed venerable.

I can distinctly remember the shabby old house in which they lived, only a few steps from their cousins' home. I can recall Miss Alcott herself as she took part in all the bright goings-on of the village,— the private theatricals, the Shakespeare club, the endless fun and frolic of those days.

She had even then written several articles; indeed, I believe that her first novel, "Moods," had seen the light, though it was then unpublished. This was the book which went through such tribulation, being the identical one which Amy nearly destroyed in her fit of revenge mentioned in "Little Women." The heroine excited my interest by her views on the subject of early rising. After being called four or five times by her stern mentor, she turned her face to the wall and remarked philosophically that she did not see any use in getting up, and she was going to lie in bed till she did!

Many of Miss Alcott's early tales and anecdotes have been preserved by her cousins, who little dreamed then of the fame which awaited her. Some of her writings which would now be enthusiastically greeted fell flat and unappreciated. Even her own family did not then fully recognize her surpassing talents as a story-writer. One staunch little cousin stood by her through thick and thin, and fought bravely for her, until one day her faith was justified.

The two cold, disagreeable winters which Miss Alcott mentions as being the extent of their stay in Walpole were filled with many interesting events.

The "conversations" or *conversaziones,* which were afterward carried out in Boston and elsewhere had here their origin. Once a week a devoted band of so-called "Æsthetics" struggled up the long, steep hill which led to the home of Dr. [Henry Whitney] Bellows, where these solemn gatherings were held. At these meetings, Mr. Alcott was nearly the sole performer, Dr. Bellows being the only person brave enough to add his word. What might be the meaning of his utterance, no man could fathom; but every one sat and listened in awe-struck silence.

Several years afterward, he renewed these meetings in Concord and elsewhere near Boston; and perhaps it will not be out of place to mention a tale told me by a friend about these gatherings.

A course of ten conversations was to be given in Salem, I think, and my friend purchased a ticket for the vast sum of ten dollars. The first conversation had for its subject, "Love," and many young persons flocked thither to learn what the great philosopher had to say on this important topic.

He began in his usual far-off fashion, talking in a beautiful, mystical way of the spiritual meaning of this most common word. Finally descending from his heights of inspiration, he pointed his long, thin finger impressively toward my friend, and said slowly and solemnly, "Now what does that young lady in blue think about love?" A dreadful silence ensued, and never more was that young woman seen in those classic halls.

Two years after the Alcotts' stay in Walpole, Lizzie, the original of the exquisite picture of Beth in "Little Women," sickened and died at her home in Concord.

The short sketch of the family which follows is taken in part from information given by near and dear friends and relatives, in part from personal recollection.

The father of A. Bronson Alcott was the son of a Connecticut farmer of whom nothing is known save that, he was the parent of one of the wonders of the world. Mr. Alcott early left the paternal roof and began his career as a peddler, taking the South as his field of action, peddling good tidings of all kinds, carrying his books everywhere and reading them too, doing his best to raise the benighted African race at the same time that he was procuring a scanty sustenance for himself. He returned North to Boston a few years afterward, and there fell in love with Miss Abby May, who afterward became his wife. They were both in sympathy in the great work of helping on mankind.

Fortunately, Mrs. Alcott possessed a greater degree of practical common sense than her husband. After their marriage they went to German-town, Pennsylvania, where they remained two years, during which period Louisa was born, Nov. 29, 1832.

Not long afterward, Mr. Alcott moved to Boston, where he opened a school in Tremont Temple. This most remarkable school has been very pleasantly described by Miss Peabody in her "Record of a School." She was his sole assistant, and indeed it was here that she really began her kindergarten teaching.

It was Mr. Alcott's theory that everything which the eyes of his pupils rested upon should be beautiful or noble, and suggest fine or great thoughts. Consequently, he had a beautiful room, thoroughly simple in its furniture, but fine in proportion, and exquisite in finish. In each of the four corners was a bust of some grand human being,— Socrates, Shakespeare, Milton, and one other. Over the platform, above his head, was a fine cast of the head of Christ; over that a head of Plato. Around his seat were chairs arranged in circular fashion, so that each occupant might have his eyes fixed directly upon the teacher. He collected all his scholars about him, and began with a short talk on some suggestive topic, or a reading from some fine book. Then he would question the pupils, drawing answers from each one, until the class was alive with interest.

His theories with regard to development and punishment were singular but suggestive. Punishment, he said, should never be inflicted except as a reminder. Taken in any other way, punishment was coarse and brutal.

Thus it is related that one of the boys was found guilty of some misdemeanor. Mr. Alcott called him up, and after talking gently with the offender, gave him a ruler and bade him apply it to his teacher. The boy hesitated, and drew back, but Mr. Alcott was firm; and the boy after administering one or two faint blows with a burst of tears begged Mr. Alcott to beat *him*,—"anything, indeed, rather than that."

Another instance is mentioned in which a refractory girl was punished through the vicarious suffering of her best-beloved, most intimate friend. The youthful sinner was perfectly heart-broken and was never known to sin again.

Mr. Alcott's school flourished for some time until some of his pro-slavery patrons withdrew their children because a negro boy had been retained by the teacher in spite of all remonstrances.

When Miss Alcott was about ten years old, the family moved to Harvard, Mass., and there in an old farm-house, with three or four other families, they founded what Miss Alcott describes under the name of the "Arcadian Club." In an article in the *Atlantic* called "Transcendental Wild Oats," Miss Alcott vividly sets forth this strange experience. I remember well hearing Mrs. Alcott as she related to my aunt, of sainted memory, the story of this community. I was a child of twelve or fourteen, but I used to steal in and sit unperceived while these stories were being told.

This attempt to establish a Community at Harvard has often been confounded with the "Brook Farm" experiment, immortalized by Hawthorne in his "Blithedale Romance." But it was much less pretentious in form and in numbers, consisting of only four families who held their goods in common. As they had forsworn all the luxuries and vanities of life, and most of the comforts thereof, they proposed to procure what little they needed,— namely, the fruits of the earth,—by the sweat of their brow. The men were to raise the needed fruits and vegetables, corn, wheat, etc. Animal food was not allowed to the followers of Alcott. The women were supposed to take their turn in the cares of the household, each serving a week.

Mrs. Alcott, being the only person not of an aesthetic cast of mind, appears to have had *her* turn nearly every week. Indeed, I imagine that some of the labors of the men fell upon her. One cannot imagine the spiritual-minded leader descending to the contemplation of kindling-wood, or the digging of potatoes.

After this strange experience, Mr. Alcott next took up his abode in Concord. Here we learn of the wonderful stories which Louisa used to tell her sisters and her young friends. Here passed much of that bright and joyous living of which we read in the first part of "Little Women." Here was the "attic" to which "Jo" retired to express her enthusiasm or indignation on paper. Here also were the meetings of the "Pickwickian Club," so well described in the same book. From this spot and from the memories connected with it doubtless came much of the inspiration which produced her books.

When Miss Alcott was sixteen, her father moved to Boston, and there our authoress began to teach. Her writing went on at the same time, and many were the little effusions which came from her pen, never to be known to the world.

When the war broke out, in 1861, she was filled with enthusiasm, went to Washington, and took her place as a nurse. She did not long remain there, for she was taken sick with a typhoid fever which nearly cost her her life, and from which she never fully recovered. Soon afterward "Hospital Sketches" appeared to the world, and was very favorably received.

No book of hers has had anything like the power of "Little Women"; probably for the reason that in that one book were written all the beautiful real experiences of her life, and later stories were only variations.

During the last twenty years the Alcotts have made their home in Concord, but there have been frequent absences in Europe and elsewhere. Always they seemed to turn back with loving hearts to their old abiding-place.

For the last five years Miss Alcott has been more or less of an invalid. Still, no one save the few who knew her best could guess the suffering which she concealed under a bright smile or a "dreadful" pun. Her cousin, who resembles her in many particulars, has often told the "good things" that Louisa would utter while undergoing spasms of pain.

The family of six whom we first knew in "Little Women" has been fast broken up. First angelic little Beth, then the dear Marmee, and in 1879, May, Mrs. Nieriker. A few weeks ago, all that was left of this loving group was gathered together in their house in Louisburg Square, Boston, under the tender care of Mrs. Pratt, the Meg of our memory. Here was Mr. Alcott, a confirmed invalid for five years, paralyzed in body and speech. Here were Meg's two children, Daisy and Demi (only these were two little boys); here was sister May's little girl, Louisa, and here occasionally was Miss Alcott herself. A little later, two more bright spirits from the midst of this loving group went up to join the "choir invisible."

Every Other Sunday 3 (15 April 1888): 122–23.

From *Louisa May Alcott: Her Life, Letters and Journals* (1889)

EDNAH DOW CHENEY

Ednah Dow Cheney (1824–1904), writer, reformer, abolitionist, suffragist, is best known for her biography, *Louisa May Alcott: Her Life, Letters and Journals* (1889), which would remain the standard edition of Alcott's private writings for almost a century. Ironically, Cheney knew and appreciated Bronson Alcott more than she did Louisa May.

Born Ednah Dow Littlehale in Boston, the youngest daughter of a merchant who had made his fortune in the West Indian trade, she was a student of Margaret Fuller and first met Bronson at his initial series of conversations given at West Street, Boston, in 1848. She was twenty-four, just seven years older than Anna, when Bronson was introduced to her. She later began to transcribe his conversations, and in July 1851, Bronson recorded his thoughts about her in his journal: "She came—the maiden and passed the morning; a long and lavish morning with me, and left me the principal owner of a heart green with youthful regards." He then quoted the poet Herbert: "And now in age I find again / After so many deaths, I live I write / I once more smell the dew & rain." Other similar passages followed in Bronson's journals over the next few years. Clearly, he was captivated by her and she by him. However, no direct evidence of a romantic relationship exists; most of Cheney's private writings were destroyed before her death.

In 1853, she married the Boston artist Seth Wells Cheney, a widower and fourteen years her senior. Already suffering from tuberculosis at the time of their marriage, Seth Cheney died in 1856, leaving Ednah with their one-year-old daughter, Margaret. She remained unmarried the rest of her life, taking up various causes and reforms. She continued her contact with the Alcotts, speaking several times at the Concord School of Philosophy. In 1888, she published *Louisa May Alcott: The Children's Friend* as a memorial and keepsake for young readers. With the success of this volume and with the family's permission (primarily that of Anna Alcott Pratt, to whom the book is dedicated), Cheney published the "authorized" biography under the Roberts Brothers imprint the following year. This work would lead the way in establishing Louisa May as "Duty's child," who struggled long and hard for her family. The following personal description of Louisa May, along with the other family members, forms the concluding chapter of Cheney's biography, and it could have been written only by someone who knew the Alcotts well.

Miss Alcott's appearance was striking and impressive rather than beautiful. Her figure was tall and well-proportioned, indicating strength and activity, and she walked with freedom and majesty. Her head was large, and her rich brown hair was long and luxuriant, giving a sense of fulness and richness of life to her massive features. While thoroughly unconventional, and even free and easy in her manner, she had a dignity of deportment which prevented undue liberties, and made intruders stand in awe of her. Generous in the extreme in serving others, she knew her own rights, and did not allow them to be trampled on. She repelled "the spurns that patient merit of the unworthy takes" and had much of the Burns spirit that sings "A man's a man for a' that" in the presence of insolent grandeur.

Miss Alcott always took her stand not for herself, but for her family, her class, her sex. The humblest writer should not be imposed upon in her person; every woman should be braver and stronger from her attitude. She was careless of outward distinctions; but she enjoyed the attentions which her fame brought her with simple pleasure, and was delighted to meet bright, intelligent, distinguished people, who added to her stores of observation and thought. She had the rare good fortune, which an heir of millions might envy, of living all her life in the society of the noblest men and women. The Emersons, the Thoreaus, the Hawthornes, and Miss Elizabeth Peabody were the constant companions of her childhood and youth. It was from them that her standard of character was formed, and she could never enter any circle higher than that in which she had breathed freely from a child. She was quite capable of hero-worship, but her heroes were few.

With all her imagination and romance, Miss Alcott was a tremendous destroyer of illusions; she remorselessly tore them away from herself, persisting in holding a lens before every fault and folly of her own, and she did the same for those she loved best. Only what was intrinsically noble and true could stand the searching test of her intellectual scrutiny and keen perception of the incongruous and ridiculous.

This disposition was apparent in Louisa's relation to her father, whom she did not always fully understand. Perhaps he had a perception of this when he wrote —

"I press thee to my heart, as Duty's faithful child."

She had little sympathy with his speculative fancy, and saw plainly the impracticability of his schemes, and did not hesitate to touch with light and kindly satire his little peculiarities; yet in her deepest heart she gave him not only affection, but deep reverence. She felt the nobility and grandeur of his mind and heart. In "Little Women" the portrait of the father is less vivid and less literal than that of any other member of the family, and is scarcely recognizable; but it was impossible to make the student and idealist a part of the family life as she painted it, — full of fun, frolic, and adventure. In the second part she has taken pains to make up for this seeming neglect, and pays homage to the quiet man at the end of the house, whose influence was so potent and so sweet over all within it.

Mrs. Alcott was a rich and noble nature, full of zeal and impulse, daily struggling with a temper threatening to burst out into fire, ready to fight like a lioness for her young, or to toil for them till Nature broke down under the burden. She had a rich appreciation of heroism and beauty in all noble living, a true love of literature, and an overflowing sympathy with all suffering humanity, but was also capable of righteous indignation and withering contempt. To this mother, royal in her motherhood, Louisa was bound by the closest ties of filial love and mutual understanding. She early believed herself to be her mother's favorite child, knew she was close to her heart, her every struggle watched, her every fault rebuked, every aspiration encouraged, every effort after good recognized. I think Louisa felt no pride in this preference. She knew that she was dear to her mother, because her stormy, wayward heart was best understood by her; and hence the mother, wiser for her child than for herself, watched her unfolding life with anxious care. Throughout the childish journal this relation is evident: the child's heart lies open to the mother, and the mother can help her because she understands her, and holds sacred every cry of her heart.

Such a loving relation to a mother — so rich, so full, so enduring — was the greatest possible blessing to her life. And richly did Louisa repay the care.

From her earliest years she was her mother's confidante, friend, and comforter. Her dream of success was not of fame and glory, but of the time when she could bring this weary pilgrim into "that chamber whose name is Peace," and there bid her sit with folded hands, listening to the loving voices of her children, and drinking in the fulness of life without care or anxiety.

And it all came true, like the conclusion of a fairy story; for good fairies had been busy at work for many years preparing the way. Who that saw that mother resting from her labors, proud in her children's success, happy in her husband's contentment, and in the love that had never faltered in the darkest days, can ever forget the peace of her countenance, the loving joy of her heart.

The relation of Miss Alcott to her older sister was of entire trust and confidence. Anna inherited the serene, unexacting temper of her father, with much of the loving warmth of her mother. She loved to hide behind her gifted sister, and to keep the ingle-side warm for her to retreat to when she was cold and weary. Anna's fine intellectual powers were shown more in the appreciation of others than in the expression of herself; her dramatic skill and her lively fancy, combined with her affection for Louisa, made her always ready to second all the plans for entertainment or benevolence. She appears in her true light in the sweet, lovable Meg of "Little Women;" and if she never had the fame and pecuniary success of her sister, she had the less rare, but equally satisfying, happiness of wifehood and motherhood. And thus she repaid to Louisa what she had so generously done for the family, by giving her new objects of affection, and connecting her with a younger generation.

Louisa was always very fond of boys, and the difference of nature gave her an insight into their trials and difficulties without giving her a painful sense of her own hard struggles. In her nephews she found objects for all her wise and tender care, which they repaid with devoted affection. When boys became men, "they were less interesting to her; she could not understand them."

Elizabeth was unlike the other sisters. Retiring in disposition, she would gladly have ever lived in the privacy of home, her only desire being for the music that she loved. The father's ideality was in her a tender religious feeling; the mother's passionate impulse, a self-abnegating affection. She was in the family circle what she is in the book,—a strain of sweet, sad music we long and love to hear, and yet which almost breaks the heart with its forecasting of separation. She was very dear to both the father and mother, and the picture of the father watching all night by the marble remains of his child is very touching. He might well say,—

"Ah, me! life is not life deprived of thee."

Of the youngest of all,—bright, sparkling, capricious May,— quick in temper, quick in repentance, affectionate and generous, but full of her own plans, and quite inclined to have the world go on according to her fancies,—I have spoken elsewhere. Less profound in her intellectual and religious nature than either of her sisters, she was like a nymph of Nature, full of friendly sportiveness, and disposed to live out her own life, since it might be only a brief summer day. She was Anna's special child, and Louisa was not always so patient with her as the older sister; yet how well Louisa understood her generous nature is shown by the beautiful sketch she has made of her in "Little Women." She was called the lucky one of the family, and she reaped the benefit of her generous sister's labors in her opportunities of education.

From *Louisa May Alcott: Her Life, Letters and Journals* (Boston: Roberts Brothers, 1889), pp. 388–93.

"Recollections of Louisa May Alcott" (1892)

MARIA S. PORTER

> Maria S. Porter was friends with Alcott for approximately twenty years before her death. She was married to Charles Porter of Lynn, Massachusetts, and was herself interested in abolition and women's rights. When Porter was elected a member of the Melrose school committee in 1874, Alcott wrote to her that she hoped "that the first thing you . . . propose . . . will be to reduce the salary of the head master of the High School, and increase the salary of the first woman assistant, whose work is quite as good as his, and even harder, to make the pay equal" (*Selected Letters,* 189). Porter was, as she asserts here, the last person to whom Alcott wrote just before her death. Carrying forward the theme of "Duty's child" that Cheney established, Porter, while highlighting events in Alcott's life, offers many reflective comments by Alcott herself. Porter, who spent time with Alcott during her many stays at the Bellevue Hotel in Boston, gives readers more of a portrait of an older Alcott than many of the recollections published soon after the author's death.

No name in American literature has more thrilled the hearts of the young people of this generation than that of Louisa May Alcott. What a life of beneficence and self-abnegation was hers! How distinctively was her character an outcome of the best New England ancestry. In her veins ran the blood of the Quincys, the Mays, the Alcotts, and the Sewalls. What better inheritance could one have? and after all how important a factor in life is heredity! One is so enriched, strengthened, and upborne by a good ancestry, or sometimes, alas! so handicapped, baffled, and utterly defeated in the conflicts of life by bad hereditary influence, that when one has so fine an inheritance as was Louisa Alcott's, one should be thankful for it and rejoice in it as she did.

In looking back upon Miss Alcott's life, heroic and faithful to the end, it is the woman who interests us even more than the writer, whose phenomenal success in touching the hearts of old and young is known so well the world over. "Do the duty that lies nearest," was her life motto, and to its fulfilment were given hand and brain and heart. Helen Hunt Jackson once wrote of her:

"Miss Alcott is really a benefactor of households." Truer words were never written. She was proud of her ancestors.

I remember a characteristic expression of hers as we sat together one morning in June, 1876, in the old South Meeting House, where was assembled an immense audience, stirred to a white heat of patriotic enthusiasm by the fervid eloquence of Wendell Phillips, whose plea to save that sacred landmark from the vandals who were ready to destroy it can never be forgotten. At the conclusion of Phillips's speech she turned to me, her face aglow with emotion, and said: "I am proud of my foremothers and forefathers, and especially of my Sewall blood, even if the good old judge did condemn the witches to be hanged." After a moment of silence she added: "I am glad that he felt remorse, and had the manliness to confess it. He was made of the right stuff." Of this ancestor, Whittier wrote in "The Prophecy of Samuel Sewall:"

> "Stately and slow with solemn air,
> His black cap hiding his whitened hair,
> Walks the Judge of the great Assize,
> Samuel Sewall, the good and wise;
> His face with lines of firmness wrought
> He wears the look of a man unbought."

Of the name of Quincy, Oliver Wendell Holmes has written in "Dorothy Q":

> "Look not on her with eyes of scorn,
> Dorothy Q was a lady born!
> Ay! since the galloping Normans came,
> England's annals have known her name;
> And still to the three-hilled rebel town
> Dear is that ancient name's renown,
> For many a civic wreath they won,
> The youthful sire and the gray-haired son."

Miss Alcott began to write at a very early age. Her childhood and early girlhood were passed in the pure sweet atmosphere of a home where love reigned. Louisa and her sister Anna were educated in a desultory and fragmentary manner, or, perhaps one should say, without system. Mr. and Mrs. Alcott, the two Misses Peabody, Thoreau, Miss Mary Russell, and Mr. Lane had a share in their education. Mrs. Hawthorne taught Anna to read, and I think Louisa once spoke of her to me as her own first teacher.

Mrs. Alcott was a remarkable woman, a great reader, with a broad, practical mind, deep love of humanity, wide charity, untiring energy, and a highly sensitive organization, and she was married to a man whom she devotedly loved, who was absolutely devoid of practical knowledge of life, and who was an idealist of the extremest type. With the narrowest means, her trials, perplexities, and privations were very great, but she bore them all with heroic courage and fidelity, and with unwavering affection for her husband. Louisa early recognized all this. She soon developed the distinguishing traits of both father and mother. Emerson, soon after he made Mr. Alcott's acquaintance, recognized his consummate ability as a conversationalist, and was through life his most loyal friend. Louisa was very proud of her father's intellectual acquirements, and it was most interesting to hear her tell of the high tributes paid him by some of the great thinkers of the age. In a note to me in October, 1882, just after her father had been stricken with paralysis, she wrote:

"My poor, dear father lies dumb and helpless. He seems to know us all—and it is so pathetic to see my handsome, hale, active old father changed at one fell blow into this helpless wreck. You know that he wrote those forty remarkable sonnets last winter, and these, with his cares as Dean of the School of Philosophy and his many lectures there, were enough to break down a man of eighty-three years, I continually protested and warned him against overwork and taxation of the brain, but 'twas of no avail. Wasn't I doing the same thing myself? I did not practise what I preached, and indeed I have great cause for fear that I may be some day stricken down as he is. He seems so tired of living; his active mind beats against the prison bars. Did I ever tell you what Mr. Emerson once said of him to me? 'Louisa, your father could have talked with Plato.' Was not that praise worth having? Since then I have often in writing addressed him as 'My dear old Plato.'"

Just after the publication of the Correspondence of Carlyle and Emerson, I found her reading it one day. Her face was radiant with delight as she said: "Let me read you what Emerson wrote to Carlyle just before father went to England. 'I shall write again soon, for Bronson Alcott will probably go to England in about a month, and him I shall surely send you, hoping to atone by his great nature for many smaller ones that have craved to see you.'" Again she read: "He is a great man and is made for what is greatest." . . . "Alcott has returned to Concord with his wife and children and taken a cottage and an acre of ground, to get his living by the help of God and his own spade. I see that some of the education people in England have a school called 'Alcott House,' after my friend. At home here he is despised and rejected of men as much as ever was Pestalozzi. But the creature thinks and talks and I am proud of my neighbor.'"

Carlyle's estimate of Alcott, although not as high as Emerson's, was a fairly appreciative one. He wrote to Emerson after Alcott's visits to him:

"He is a genial, innocent, simple-hearted man, of much natural intelligence and goodness, with an air of rusticity, veracity, and dignity withal, which in many ways appeals to me. The good Alcott, with his long, lean face and figure, his gray worn temples and mild radiant eyes, all bent on saving the world by a return to the Golden Age; he comes before one like a kind Don Quixote, whom nobody can even laugh at without loving."

Louisa, after reading these extracts, taken from different parts of the books, said with emphasis: "It takes great men like Emerson and Carlyle and Thoreau to appreciate father at his best." She always spoke with great freedom and frankness of her father's lack of practical ability; and very pathetic were some of the stories she told of her own early struggles to earn money for the family needs; of her strivings to smother pride while staying with a maternal relative who had offered her a home for the winter while she was teaching in a small private school in Boston; and of her indignation when Mr. Fields said to her father, who had taken a story of hers to him to read with the hope that it might be accepted for the *Atlantic:* "Tell Louisa to stick to her teaching; she can never succeed as a writer!" This message, she said, made her exclaim to her father: "Tell him I will succeed as a writer, and some day I shall write for the *Atlantic!*" Not long afterward a story of hers was accepted by the *Atlantic* and a check for fifty dollars sent her. In telling me of this she said: "I called it my happy money, for with it I bought a second-hand carpet for our parlor, a bonnet for Anna, some blue ribbons for May, some shoes and stockings for myself, and put what was left into the Micawber Railroad, the Harold Skimpole Three Per Cents, and the Alcott Sinking Fund."

One merry talk about the experiences of her girlhood and early womanhood, with several pathetic and tragic stories, one beautiful moonlight summer evening, as we floated down the Concord River, made a profound impression on me, and I recall the stories with great distinctness.

"When I was a girl of eighteen or thereabouts," she said, "I had very fine dark brown hair, thick and long, almost touching the floor as I stood. At a time when the family needs were great, and discouragement weighed heavily upon us, I went to a barber, let down my hair, and asked him how much money he would give me for it. When he told me the sum, it seemed so large to me that I then and there determined I would part with my most precious possession if during the next week the clouds did not lift."

This costly gift, however, was not laid upon the family altar by the heroic girl. A friend who was ever ready to extend an unobtrusive helping hand when it was needed came to the rescue. Louisa, in relating this, said: "That was not the first time he had helped father, nor was it indeed the last."

Another incident that she told me that same evening in her inimitable way, with its amusing and pathetic details, revealed to me how supreme was her loyalty and devotion to her family, and above all to her mother.

In 1850, when Louisa was eighteen years of age, Mrs. Alcott had, with the advice of friends, taken a position as visitor to the poor in Boston. She had also opened an intelligence office, where she often assisted gentlefolk reduced from affluence to poverty, to situations where, without an entire sacrifice of pride, they could earn an honest independence. One day as Louisa was sitting in the office sewing on some flannel garments for the poor, under her mother's supervision, a tall man, evidently from his garb a clergyman, entered and said that he came to procure a companion for his invalid sister and aged father. He described the situation as a most desirable one, adding that the companion would be asked to read to them and perform the light duties of the household that had formerly devolved upon his sister, who was a martyr to neuralgia. The companion would be in every respect treated as one of the family, and all the comforts of home would be hers.

Mrs. Alcott, who in spite of many bitter experiences in the past never lost her faith in people and was rather too apt to take them for what they seemed to be, tried to think of some one who would be glad of so pleasant a home as described. She turned to Louisa and asked her if she could suggest any one. The reply came at once: "Only myself!" Great was her mother's surprise, and she exclaimed: "Do you really mean it, dear?" "I really do, if Mr. R—— thinks I would suit." The clergyman smiled and said, "I am sure you would, and I feel that if we can secure you, we shall be most fortunate."

When Mrs. Alcott had recovered from her surprise, she prudently asked him what wages would be paid. The smooth reply was that the word "wages" must not be used, but any one who lent youth and strength to a feeble household would be paid and well paid, and with another smile he took his leave. Then Mrs. Alcott asked: "Are you in earnest in engaging to go out for a month to live with these utter strangers?"

"Of course I am," said Louisa. "Why not try the experiment? It can but fail, as the teaching and sewing and acting and writing have. I do house-work at home for love; why not there for money?"

"But you know, dear," her mother replied, "it is going out to service, even if you are called a companion."

"I don't care. Every kind of work that is paid for is service. It is rather a downfall to give up trying to be a Siddons or a Fanny Kemble, and become a servant, at the beck and call of people; but what of it?" "All my highly respectable relatives," said Louisa, "held up their hands in holy horror when I left the paternal roof to go to my place of servitude, as they called it, and said: 'Louisa Alcott will disgrace her name by what she is doing.' But despite the lamentations and laughter of my sisters, I got my small wardrobe ready, and after embracing the family with firmness started for my new home."

She had promised to stay four weeks; but, after a few days, she found that instead of being a companion to the invalid sister, who was a nonentity, while the father passed his days in a placid doze, she was called upon to perform the most menial services, made a mere household drudge, or, to use her own expression, "a galley slave." "Then," said she, "I pocketed my pride, looked the situation squarely in the face, and determined I would stay on to the bitter end. My word must be as good as my bond." By degrees all the hard work of the family was imposed upon her, for the sister was too feeble to help or even to direct in any way, and the servant was too old to do anything but the cooking, so that even the roughest work was hers. Having made up her mind to go when the month was over, she brought water from the well, dug paths in the snow, split kindlings, made fires, sifted ashes, and was in fact a veritable Cinderella. "But," said she, "I did sometimes rebel, and being a mortal worm, I turned now and then when the clergyman trod upon me, especially in the matter of boot-blacking,—that was too much for my good blood to bear! All the Mays, Sewalls, and Alcotts of the past and present appeared before my mind's eye; at blacking boots I drew the line and flatly refused. That evening I enjoyed the sinful spectacle of the reverend bootblack at the task. Oh, what a long month that was! And when I announced my intention of leaving at its end, such dismay fell upon the invalid sister, that I consented to remain until my mother could find a substitute. Three weeks longer I waited. Two other victims came, but soon left, and on departing called me a fool to stay another hour. I quite agreed with them, and when the third substitute came, clutched my possessions, and said I should go at once. The sister wept, the father tremblingly expressed regret, and the clergyman washed his

[63]

hands of the whole affair by shutting himself in his study. At the last moment, Eliza, the sister, nervously tucked a small pocket-book into my hand, and bade me good-by with a sob. The old servant gave me a curious look as I went away, and exclaimed: 'Don't blame us for anything; some folks is liberal and some ain't!' So I left the house, bearing in my pocket what I hoped was, if not a liberal, at least an honest return for seven weeks of the hardest work I ever did. Unable to resist the desire to see what my earnings were, I opened my purse—and beheld four dollars! I have had many bitter moments in my life, but one of the bitterest was then, when I stood in the road that cold, windy day, with my little pocket-book open, and looked from my poor, chapped, grimy chillblained hands to the paltry sum that had been considered enough to pay for the labor they had done. I went home, showed my honorable wounds, and told my tale to the sympathetic family. The four dollars were returned, and one of my dear ones would have shaken the minister, in spite of his cloth, had he crossed his path."

This experience of going out to service at eighteen made so painful an impression upon her that she rarely referred to it, and when she did so it was with heightened color and tearful eyes.

Long years before she wrote her story called "Transcendental Wild Oats," she had told me in her humorous way of the family experiences at "Fruitlands," as the community established by Mr. Alcott and his English friend, Mr. Lane, was called. In 1843, when Louisa was eleven years of age, these idealists went to the small town of Harvard, near Lancaster, Massachusetts, to carry out their theories. Mr. Lane was to be the patriarch of the colony of latter-day saints. Louisa, in speaking of her father's connection with this movement, said: "Father had a devout faith in the ideal. He wanted to live the highest, purest life, to plant a paradise where no serpent could enter. Mother was unconverted, but true as steel to him, following wherever his vagaries led, hoping that, at last she might, after many wanderings, find a home for herself and children."

The diet at Fruitlands was strictly vegetarian; no milk, butter, cheese, or meat could be eaten or tasted even within the holy precincts—nothing that had caused death or wrong to man or beast. The garments must be of linen, because those made from wool were the result of the use of cruel shears to rob the sheep of their wool, and the covering of the silk-worms must be despoiled to make silken ones. The bill of fare was bread, porridge, and water for breakfast; bread, vegetables, and water for dinner; bread, fruit, and water for supper. They had to go to bed with the birds, because candles, for conscientious reasons, could not be burnt,—the "inner light" must be all-sufficient; sometimes pine knots were used when absolutely necessary. Meanwhile, the philosophers sitting in the moonlight built with words a new heaven and a new earth, or in the starlight wooed the Oversoul, and lived amid "metaphysical mists and philanthropic pyrotechnics." Mr. Alcott revelled in the "Newness," as he was fond of calling their new life. He fully believed that in time not only Fruitlands, but the whole earth would become a happy valley, the Golden Age would come; and toward this end he talked, he prophesied, he worked with his hands; for *he* was in dead earnest, his was the enthusiasm of a soul too high for the rough usage of this work-a-day world."

In the meanwhile, with Spartan fortitude Mrs. Alcott bore the brunt of the household drudgery. How Louisa's eyes would twinkle as she described the strange methods at Fruitlands! "One day in autumn mother thought a northeast storm was brewing. The grain was ripe and must be gathered before the rain came to ruin it. Some call of the Oversoul had wafted all the men away, and so mother, Anna, a son of Mr. Lane's, and I must gather the grain in some way. Mother had it done with a clothes-basket and a stout Russia linen sheet. Putting the grain into the basket we emptied it upon the sheet, and taking hold of the four corners carried it to the barn."

During the summer, Mr. Emerson visited them and wrote thus in his journal:

"The sun and the sky do not look calmer than Alcott and his family at Fruitlands. They seem to have arrived at the fact—to have got rid of the show, and so are serene. Their manners and behavior in the house and in the field are those of superior men,—of men of rest. What had they to conceal? What had they to exhibit? And it seemed so high an attainment that I thought—as often before, so now more, because they had a fit home or the picture was fitly framed,—that those men ought to be maintained in their place by the country for its culture. Young men and young maidens, old men and women should visit them and be inspired. I think there is as much merit in beautiful manners as in hard work. I will not prejudge them successful. They look well in July; we will see them in December."

But alas! Emerson did not see the idealists in December. When the cold weather came on, the tragedy for the Alcott family began. Some of those who had basked in the summer sunshine of the "Newness" fled to "fresh fields and pastures new" when the cold and dark days came. Mr. Lane, in whose companionship Mr. Alcott had enjoyed so much, left to join the Shakers, where he soon found the order of things reversed for him, as it was all work and no play with the brethren and sisters there. Mr. Alcott's strength and spirits were exhausted. He had assumed more than his share of responsibility, and a heavy weight of suffering and debt was laid upon him. The experiment had ended in disastrous failure,—his Utopia had vanished into thin air. His strange theories had alienated many of his old friends; he was called a visionary, a fool, a madman, and some even called him unprincipled. What could he do for his family? Then it was that his wife, whose loyalty was supreme, whose good sense and practical views of life had shown her from the beginning what would be the outcome of the experiment—then it was that her strong right arm rescued him. He was cherished with renewed love and tenderness by wife and children, who always remembered with pain this most bitter of all their experiences, and could never refer to it without weeping. Louisa, in recalling it, would say: "Mother fought down despondency and drove it from the household, and even wrested happiness from the hard hand of fate."

After Mr. Alcott had rallied from the depression caused by the failure at Fruitlands, he went back to Concord with his family and worked manfully with his hands for their support; he also resumed his delightful conversations, which in those days of transcendentalism had become somewhat famous. When a young girl, I attended them with my mother at the house of the Unitarian clergyman in Lynn. The talks of Mr. Alcott and the conversations that followed were most interesting—unlike anything that had been heard in Boston or its vicinity in those days. Afterward Ralph Waldo Emerson and Thoreau used to come and give us in parlors "Lectures on Transcendentalism," as they were called.

The busy years rolled on for Louisa, who exerted herself to the utmost to be the family helper in sewing, teaching, and writing. After her stories were accepted by the *Atlantic*, it became for her smooth sailing. One day, as Mr. Alcott was calling upon Longfellow, the poet took up the last *Atlantic* and said, "I want to read to you Emerson's fine poem on Thoreau's flute." As he began to read Mr. Alcott interrupted him, exclaiming with delight: "My daughter Louisa wrote that!" In telling me of this, Louisa said: "Do you wonder that I felt as proud as a peacock when father came home and told me?" This occurred before the names of the writers were appended to their contributions to the magazine.

Miss Alcott made two visits to Europe, travelling quite extensively and meeting many distinguished people. She was always an ardent admirer of the writings of Dickens, and she had the great pleasure of meeting him in London and hearing him read. All the characters in his books were like household friends to her; she never tired of talking about and quoting them. Her impersonation of Mrs. Jarley was inimitable; and when I had charge of the representation of "The Old Curiosity Shop" at the author's carnival held at Music Hall, in aid of the Old South Preservation Fund, I was so fortunate as to persuade her to take the part of Mrs. Jarley in the waxwork show. It was a famous show,—never to be forgotten. People came from all parts of New England to see Lóuisa Alcott's Mrs. Jarley, for she had for years been famous in the part whenever a deserving charity was to be helped in that way. Shouts of delight and peals of laughter greeted her original and witty descriptions of the "figgers" at each performance, and it was repeated every evening for a week.

One day during her last illness I received a note from her, in which she wrote:

"A poor gentlewoman in London has written to me, because she thinks after reading my books, that I loved Dickens's writings, and must have a kind heart and generous nature, and, therefore, takes the liberty to write and ask me to buy a letter written to her by Charles Dickens, who was a friend of hers. Such is her desperate need of money that she must part with it, although it is very precious to her. She has fourteen children, and asks five pounds for the letter. Now, I don't want the letter, and am not well enough to see or even write to any one about buying it from her; will not you try and do it for me? 'If at first you don't succeed, try, try again.' I'll add something to whatever you get for it. Remember the poor thing has fourteen children, and has been reduced from affluence to poverty."

The letter could not be sold for the price named, nor indeed to any one at its proper value, so Miss Alcott returned it and sent the price asked for it by the next steamer. This is only one of the many generous acts of sympathy of which I knew.

The Alcotts were always Anti-Slavery people. Mrs. Alcott's brother, Samuel J. May, and her cousin, Samuel E. Sewall, were the staunchest supporters of Garrison in the early struggles. Mr. Alcott was the firm friend of that intrepid leader in the war against slavery. Nearly all the leading Abolitionists were their friends,—Lucretia Mott, the Grimké sisters, Theodore

Weld, Lydia Maria Child, Wendell Phillips, Theodore Parker, Miss Peabody, and others of that remarkable galaxy of men and women who in those benighted years were ranked as fanatics by the community at large. When the mob-spirit reigned in Boston and Garrison was taken to a jail in the city to protect him from its fury and save his life, Mr. and Mrs. Alcott were among the first to call upon him to express their sympathy.

When the war came, the Alcotts were stirred to a white heat of patriotism. Louisa wrote:

"I am scraping lint and making blue jackets for our boys. My May blood is up. I must go to the front to nurse the poor helpless soldiers who are wounded and bleeding. I must go, and good-by if I never return."

She did go and came very near losing her life; for while in the hospital she contracted a typhoid fever, was very ill, and never recovered from its effects; it can be truly said of her she gave her life to her country. One of her father's most beautiful sonnets was written in reference to this experience. He refers to her in this as "duty's faithful child."

During her experience as a hospital nurse she wrote letters home and to the *Commonwealth* newspaper. From these letters a selection was made and published under the title of "Hospital Sketches." To me this is the most interesting and pathetic of all of Miss Alcott's books. With shattered health she returned to her writing and her home duties. Slowly but surely she won recognition; but it was not until she had written "Little Women," that full pecuniary success came.

Miss Alcott had the keenest insight into character. She was rarely mistaken in her judgment of people. She was intolerant of all shams, and despised pretentious persons. Often in her pleasant rooms at the Bellevue have I listened to her estimates of people whom we knew. She was sometimes almost ruthless in her denunciation of society, so-called. I remember what she said as we sat together at a private ball, where many of the butterflies of fashion and leaders of society were assembled. As with her clear, keen eyes she viewed the pageant, she exclaimed: "Society in New York and in Boston, as we have seen it to-night, is corrupt. Such immodest dressing, such flirtations of some of these married women with young men whose mothers they might be, so far as age is concerned, such drinking of champagne—I loathe it all! If I can only live long enough I mean to write a book whose characters will be drawn from life. Mrs.—— (naming a person present) shall be prominent as the society leader, and the fidelity of the picture shall leave no one in doubt as to the original."

She always bitterly denounced all un-womanliness. Her standard of morality was a high one, and the same for men as for women. She was an earnest advocate of woman suffrage and college education for girls, because she devoutly believed that woman should do whatever she could do well, in church or school or State. When I was elected a member of the school committee of Melrose in 1873, she wrote:

"I rejoice greatly thereat, and hope that the first thing that you and Mrs. Sewall propose in your first meeting will be to reduce the salary of the head master of the High School, and increase the salary of the first woman assistant, whose work is quite as good as his, and even harder; to make the pay equal. I believe in the same pay for the same good work. Don't you? In future let woman do whatever she can do; let men place no more impediments in the way; above all things let's have fair play,—let *simple justice* be done, say I. Let us hear no more of 'woman's sphere' either from our wise (?) legislators beneath the gilded dome, or from our clergymen in their pulpits. I am tired, year after year, of hearing such twaddle about sturdy oaks and clinging vines and man's chivalric protection of woman. Let woman find out her own limitations, and if, as is so confidently asserted, nature has defined her sphere, she will be guided accordingly—but in heaven's name give her a chance! Let the professions be open to her; let fifty years of college education be hers, and then we shall see what we shall see. Then, and not until then, shall we be able to say what woman can and what she cannot do, and coming generations will know and be able to define more clearly what is a 'woman's sphere' than these benighted men who now try to do it."

During Miss Alcott's last illness she wrote:

"When I get upon my feet I am going (D.V.) [1] to devote myself to settling poor souls who need a helping hand in hard times."

Many pictures and some busts have been made of Miss Alcott, but very few of them are satisfactory. The portrait painted in Rome by Healy is, I think, a very good one. The bas-relief by Walton Ricketson, her dear sculptor friend, is most interesting and has many admirers. Ricketson has also made a bust of Mr. Alcott for the Concord Library, which is exceedingly good, much liked by the family, and so far as I know, by all who have seen it. Of the photographs of Miss Alcott only two or three are in the least satisfactory, notably the full length one made by Warren many years ago, and also one by Allen and Rowell. In speaking of her pictures she once said: "When I don't look like the tragic muse, I look like a smoky relic of the Boston fire." Mr. Ricketson is now at work upon a bust of her, a photograph of which, from the clay, accompanies this article. In a letter to me in reply to one written after I had seen the bust in his studio at Concord, Mr. Ricketson writes:

"I feel deeply the important task I have to do in making this portrait, since it is to give form and expression to the broad love of humanity, the fixed purpose to fulfil her mission, the womanly dignity, physical beauty, and queenly presence which were so perfectly combined in our late friend, and all so dominated by a fine intellectuality. To do this and satisfy a public that has formed somewhat an idea of her personal appearance is indeed a task worthy of the best effort. I certainly have some advantages to start with. The medallion from life modelled at Nonquitt in 1886, and at that time considered the best likeness of her, is invaluable, as the measurements are all accurate. I also have access to all the photographs, etc., of the family, and the criticisms of her sister, nephews, and friends, and my long and intimate acquaintance. I feel this to be the most important work I have as yet attempted. I intend to give unlimited time to it, and shall not consider it completed until the family and friends are fully satisfied. The success of the bust of the father leads me to hope for the same result in the one of his beloved daughter."

Miss Alcott always took a warm interest in Mr. Elwell, and assisted him towards his education in art in early life.

Miss Alcott had a keen sense of humor, and her friends recall with delight her sallies of wit and caustic descriptions of the School of Philosophy, the "unfathomable wisdom," the "metaphysical pyrotechnics," the strange vagaries of some of the devotees. She would sometimes enclose such nonsense rhymes as these to her intimate friends:

> "Philosophers sit in their sylvan hall
> And talk of the duties of man,
> Of Chaos and Cosmos, Hegel and Kant,
> With the Oversoul well in the van;
> All on their hobbies they amble away,
> And a terrible dust they make;
> Disciples devout both gaze and adore,
> As daily they listen, and bake!"

The "sylvan hall" was, as I know from bitter experience while attending the sessions of the School of Philosophy, the hottest place in historic old Concord.

Sometimes Miss Alcott would bring her nonsense rhymes or "jingles," as she called them, to the club, and read at our pleasant club-teas, amid shouts of merriment followed by heartiest applause. . . .

From the time that the success of "Little Women" established her reputation as a writer, until the last day of her life, her absolute devotion to her family continued. Her mother's declining years were soothed with every care and comfort that filial love could bestow; she died in Louisa's arms, and for her she performed all the last offices of affection,—no stranger's hands touched the beloved form. The most beautiful of her poems was written at this time, in memory of her mother, and was called "Transfiguration." A short time after her mother's death, her sister May, who had married Mr. Ernest Nieriker, a Swiss gentleman, living in Paris, died after the birth of her child. Of this Louisa wrote me in reply to a letter of sympathy:

"I mourn and mourn by day and night for May. Of all the griefs in my life, and I have had many, this is the bitterest. I try so hard to be brave, but the tears will come, and I go off and cry and cry; the dear little baby may comfort Ernest, but what can comfort us? May called her two years of marriage perfect happiness, and said: 'If I die when baby is born, don't mourn, for I have had in these two years more happiness than comes to many in a lifetime.' The baby is named for me, and is to be given to me as my very own. What a sad but precious legacy!"

The little golden-haired Lulu was brought to her by its aunt, Miss Sophie Nieriker, and she was indeed a great comfort to Miss Alcott for the remainder of her life.

In 1885, Miss Alcott took a furnished house on Louisburg Square in Boston, and although her health was still very delicate she anticipated much quiet happiness in the family life. In the autumn and winter she suffered much from indigestion, sleeplessness, and general debility. Early in December she told me how very much she was suffering, and added: "I mean if possible to keep up until after Christmas, and then I am sure I shall break down." When I went to carry her a Christmas gift, she showed me the Christmas tree, and seemed so bright and happy that I was not prepared to hear soon after that she had gone out to the restful, quiet of a home in Dunreath Place,

[71]

at the Highlands, where she could be tenderly cared for under the direction of her friend, Dr. Rhoda Lawrence, to whom she dedicated one of her books. She was too weak to bear even the pleasurable excitement of her own home, and called Dr. Lawrence's house, "Saint's Rest." The following summer she went with Dr. Lawrence to Princeton, but on her return in the autumn her illness took an alarming character, and she was unable to see her friends, and only occasionally the members of her family. On her last birthday, November 29th, she received many gifts, and as I had remembered her, the following characteristic letter came to me, the last but one that she sent me:

"Thanks for the flowers and for the kind thought that sent them to the poor old exile. I had seven boxes of flowers, two baskets, and three plants, forty gifts in all, and at night I lay in a room that looked like a small fair, with its live tables covered with pretty things, borders of posies, and your noble roses towering in state over all the rest. That red one was so delicious that I revelled in it like a big bee, and felt it might almost do for a body—I am so thin now. Everybody was very kind, and my solitary day was made happy by so much love. Illness and exile have their bright side, I find, and I hope to come out in the spring a gay old butterfly. My rest-and-milk-cure is doing well, and I am an obedient oyster since I have learned that patience and time are my best helps."

In February, 1887, Mr. Alcott was taken with what proved to be his last illness. Louisa knew that the end was near, and as often as she was able came into town to see him. On Thursday morning, March 2d, I chanced to be at the house, where I had gone to inquire for Mr. Alcott and Louisa. While talking with Mrs. Pratt, her sister, the door opened, and Louisa, who had come in from the Highlands to see her father, entered. I had not seen her for months, and the sight of her thin, wan face and sad look shocked me, and I felt for the first time that she was hopelessly ill. After a few affectionate words of greeting she passed through the open doors of the next room. The scene that followed was most pathetic. There lay the dear old father, stricken with death, his face illumined with the radiance that comes but once,—with uplifted gaze he heeded her not. Kneeling by his bedside, she took his hand, kissed it and placed in it pansies she had brought, saying, "It is Weedy" (her pet name). Then after a moment's silence she asked: "What are you thinking of, dear?" He replied, looking upward, "Up there; you come too!" Then with a kiss she said, "I wish I could go," bowing her head as if in prayer. After a little came the "Good-by," the last kiss, and like a shadow she glided

[72]

from the room. The following day I wrote her at the "Saint's Rest," enclosing
a photograph of her sister May, that I found among some old letters of her
own. Referring to my meeting with her the day before, I said:

"I hope you will be able to bear the impending event with the same brave
philosophy that was yours when your dear mother died."

She received my note on Saturday morning, together with one from her
sister. Early in the morning she replied to her sister's note, telling of a dull
pain and a weight like iron on her head. Later, she wrote me the last words
she ever penned; and in the evening came the fatal stroke of apoplexy, followed by unconsciousness. Her letter to me was as follows:

"Dear Mrs. Porter:—Thanks for the picture. I am very glad to have it. No
philosophy is needed for the impending event. I shall be very glad when the
dear old man falls asleep after his long and innocent life. Sorrow has no place
at such times, and death is never terrible when it comes as now in the likeness
of a friend.

"Yours truly, L. M. A.

"P.S. I have another year to stay in my 'Saint's Rest,' and then I am promised twenty years of health. I don't want so many, and I have no idea I shall
see them. But as I don't live for myself, I hold on for others, and shall find
time to die some day, I hope."

Mr. Alcott died on Sunday morning, March 4, and on Tuesday morning,
March 6, death, "in the likeness of a friend," came to Louisa. Mr. Alcott's funeral took place on Tuesday morning and many of the friends there assembled were there met with the tidings of Louisa's death. Miss Alcott had
made every arrangement for her funeral. It was her desire that only those near
and dear to her should be present, that the service should be simple, and that
only friends should take part. The services were indeed simple, but most impressive. Dr. Bartol, the lifelong friend of the family, paid a loving and simple
tribute to her character, as did Mrs. Livermore. Mrs. Cheney read the sonnet written by Mr. Alcott, which refers to her as "Duty's faithful child," and
Mrs. Harriet Winslow Sewall, a dear cousin, read tenderly the most beautiful of Louisa's own poems, "Transfiguration," written, as I have said, in
memory of her mother. That was all.

1. "D.V." is an abbreviation from the Latin "Deo Volente," meaning "God willing."

The New England Magazine 6 (March 1892): 3–19.

"A Foreword by Meg" (1893)

ANNA ALCOTT PRATT

When an admirer wrote Louisa May that she had acted in a production of "The Witch's Curse," from *Little Women,* Alcott responded: "The original libretto still exists, written in an old account book, with stage directions, which would convulse any manager, and a list of properties and costumes seldom surpassed. . . . My acting days are over, but I still prance now and then with my boys, for in spite of age, much work, and the proprieties, an occasional fit of the old jollity comes over me, and I find I have not forgotten how to romp as in my Joian days" (*Selected Letters,* 182).

While Anna, in this preface, recalls the plays that the real March sisters presented for family and friends at Hillside in Concord, both of the older Alcott girls participated in numerous dramatic performances in Concord during the 1850s and 1860s and in Walpole, New Hamsphire, where they spent the summer of 1855. As early as 1850, Louisa confessed that "Anna wants to be an actress, and so do I. We could make plenty of money perhaps, and it is a very gay life. Mother says we are too young, and must wait. A. acts often splendidly. I like tragic plays. . . . We get up fine ones, and make harps, castles, armor, dresses, water-falls, and thunder, and have great fun" (*Journals,* 63–64).

In the good old times, when "Little Women" worked and played together, the big garret was the scene of many dramatic revels. After a long day of teaching, sewing, and "helping mother," the greatest delight of the girls was to transform themselves into queens, knights, and cavaliers of high degree, and ascend into a world of fancy and romance. Cinderella's godmother waved her wand, and the dismal room became a fairy-land. Flowers bloomed, forests arose, music sounded, and lovers exchanged their vows by moonlight. Nothing was too ambitious to attempt; armor, gondolas, harps, towers, and palaces grew as if by magic, and wonderful scenes of valor and devotion were enacted before admiring audiences.

Jo, of course, played the villains, ghosts, bandits, and disdainful queens; for her tragedy-loving soul delighted in the lurid parts, and no drama was perfect in her eyes without a touch of the demonic or supernatural. Meg loved the sentimental rôles, the tender maiden with the airy robes and flowing locks, who made impossible sacrifices for ideal lovers, or the cavalier, singing soft serenades and performing lofty acts of gallantry and prowess. Amy was the fairy sprite, while Beth enacted the page or messenger when the scene required their aid.

But the most surprising part of the performance was the length of the cast and the size of the company; for Jo and Meg usually acted the whole play, each often assuming five or six characters, and with rapid change of dress becoming, in one scene, a witch, a soldier, a beauteous lady, and a haughty noble. This peculiar arrangement accounts for many queer devices, and the somewhat singular fact that each scene offers but two actors, who vanish and reappear at most inopportune moments, and in a great variety of costume. Long speeches were introduced to allow a ruffian to become a priest, or a lovely damsel to disguise herself in the garb of a sorceress; while great skill was required to preserve the illusion, and astonish the audience by these wonderful transformations.

The young amateur of to-day, who can easily call to her aid all the arts of the costumer and scene-maker, will find it hard to understand the difficulties of this little company; for not only did they compose their plays, but they were also their own carpenters, scene-painters, property-men, dress-makers, and managers. In place of a well-appointed stage, with the brilliant lights and inspiring accessories of a mimic theatre, the "Little Women" had a gloomy garret or empty barn, and were obliged to exercise all their ingenuity to present the scenes of their ambitious dramas.

But it is surprising what fine effects can be produced with old sheets, bright draperies, and a judicious arrangement of lights, garlands and picturesque properties; and Jo's dramatic taste made her an admirable stage-manager. Meg was especially handy with saw and hammer, and acted as stage-carpenter,—building balconies, thrones, boats, and towers after peculiar designs of her own. Bureaus, tables, and chairs, piled aloft and arched with dark shawls, made dungeon walls and witch's cave, or formed a background for haunted forest and lonely glen. Screens of white cloth furnished canvas on which little Amy's skilful hand depicted palace halls, or romantic scene for lovers' tryst; and Beth's deft fingers were most apt in constructing properties for stage adornment, and transforming the frailest material into dazzling raiment. For the costumes were a serious consideration. No money could be spared from the slender purse to supply the wardrobes of these aspiring actors, and many were the devices to clothe the little company.

Thus a robe in one scene became a cloak in the next, and the drapery of a couch in the third; while a bit of lace served as mantle, veil, or turban, as best suited the turn of the play. Hats covered with old velvet, and adorned with feathers plucked from the duster, made most effective headgear for gay cavalier or tragic villain. From colored cotton were manufactured fine Greek tunics and flowing trains; and remarkable court costumes were evolved from an old sofa-covering, which had seen better days, and boasted a little gold thread and embroidery.

Stars of tin, sewed upon dark cambric, made a suit of shining armor. Sandals were cut from old boots. Strips of wood and silver paper were fashioned into daggers, swords, and spears, while from cardboard were created helmets, harps, guitars, and antique lamps, that were considered masterpieces of stage art.

Everything available was pressed into service; colored paper, odds and ends of ribbon, even tin cans and their bright wrappings were treasures to the young actors, and all reappeared as splendid properties.

At first a store of red curtains, some faded brocades, and ancient shawls comprised the stage wardrobe; but as the fame of the performances spread abroad, contributions were made to the little stock, and the girls became the proud possessors of a velvet robe, a plumed hat adorned with silver, long yellow boots, and a quantity of mock pearls and tinsel ornaments.

Such wealth determined them to write a play which should surpass all former efforts, give Jo a chance to stalk haughtily upon the stage in the magnificent boots, and Meg to appear in gorgeous train and diadem of jewels.

"The Witch's Curse" was the result, and it was produced with astounding effect, quite paralyzing the audience by its splendid gloom. Jo called it the "lurid drama," and always considered it her masterpiece. But it cost hours of thought and labor; for to construct a dungeon, a haunted chamber, a cavern, and a lonely forest taxed to the uttermost the ingenuity of the actors. To introduce into one short scene a bandit, two! cavaliers, a witch, and a fairy spirit—all enacted by two people—required some skill, and lightning change of costume. To call up the ghostly visions and mysterious voices which should appall the guilty Count Rodolpho, was a task of no small difficulty. But inspired by the desire to outshine themselves, the children accomplished a play full of revenge, jealousy, murder, and sorcery, of all which indeed they knew nothing but the name.

Hitherto their dramas had been of the most sentimental description given to the portrayal of woman's devotion, filial affection, heroism, and self-sacrifice. Indeed, these "Comic Tragedies" with their highflown romance and fantastic ideas of love and honor, are most characteristic of the young girls whose lives were singularly free from the experiences of many maidens of their age.

Of the world they knew nothing; lovers were ideal beings, clothed with all the beauty of their innocent imaginations. Love was a blissful dream; constancy, truth, courage, and virtue quite every-day affairs of life. Their few novels furnished the romantic element; the favorite fairy-tales gave them material for the supernatural; and their strong dramatic taste enabled them to infuse both fire and pathos into their absurd situations.

Jo revelled in catastrophe, and the darker scenes were her delight; but she usually required Meg to "do the love-part," which she considered quite beneath her pen. Thus their productions were a queer mixture of sentiment and adventure, with entire disregard of such matters as grammar, history, and geography,—all of which were deemed of no importance by these aspiring dramatists. . . .

"A Foreword by Meg," *Comic Tragedies Written by "Jo" and "Meg" and Acted by the "Little Women"* (Boston: Roberts Brothers, 1893), pp. 7–13.

From *Sketches from Concord and Appledore* (1895)

FRANK PRESTON STEARNS

Frank Preston Stearns was the son of Major George Luther Stearns and Mary Preston Stearns, who had long been friends with Bronson Alcott. Stearns was a student at Frank Sanborn's academy in Concord during the early 1860s. After graduation from Harvard, he became an authority on Italian art, publishing several books on the subject. Many of the students at Sanborn's school were near contemporaries with May Alcott and thus often discussed in the sisters' letters. In March 1860, Sanborn's students presented a masquerade ball at the Concord Town Hall, and Louisa, after sewing May's first ball dress, reported to her friend Alf Whitman: "Frank Stearns was Alcibiades in a real Greek dress gorgeous to behold" (*Selected Letters*, 50).

Since his parents were longtime friends of the family (both were staunch abolitionists), Stearns offers an insider's view of the Alcotts, especially Louisa, often giving intimate scenes with the vividness of a polished writer. His accounts of the entertaining nights in the Alcott home when the school boys would "talk with the ladies" and his recollection of the plays Louisa acted in reveal Alcott before the fame of *Little Women* and give rare insight into the personal Louisa. Stearns goes far to demythologize the famous author, who, in his words, "had no proclivity for paddling up and down Concord River in search of ideas."

Mr. Alcott's house in Concord was situated on the Lexington road about three-quarters of a mile from the village centre. It was the best-looking house almost in the town, being of simple but faultless architecture, while the others were mostly either too thin or too thick, or out of proportion in some way. It lacked a coat of fresh paint sometimes, but this was to its advantage from an artistic point of view. Fine old elm-trees shaded the path in front of it, and across the road a broad level meadow stretched away to Walden woods. In the rear it was half surrounded by low pine-wooded hills, which protected it from the north-easterly storms and the cold draughts of winter. Mr. Alcott had quite a genius for rustic architecture, as is proved by the summer-house which he and Thoreau built for Emerson, and the fences, seats and arbors with which he adorned his little place added a final charm to the rural picture. In summer nights the droning of the bittern could be heard across the meadows, and woodcock came down familiarly from the hills to look for worms in the vegetable-garden. The snow melted here in Spring and the grass grew green earlier than in other places. It was the fitting abode and haven of rest for a family that had found the conflict of life too hard for them.

Within the house was as pleasant as without. There is no better decoration for a room than a good library, and though Mr. Alcott's books were not handsomely bound one could see at a glance they were not of a common sort. They gave his study an air of distinction, which was well carried out by the refined look and calm demeanor of its occupant. The room opposite, which was both parlor and living-room, always had a cheerful homelike appearance; and after the youngest daughter May entered on her profession as a painter, it soon became an interesting museum of sketches, water-colors and photographs. I remember an engraving of Murillo's Virgin, with the moon under her feet, hanging on the wall, and some excellent copies of Turner's water-color studies. The Alcotts were a hospitable family, not easily disturbed by callers, and ready to share what they had with others. The house had a style of its own.

How Emerson accomplished what he did, with his slight physique and slender strength, will always be one of the marvels of biography. His is the only instance, I believe, on record of a man who was able to support a family by writing and talking on abstract subjects. It is true he inherited a small property, enough to support a single man in a modest way, and without this his career would not have been possible; but the main source of his income was winter lecturing—a practice which evidently killed Theodore Parker, naturally a strong and powerful man. Yet he was not satisfied with this, but wished also to provide for others who had no claims of relationship upon him. His generous efforts in behalf of Carlyle have long since been made public; but the help he gave Mr. Alcott will probably never be known. Least of all would Emerson have wished it to be known. One can imagine that he said to himself: "Here is a man of rare spiritual quality, with whom I am in the closest sympathy: I cannot permit him to suffer any longer." So after the philosophic school in the Masonic Temple had come to an end, he invited him to Concord and cared for him like a brother. Mr. Alcott deserved this, for though he was not more a philosopher than Thoreau was a naturalist, equally with Thoreau he was a character. The primal tenet in his creed was like the ancient mariner's, to harm neither man nor bird nor beast; and he exemplified this doctrine with incredible consistency for full fifty years. He lived a blameless life. Many laughed at him for his unpractical theories; but the example of one such man, even in a reactionary way, is worth more to the community than the practical efforts of ten ordinary men. He has besides the distinction of being the person, whom, during the middle portion of his life, Emerson most liked to converse with.

Froude the historian calls Charles the Fifth one of nature's gentlemen: so was Mr. Alcott. It is easy to distinguish the man whose behavior is an emanation of himself from people of well-bred manners or of cultivated manners. Well-bred manners come from habit and association, and though always pleasant may be nothing more than a superficial varnish; while cultivated manners imply a certain amount of self-restraint. No man was ever more free from formality or affectation. He was neither condescending to inferiors nor would he yield ground to those who considered themselves above him, but met all people on the broad equality of self-respect. He was always most respected where society was most polite and refined. Neither was he lacking in personal courage. During the Anthony Burns excitement in Boston in 1852, he took a prominent position among the rescuers, and if a collision of the guards had taken place he would likely have been killed.

He had a fine philosophical mind, and if it had only been trained properly in early life he might have won a distinguished place among metaphysicians. That however was hardly possible in the America of that time. He was not a philosopher in the modern sense, but he was in the ancient sense—a disciple of Pythagoras, dropped down from the pure Grecian sky into the restless turmoil of the nineteenth century. He wished to discover everything anew for himself, instead of building upon the discoveries of others. His conversations, usually in the parlors of some philanthropic gentlemen, were made up partly of Pythagorean speculation and partly of fine ethical rhapsody which sometimes rose to genuine eloquence. They served to interest neophytes in the operations of their own minds, and the more experienced found much the same satisfaction in it as in Emerson's discourses. He was an excellent speaker; confident, quick-witted and conciliatory. I remember a very eloquent address that he delivered at an anniversary meeting in 1868, and at an anti-slavery convention, where Garrison and Phillips fell out, Mr. Alcott made the best speech of the occasion, discriminating between the two leaders in a just and sensible manner.

He was memorable for shrewd observations. He said once to a lady who was fretting because the clergyman did not come in time, "Meanwhile, Mrs. D., there is providence." Of a good-humored young radical who wished to make war on all conventional forms, religious and political parties, he remarked, "Unless our friend changes his ideas he will not be the happy man at forty that he is now;" and the saying came true. If we are to judge the value of Alcott's thought by the constant cheerfulness and contentment of his daily life, his ideas must have been of an excellent quality. His flowing white hair, and the calmness and purity of his aspect, gave him quite an apostolic look; and once while visiting at the house of a friend, a certain small boy—the same for whom John Brown afterwards wrote his autobiography of a boy—asked his mother if that man was one of Christ's disciples. Such was the father of "Little Women."

The Alcotts received their friends weather permitting on Monday evenings, and some favored youths of Mr. Sanborn's school would go there to play whist, make poker-sketches, and talk with the ladies; while Mrs. Alcott, who had played with the famous automaton in her younger days, would have a quiet game of chess with some older person in a corner. Louisa usually sat by the fire-place, knitting rapidly with an open book in her lap, and if required to make up a table would come forward with a quiet look of resignation and some such remark as "You know I am not a Sarah Battles." Then after a while her love of fun would break forth, and her bright flashes of wit would play about the heads of all who were in the room. Just after ten Mr. Alcott would come in with a dish of handsome apples and his wife produce some ginger cakes; a lively chat for fifteen or twenty minutes would follow, and then the guests would walk home. It was in this way Louisa acquired that stock of information about young people and their affairs which she made such good use of afterwards. Human nature to the poet and novelist is like a Calumet and Hecla mine which never becomes exhausted.

Louisa Alcott resembled her mother in figure, features and color, and in her ardent and impulsive temperament. In the greater number of families the eldest child resembles the father; the second and third are more like their mother, and the fifth (if there be so many) is often like the grandparents. In the Alcott family however it was just the reverse of this, for May the youngest daughter was the only one like her father, inheriting the artistic side of his nature, instead of the philosophical. Neither did Louisa resemble her grandmother's family, the Sewalls. She was emphatically a May, and the best of all the Mays, though there have been many of them who were excellent. I think she was indebted to her father for her enterprising spirit and keen sense of character. Mr. Alcott knew the people of Concord much better than they understood him, and was always most interesting when he talked of the distinguished people with whom he had been acquainted. May was fond of society, and a walk to and from the school dances cold winter nights; and then ready next morning for a skating party on Walden pond; but she said her sisters had little entertainment in their youth, dressing always in the plainest manner and practising a stoical self-denial. Louisa liked to look at other people dancing, and generally it made her happy to see the young folks enjoy themselves. This shows the true woman in her. The portrait she has given of herself as Jo in "Little Women" is not to be taken too literally. Like Thackeray in "Pendennis" she has purposely left out the noble side of her nature,—for indeed that was only disclosed at rare intervals and for those who had eyes to see. She had the strongest features of the family, and a quick decisive manner which was sometimes mistaken for arrogance.

Louisa and her sister Annie (now Mrs. Pratt) were excellent actresses, and were always in demand when private theatricals were on foot. To see them perform in the "Two Buzzards" with her sister and F. B. Sanborn was a treat of the first order. I can hear Louisa now saying, "Brother Benjamin, brother Benjamin!" in a scene of which all the rest is gone from my memory. Another favorite *rôle* of hers was Dickens' character of Sarah Gamp in the nocturnal interview with her friend Betsy Prig. As Mrs. Jarley exhibiting her wax tableaux she was inimitable. She did it with a snap. Once she was called upon to assist at an entertainment given at the house of the village blacksmith: she invented a charade which was both novel and appropriate. She arranged her father to look like the Boston statue of Franklin—and the resemblance was a very striking one—and then came in with another gentleman in a travelling dress, and surveyed and criticized him. When she said, "He seems to have rather a brassy expression," Mr. Alcott could scarcely hold his face. This was the first part: the second consisted of the scene from the "Two Buzzards" already mentioned, and for the third a witty dialogue about Mr. Sanborn's school. As more than half of the audience was composed of Mr. Sanborn's pupils this charade produced a great effect.

Her acting had this peculiarity, that she seemed to always to be herself and the character she was representing at the same time. This is the case also with some professional actors and actresses, notably with Madame Ristori and Edwin Booth: but it is not the finest kind of acting.

The anti-slavery conflict and the civil-war with which it ended appealed strongly to her ardent and sympathetic nature; and this finally resulted in her enlisting as a nurse to tend the wounded soldiers. Her lively and picturesque "Hospital Sketches" written at Washington for the "Boston Commonwealth" are the echo of this period. Very few passed through that crisis without bearing the scars of it for life, and the fever which Louisa Alcott contracted in the camp sapped her vitality and probably shortened her days. She was one of the veterans, and deserved a pension.

While she was convalescing she said to a friend who condoled with her on her misfortunes, "The loss of my hair was the worst of it" (this had been cut off by order of the doctor); "I felt as if that were a disgrace." When some one asked her how she amused herself she replied, "I think out sketches of stories and put them away in little pigeon-holes in my brain for future use."

On the Fourth of July 1864 there was an evening-party at the house of Hon. E. R. Hoar, and nearly at the close of it Miss Alcott came to me with a humorous twinkle in her eye and said: "A few of us are going to have a picnic to-morrow at Conantum"—a picturesque bluff owned by one Conant, about three miles up the river—"and Mrs. Austin and I have engaged a boat for the occasion and are now looking for a muscular heathen to row it. Will you come?" Nothing could have pleased me better; so next morning we all started in the best of spirits. There was however a head wind, the boat was without a rudder, and the Concord River is very crooked. I think Miss May Alcott was also in the party. I found it terribly hard rowing, and finally exclaimed, "This is the darnedest boat I ever pulled." "Frank," said Louisa, "never say darn. Much better to be profane than vulgar. I had rather live in hell than in some places on earth. Strong language, but true. Here, take some cold tea." She had a claret-bottle full of this beverage, and gave me a good drink of it. Her vigorous piece of common-sense was also very refreshing, and Conantum being now in sight, Miss Alcott and her sister insisted on landing at the next bridge, leaving Mrs. Austin and myself to continue the way alone. Unluckily there was no one now to care for the bottle of cold tea, and rolling about in the stern of the boat the cork came out and the tea was spilled. This was a severe loss to Miss Alcott who was not yet strong enough for an all-day picnic, and when I explained it to her she said, "Don't talk to me. I know you college-boys. That cork never came out by accident. You drank the tea yourself, and now in what way I am going to punish you for it I cannot tell." With such biting humor she partly relieved and partly concealed her just vexation.

Characteristic writers are commonly the last to be appreciated, and Miss Alcott's first novel did not meet with an encouraging reception from the public. Some tender critics even complained that the story was subversive of conservative morality. "I cannot help that," Louisa remarked in her emphatic manner, "I did not make morality or human nature, and am not responsible for either: but people who are given to moods act as I have described; sometimes they like one person and sometimes another." Perhaps she was thinking not so much of moody natures as of those contradictory characters who have inherited the traits of very dissimilar ancestors. She wrote another novel which she herself liked much better and had great hopes of, which was lost in some miraculous way by her publisher Mr. Fields. He paid her for it what many people would consider a handsome compensation—exactly the sum that Stuart Mill paid Carlyle for burning up the first volume of his "French Revolution"—but it was a trying affair for both sides. How so bulky an object as a novel in manuscript could have been lost without its falling into the hands of some person who knew what to do with it, is most difficult to imagine.

That so many of the world's benefactors are doomed to incalculable torments here on earth may be a good argument for immortality, but for Divine Providence it is no better evidence than the Lisbon earthquake which so startled the optimists and thinking men of the last century. There is no telling why this is so; for misfortune falls upon the just as well as the unjust, and often no human foresight can prevent it. Louisa Alcott supposed that she was nearly well of her fever when inflammatory-rheumatism set in. The worst of this was the loss of sleep which it occasioned. Long continued wakefulness is a kind of nervous cremation, and resembles in its physical effect the perpetual drop of water on the head with which the Spanish inquisitors used to torment their heretics. Any mental agitation makes the case very much worse, and it requires great self-control to prevent this. It was melancholy to behold her at that time. Her pallid face, the dark rings about her eyes, and her dreary, hopeless expression might have penetrated the most obdurate heart. "I don't suppose it is going to kill me" she said, "but I shall never get over it.

I go to bed at nine o'clock and think steadily of the wood-box in order to keep my mind from more serious subjects."

It is not always darkest before dawn, especially when the moon is on its last quarter, but happily it was so in this instance. Three years later she was in much better health, and had published "Little Women." First the young people read it; then their fathers and mothers; and then the grandparents read it. Grave merchants and lawyers meeting on their way down town in the morning said to each other, "Have you read 'Little Women'"; and laughed as they said it. The clerks in my office read it, so also did the civil engineer, and the boy in the elevator. It was the rage in '69 as "Pinafore" was in '78. It was re-published in London,—a rare compliment for a book of its kind.

Rumors of this unusual success had reached the little household in Concord and filled their home with pleasant expectations; but they had no idea of the extent of it. The evening papers announced on the night before Christmas that Miss Alcott's publishers had sent her that day a very large cheque. There were many glad hearts at this news beside those in the Alcott family; where, I fancy, tears and prayers were not wanting to complete the sacrament. The long struggle was ended, and peace and rest had come at last. Louisa had won a glorious victory, and the laurel wreath was on her brow.

The style of "Little Women" is not classic; but as Goldsmith says in his preface to the "Vicar of Wakefield," "It matters not." It filled a vacant place in American and perhaps also in English literature, and must continue to fill it. Novelists usually take up their characters at the age of twenty-one, or somewhere in the twenties, and there have also been many excellent books written for children; but to describe the transition period between fifteen and twenty there had not as yet been anything adequate—if we partially except Thomas Hughes' sketches of life at Rugby and Oxford. It is a period of life which deserves much more consideration than it often receives. It is the integrating period, during which we make our characters and form those habits of thought and action which mainly determine our destiny. The bloom of youth may conceal this internal conflict, but it is there none the less, and frequently a very severe one. "You have no idea how many trials I have," I once heard a schoolgirl of sixteen say, the perfect picture of health and happiness; and those who remember well their own youth will not be inclined to laugh at this. The tragedy of childhood is the commonest form of tragedy; and youth is a melodrama in which pathos and humor are equally mingled. Those who by some chance have escaped this experience and have had the path of early life made smooth for them, may grow to be thrifty trees but are not likely to bear much fruit. It is for her clear perception of these conditions and her skill and address in dealing with them that Miss Alcott deserves the celebrity that is now attached to her name. Her simple pictures of domestic country life are drawn with a firm and confident hand. They stand out in strong relief, and take their color from her own warm-hearted womanly nature. Her characters act unconsciously before us as if we looked at them through a window. In American fiction "Little Women" holds the next place to the "Scarlet Letter" and "Marble Faun."

There is one of Boccaccio's stories which differs so much from the others in closeness of statement and fulness of detail that it is judged to have been an experience of his own. As the critics say, he knew too much about his subject: Louisa Alcott wisely avoided this error. Her characters are always real, but,—in her best work at least,—not realistic. There are people in natural life, full of peculiarities, whom it would take pages to describe, while others can be hit off in a few sentences. Miss Alcott knew that characters of a few simple traits were best suited to her purpose; and she was too good an artist to imitate her model. Her impersonation of herself as Jo was pretty near the truth, but Beth, Amy, and Meg only resemble her sisters in a very general way. If the book were more of a biography it would not be good fiction. Some of the incidents in it were taken from her own or the family experiences, but more are either imaginary or conventional. It is said that her primary intention was to leave Jo in a state of single blessedness, and that Roberts Brothers fairly declined to publish the second volume unless she was married off to somebody. Thus originated the episode of the German Professor, one of the best in the story. Laurie was supposed to have been taken from Julian Hawthorne, because he lived in the next house and was rather an attractive kind of boy. Louisa herself said there was no ground for this: and yet Laurie seems to me a good deal like him.

I remember meeting her at the Radical club in Boston in January 1868, and her drawing me into a corner where she told me that she was writing a book for young people and would like to know about the game of cricket. This fixes the time pretty closely when "Little Women" was begun. She was frequently to be seen at the meetings of the Radical club, afterwards called the Chestnut Street club, where her father was one of the leading members. She did not care for lectures, but greatly enjoyed listening to the discussion of learned and thoughtful men. It was an era of large designs and great mental activity; and in such periods the best literary work is always accomplished. Once she said (in her father's presence), "It requires three women to take care of a philosopher, and when the philosopher is old the three women are pretty well used up." But at another time she said, "To think of the money I make by writing this trash, while my father's words of immortal wisdom only bring him a little celebrity." She honored her father, and lived more for him than for anybody else, including herself.

Her journey through Europe was like a triumphal procession. Doors were opened to her everywhere; not the palace of the Rothschilds or the apartments of the ex-Queen of Naples, but those of distinguished artists and literary people. Mr. Healy, the best American painter in Rome, requested permission to paint her portrait. This she consented to, and was rather surprised when he afterwards presented it to her. "I wondered," she said while we were looking at the picture, "what was going to come next; when one day Mr. Healy's daughter appeared with a novel in manuscript which she wished I would give an opinion of. I found it to be good and sent it to my London publisher, who happily published it for her." Posterity ought to be grateful for Healy's little manoeuvre.

The same attentions followed her on her return to Boston; but she did not care for them. She had learned that the satisfaction of good work is the only one which we never have to regret. She was busy with plans for the future, considering especially how she might order and arrange her affairs for the benefit of her family. Ladies whose names she had never heard, came in fine carriages and sent in their cards to her. This amused her very much. "I don't care who their grandfathers and grandmothers were," she said. "John Hancock was my great-great-grandfather, but nobody ever came to see me on his account." If she had leisure she received them; otherwise not. In her next novel, the "Old Fashioned Girl," she introduces herself with the name of Katie King, and says to her young friends: "Beware of popularity; it is a delusion and a snare; it puffeth up the heart of man, and just as one gets to liking the taste of this intoxicating draught, it suddenly faileth."

When "Little Men" was published a rather censorious critic complained that Miss Alcott's boys and girls had no very good manners, and made some inquiry after the insipid "Rollo" books which were in circulation forty years ago. It is true their manners are not of the best, but they are the Concord manners of that period. Were they otherwise they would not be true to life. Very few boys and girls of sixteen have fine manners; and even after they have acquired the art of good behavior in company they continue to act in quite a different fashion towards each other. What else can we expect of them? Exactly the same objection has been made to "School Days at Rugby"; and when some one complained of Goethe that the characters in "Wilhelm Meister" did not belong to good society he replied in verse, "I have often been in society called 'good,' from which I could not obtain an idea for the smallest poem."

Concord was large enough for Thoreau, but not for Louisa Alcott. She had no proclivity for paddling up and down Concord River in search of ideas. She had a broad cosmopolitan mind, and the slow routine of a country-town was irksome to her. She did not care for nature; and the great world was not too large a field of observation for her. Even in Rome she preferred the living image of a healthy bambino to the statue of the gladiator who has been dying in marble for so many centuries. She loved the society of people who were abreast of the times, who could give her fresh thought and valuable information. The books she read were of the most vigorous description. When some one asked her if she had read Mallock's "New Republic" she replied, "I do not read contemporary writers; only Emerson and the classics." "Louisa," said I, "you speak to my soul." "Do I?" said she, with a tenderness of feeling such as I had never noticed before. Her attachments were strong; but her resentments were of long duration.

From *Sketches from Concord and Appledore* (New York: Putnam's, 1895), pp. 69–88.

"When Louisa Alcott Was a Girl" (1898)

EDWARD W. EMERSON

The fourth and youngest child of Ralph Waldo Emerson, Edward was born in 1844. As a youth, he attended Sanborn's Concord academy. Frail health kept him from joining the Union army during the Civil War. He graduated from Harvard College in 1866 and then Harvard Medical College in 1874. That same year, Edward, returning to Concord to practice medicine, married Annie Shepard Keyes, daughter of one of Concord's leading citizens, John S. Keyes. After his father died in 1882, Edward began a career as a writer and speaker. A painter himself, he also served as an instructor at the Boston Museum of Fine Arts. He died in Concord in 1930. He is best known for his writings about his father and others in the Transcendentalist circle, such as *Henry Thoreau as Remembered by a Young Friend* (1917) and *Emerson in Concord* (1889). He also edited the centenary edition of *The Collected Works of Ralph Waldo Emerson* (12 vols.) in 1903–4.

Four years May Alcott's junior, Edward, of all the people who published reminiscences of Louisa May and her family, probably knew them the best. They had returned, after the Fruitlands disaster, to Concord in the year of his birth, and by the time Edward was thirteen years old, the Alcotts were firmly planted at Orchard House. Coming late in his own life and after the deaths of the immediate Alcott family, Edward's account, however, appears somewhat reserved, treating what he calls "this remarkable family" with the respect and dignity of a longtime friend. Despite this reverence, Edward's depiction of the Alcotts' family life illustrates why *Little Women* was and continues to be acclaimed. He pulls back the curtains of the March/Alcott home, allowing readers to experience the real "little women" growing up. The love, closeness, creativity, and fun depicted in these scenes would make anyone want to be a part of it. His recollections, along with those of Julian Hawthorne, provide a view of the Alcotts over a wide range of time that is unequaled by others who wrote about them.

In the year 1840 a remarkable family moved to Concord; high-minded, culti-vated, exceedingly poor, despised by most persons, welcomed by one or two; apparently so ill fitted to fight the world's fight that failure was sure. Yet they won, in the end, respect, recognition, success, and their name is honor-ably associated with that of the town.

The head of that family, Amos Bronson Alcott, began life as a peddler, but a call came so strongly to him, like that which Jesus gave to certain poor fishers to become teachers of a better life than they found, that he felt justified in obeying the Master's command to them: "Take no thought, saying, What shall we eat? or, What shall we drink? or, Wherewithal shall we be clothed?"

Mr. Alcott began to teach in a better sense than the schools of New En-gland then recognized. He appealed to the intellect, the conscience, the imagination, discovering for himself methods that advanced teachers strive to introduce to-day, held to these at a loss, and finally had his Boston school wrecked and was himself almost mobbed for being in advance of his day. In his school and later, on a day of public shame, he bravely espoused, even at the risk of influence and of life, the cause of the poor slaves.

It is of his family that I am to tell here, but their extraordinary nurture and home surroundings must be known to rightly value their interesting person-alities and their life together. From that life the best of lessons may be read, which may be helpful alike to those who in their youth had trials and oppor-tunities like theirs, and to those who have every advantage which they had not. In the glimpses that I shall give of this family this point is best worth heeding: that with beliefs, tastes and aims differing so widely as to make do-mestic harmony seem impossible, courage, respect for each other and love won the day, and kept father, mother and children a united family, and if with suffering, also with happiness. After the loss of his school Mr. Alcott brought his noble wife (a sister of Samuel May, justly called one of the Heralds of Free-dom) and his four little children to Concord. He gardened, let himself out for day's work to farmers, and gave conversations as opportunity offered. Be-cause of poverty, and also of his brave attempt, in a world not bred to Golden Age methods, to revive that blameless life, and live on the herb of the soil and the fruit of the tree, with water from the spring; and clothe the body in linen wrought from the blue-flowered flax, not murdering, robbing nor enslaving the animals, nor yet becoming partners in human slavery by the use of sugar, spice and cotton — all stimulants whatever were also forborne — their house-keeping was not easy for the wife to manage, and alarmingly frugal for a cold

zone. The conditions of family life were hard. As a compensation its simplicity saved time for purposes that were worth while. Mrs. Alcott made it a
rule to rise early enough in the morning to get through all the work in the
forenoon, so that after dinner was cleared away she should have a long afternoon to devote to her children. She meant that life should be rich enough in
the gifts that the woods, the flowers, the skies, stories and games and poems
had for them to make up for what they had not, so that poverty should not
darken their young lives. She was not only loving and sympathetic, but she
had a well-stored, fertile mind. From her they learned to depend on themselves for good times, and their imaginations were quickened.

.Louisa when very young used to tell fairy stories to my sister in the woods,
and later wrote others and sent them to her. These were gathered in her first
book, "Flower Fables." A great taste for acting and skill in devising and pro-
ducing wonderful romantic plays soon showed itself. Love, despair, witch-
craft, villainy, fairy intervention, triumphant right, held sway in turn. In
those days a red scarf, a long cloak, a big hat with a plume stolen from a bonnet, a paper-knife dagger, a scrap of tinsel from a button-card, a little gold
paper for Royalty, tissue paper stretched on wire hoops for fairy wings,
produced superb effects. Sheets pinned on the clothesline, a clotheshorse,
a sarsenet-cambric curtain, a few little pine trees in stands, supplemented
by proper common-sense in the audience, would give castles, enchanted
forests, caves and ladies' bowers. Barns, because of their well-known possi-
bilities for desperate but safe leaps from beams, and the advantages for dis-
appearance offered by mangers, were the first theatres. The zeal of the
mother in helping on her children's little plans appears in a touching sentence
in a story of Louisa's, where she describes the preparation for a school masquerade such as we had later. The fathers might grudge expense, "But the
mothers, whose interest in their children's pleasure is a sort of evergreen that
no frost of time can kill, sewed spangles by the bushel, made wildernesses of
tissue-paper blossom as the rose, kept tempers sweet, stomachs full, and domestic machinery working smoothly through it all by that maternal magic
which makes them the human Providences of this naughty world."

From tragedy and melodrama the girls were led to comedy by the delights
of Dickens, and thereafter they especially shone in dramatized bits of his
work. As they grew up they fully appreciated the humorous side of the
strange specimens, communists, anti-money and anti-marriage men, sun-
believers and the like, who came to their door and tarried for a time, for

[91]

Mr. Alcott had a most catholic hospitality. It was especially at Fruitlands, a Golden Age community of philosophers that wilted at winter's first frost (by no means golden, however, for poor Mrs. Alcott), that these pilgrims gathered. Thence the family, with fortunes at lowest ebb, returned to Concord, but left it in 1848 and lived for a time in Boston, and then in Walpole, New Hampshire; but Anna and Louisa tried their fortunes as teachers in Syracuse and Boston, and so saw something of the world.

In the autumn of 1857 the Alcotts returned to Concord, but in sadness, for Lizzie, the good girl of whom one of her playmates lately spoke to me as "all conscience," was fading away after an attack of scarlet fever in Walpole, where her mother had gone to the aid of a poor family afflicted with the dreadful sickness, to see that the children were not neglected. The loss of their daughter, the following spring, was, as has been well said, "the result of one of those generous acts which the Alcotts performed as constantly and as inevitably as most persons perform acts of self-interest."

At that time Mr. Sanborn's school had lately been established in Concord, which brought to town a bright company of boys and girls who were cordially received as school and play mates by those of the village. The young and brilliant master did much more than teach, for he tried to make his scholars' lives rich by all sorts of wholesome and helpful outdoor and indoor amusements. He also strove to interest them in the poetry and literature of the past, and equally in the stirring events of that exciting time when the struggle for the possession of the new states, Kansas and Nebraska, between the parties of Freedom and Slavery, and later the John Brown raid at Harper's Ferry, were rapidly bringing on the war which turned the scale for liberty. How popular that school was may be judged from the fact that, though the master was an open disciple of Theodore Parker, then regarded even by liberal churches as a dangerous subverter of religion, it counted among its pupils, besides the Concord contingent, boys and girls from Boston and its suburbs, from the farming towns around them, a Sandwich Island girl, a California boy, a daughter of advanced Philadelphia Quakers, sons of a Swedenborgian philosopher, of Missouri and Kentucky slaveholders, of a leading Kansas Free-State man, and a Baltimore fire-eater.

The Alcotts had bought a small piece of land, and a farmhouse, once good, but fallen into decay, on the "Great Road" to Boston, a mile east of the village. They made some repairs and a small addition, greatly improving its appearance, and moved into it the following summer. The situation was extremely picturesque. It was backed by a range of hills clothed in the rich green of pines relieved by a tracery of gray birch. A superb elm served as a great parasol in summer, and besides there were apple trees, pink and white in May, and red and yellow in September, which commended the place to the fruit-loving father, who called it Orchard House. In front, between the house and the wooded hills about Walden, stretched a broad meadow, said to have been an ancient bed of Concord River. A charming wood path led up a little pass among the hills behind the house, sweet with the hot breath of pine. Mr. Alcott's hands, unaided but by taste and skill, greatly beautified the place by a little terracing of the sunny slope here and there, the planting of woodbine on the porch, and the building, out of sticks cut on the place, of a rustic fence and gates, a seat around the spurs of the elm by the door, and pretty arbors and trellises out of gnarled pitch-pine boughs, over which the Concord grapevines should run, giving fragrance twice a year, fruit once, and grace all the time. Thus a far more charming effect was produced than could have been obtained with beds shaped like palm-leaves and crescents with a Turkish-rug pattern in red-leaved plants, surrounded by white, and yellow, and speckled foliage suggesting disease, blight, and even reptiles.

Appropriateness is a greater factor in beauty than is often considered — that is, harmony of furnishings and adornment with the surroundings and with the means and character of the people. So when, delighted with the real beauty of the yard, one was bid enter the unpretentious house, the effect of the rooms was unusually pleasing. A lady who remembered well their home in the days of their extreme poverty after the collapse of the Fruitlands community, said that "Even then the Alcotts' rooms were distinguished looking." Mrs. Alcott had sense and taste and was a woman of expedients. What was the secret of the pleasant effect produced on the guests on entering? First, there was light and air; second, there was rest for the eye instead of confusion; third, the things were for use for body and spirit — the furniture being plain and unpretentious, the few engravings, drawings and woodcuts good in subject and interesting, the books classics or else individual in character, and showing use. To give a few details: each window did not have two kinds of curtains, cords and tassels involved, besides shutters, wire nettings and blinds — seven lines of fortification against sun and air! The trees outside tempered the light, the blinds could help at need, and pretty muslin curtains, made out of old party dresses, did the rest. The fireplaces were for use, and not of polished tiles still virgin of the fire, which can give more adornment and cheer to a room than any furnishing. On the humble wooden mantelpiece May Alcott painted a motto, and on the summer fireboard drew Moses with the tables of the Law.

The daughters bravely did the painting of the rooms, May's copies of Halman's outlines of goddesses and heroes giving surprise and pleasure as one encountered them here and there on panel or beam or staircase. The girls also did the papering, using cheap, plain papers of quiet tints, which showed the pictures off to best advantage. The fussiness of infinite tidies, draperies, rugs, knots of ribbons and wall pockets was not there, neither did one find a spinning-wheel with an expensive ribbon around the flax next to an afternoon tea-table, a suit of armor by a hat-tree, nor Old World cooking utensils of brass in the library. Mr. Alcott's library, with its box-shelves containing in humble form the best thoughts of the world, its fireplace, plain writing-table and easy-chair, its few plaster heads of the great teachers, and strange old engravings of the wise men, looked the proper home for the benignant, silver-haired philosopher who was its greatest ornament. May's little room over the back porch, where the grapevine swung its shoots across the window, was femininely pretty and interesting, yet the effects were produced by the most inexpensive means, and on the plaster and paint she gave her pencil and brush all the liberty they cried for, as the artistic craving of her nature was now asserting itself.

Louisa, at this time twenty-five years old, wrote to a friend, "I have plans simmering, but must sweep and dust, and wash my dish-pans till I see my way." The plans, after long years of patient labor, fulfilled themselves in stories in which the very hardships and sacrifices, the growth of character, and victories over self and circumstances of the family in their early days, humanly told by her and a little changed for art's sake and propriety's, reached and moved thousands of readers, won comfort for her family, and fame and love for herself. But that all came a little later.

The Alcott girls, self-helpful, kindly and bright, came among the young people of Concord, and made themselves felt at once. But they helped their good mother and did their part at home, and however little the girls followed their father's philosophical flights or grahamite and vegetarian practices (which after they grew up they abandoned) they were a loving and loyal family. On one occasion, Mr. Alcott probably being away, a friend who called to see him found the girls shoveling in a ton of coal to the cellar. They did not flinch nor apologize for their unusual work, but said with pretended boastfulness, "See what vegetables will do. It's all vegetables!"

One evening a few months after their return to Concord, my sister and I accompanied our mother on a call on the Alcotts. Mr. Alcott was in the study, but we were cordially received by his wife, and the girls were summoned. Louisa was fine looking, had the most regular features of the family, and very handsome, wavy brown hair like her mother's. She had always a rather masculine air and a twinkle woke constantly in her eye at the comic side of things, a characteristic that carries many persons through hard experiences that crash or sour others. Her talk was always full of little catches from her favorite Dickens. I remember that her assent always took the form of "Barkis is willin'." Anna, the eldest, was plain, but so friendly and sweet-tempered a person that the beauty of expression made up for the lack of it in her features; but she had a quick sense of humor, without the ingredient of tartness that Louisa's sometimes had. Anna had a wonderful dramatic gift. May, the youngest, the darling of the family (Amy of the stories), was a tall, well-made blonde, the lower part of her face irregular, but she had beautiful blue eyes and brilliant yellow hair. She was overflowing with spirits and energy, danced well, and rode recklessly whenever she could, by rare chance, come by a saddle-horse for an hour.

Before we left, Louisa was persuaded by her mother to do something for our amusement. She disappeared and soon came in transformed. Her hair, which girls in those days wore brushed low and braided, was twisted up into a little knob on her head so tight that she could hardly wink. The broad collar, white undersleeves and hoopskirt of the day were gone, and she appeared in an ugly, scant, brown calico dress, with bloomer trousers to match, blue stockings and coarse shoes. She had a manuscript in one hand, and a pen in the other, which she thrust behind her ear and began a harangue on the "Rights of Woman," and offered and at once proceeded to read in strident tones a gem of thought which she had just turned out, called "Hoots of a Distracted Soul in the Wilderness." She then passed on to other confirmatory manuscripts that she professed to be editing—travesties on her father's writings, I think—certainly on those of my father under the name of Rolf Walden Emerboy. Mr. Alcott came in from his study to hear, and however little he could understand such manifestations of the spirit of prophecy, he seemed to feel the pride of a parent in his daughter's wit. All that I recall is the fragment of a chorus of a pæan of reform:

"Then bang the field-piece! toot the fife!
And pound the rolling drum!" etc.

Anna and May Alcott soon came to take drawing lessons at Mr. Sanborn's school, and their talent and experience in acting soon came into request. The master arranged that his scholars should meet every Friday evening through the winter term in the schoolroom, or, if necessary, in a small hall, to have a good time. Every other week we could have a dance, with early hours, no dressing up, no refreshments, the music furnished for a trifling fee by the odd and gifted ex-turnkey of the county jail, who played by ear, calling the figures smartly, and stopping short to severely correct any mistake of the dancers in cotillons, reels, "Portland Fancy," "Steamboat Quickstep," "All the Way to Boston," "Hull's Victory" and "Ladies' Triumph." The german was then hardly known in cities, and even in a liberal town like Concord the waltz was considered hardly a delicate performance, and of those who would brave public sentiment few were steady-headed enough to long continue the waltz of those days—a teetotem-spinning around the room without reversing, to the tune of "Buy a Broom." But the romping contra-dances were immensely enjoyed. On the alternate evening we had a short lecture on some literary or scientific subject, and then tableaux, charades or plays, and a great school masquerade once in the winter.

But in 1858 more ambitious theatricals were undertaken by a dramatic club of teachers, scholars and outsiders. Mr. George Bartlett was actor and manager; later he became well known from the Penobscot to the Potomac and Mississippi for his skill and taste in getting up amateur performances (which brought in thousands of dollars for the care of sick and wounded soldiers in the war, and for other good ends) with the material at hand plus mother-wit; also remembered for his hospitalities on Concord River. He was great in "Poor Pillicoddy," "The Two Buzzards," "Old Honesty," and as Mr. Bumble the beadle in the Dickens scenes, in which the Alcotts shone, Louisa as Tilly Slowboy or Sairey Gamp; Anna as Betsey Prig, but far better in the affecting part of Dot in "The Cricket on the Hearth." If Louisa could make our sides ache with laughter, Anna could cause handkerchiefs to come out and much swallowing of lumps in the throat. Poetical prologues, written for the occasion by the schoolmaster, introduced these plays with references to the town, the season and the stirring events of the times. Christmas and Yule were personified, and Columbia said her say in appropriate guise.

To keep the audience good-natured in the long waits that go with private theatricals, tableaus were introduced by George Bartlett—"The Game of Life," "Macbeth and the Witches," "Titania, Bottom and Puck," "Rebecca and Rowena"—and when there was a hitch his fertile mind, from properties close at hand, could add "The Belle of the School" (how eagerly we boys looked to see who would be chosen), or "The Flower of the Family," or "Cain and Abel"—by the brazen instrument that summoned us in after recess, a flour barrel, or a walking-stick combined with the former. Nearly all the admirable extempore amusements that Mr. Bartlett afterward described in his book were first proved among the Concord young people. Their recommendation, apart from their wit, was the absolute simplicity of the means used. But it is hard to imagine young people having better fun than we did with no expense or a very trifling cost. At the pleasant house of Doctor Bartlett, the heroic old country doctor, his bright sons and daughters and a small company of friends would cap verses, write animal alphabets, extemporize amazing charades in the easy form of "Dumb Crambo," and then, a subject being given, turn out most amusing "poems" in half an hour.

The evenings at the Alcotts' house have also left delightful memories. Although these involved a long walk, the bait was good enough to draw the girls and boys often. The hearty and motherly quality of Mrs. Alcott's welcome was something to remember. The too prevalent custom—in bad taste, too—of young girls at once retiring with their callers into a room apart from the others, was never practiced there. There was a piano, by no means too good to use, and May, in highest spirits, would swoop to the stool, and all would fall to dancing, the mother herself often joining us. One of the guests would relieve May, who then had her gay turn. Then, with or without voices, we stood by the piano and sang "Rolling Home," "Ubi sunt, O pocula," "Juanita," "Music in the Air," and "John Brown," "Marching Along," and other stirring songs fresh from the camp. Short stories on the porch might follow as twilight deepened into dark, and they were sufficiently "creepy." Perhaps chestnuts, Rhode Island greenings or Northern spies ended the evening and we went home by ten at the latest.

This was the epoch when Dr. Dio Lewis had introduced a calisthenic revival, and his classes gave great sport, in which children and elders took part.

Matches of pin-running, or, much better, of bean-bag tossing and passing between two carefully chosen sides, had passed from the classes to private houses, and were wildly exciting. We never played cards on these occasions, and let it be said that in those days to play for a prize was unheard of. We played for fun, the best of prizes, and thus there was no unwholesome excitement.

The school masquerade has been mentioned, but it was discovered that an absolutely simple and inexpensive form of this, less gay to the eye but hardly less picturesque, was even better fun and more puzzling. This was a party in which boys and girls, and men and women, came draped exactly alike in a white sheet, a white cloth with eye-slits over the face, and a pillowcase pinned tight around the scalp, entirely concealing the hair, the long end hanging down behind — a jolly entertainment, indeed.

One more picture of old times is so pleasant in memory as to call for a record. After the breaking up of the celebrated Brook Farm community two high-minded members, who, as workers and not drones, had sunk much of their property in the venture, settled in Concord and lived the rest of their days on a farm there. These were Minot Pratt and his wife. Their son, a bright and kindly young man, had acted with Anna Alcott, in "The Loan of a Lover," a charming little play but known to lead to serious results to one who takes the part of the lover, a slow, Dutch peasant, if the leading lady's part is well acted. It was so in this case, and led to a very happy marriage. Mr. Pratt, Senior, should be long remembered for the beautiful service he secretly did to this town. It was this: whenever he could spare a day from the farm he went afoot or in his wagon to some town where grew a flower which we had not, and set it out in some out-of-the-way spot in Concord wood or meadow. It is said that he increased our flora by some hundred varieties by this original beneficence. One beautiful evening under the September moon Mr. and Mrs. Pratt summoned the Concord young people to their farm for a husking. We worked gayly at the piles of bleached gold leaves and stalks to get out the livelier gold within, the lanterns shining above, and the cows beside creaking their stanchions. After an hour we passed across the moonlit yard, under the most beautiful elm in Middlesex, into the house, where we washed our hands and brushed our clothes, and were then invited into the kitchen to supper by our hostess. There was a long table with a white cloth. In the centre in a shining milk-pan was a mountain of white-blossomed popcorn, flanked by candles placed in sockets cut in the small ends of huge orange carrots. Next were baskets of apples, crimson and yellow and green, round towers of brown bread and fragrant soft gingerbread, with fresh cheese near by. Then there were candelabras made of inverted multiplex rutabagas, and here and there gleamed the tanned, yellow faces of pumpkin pies. The room was decorated with autumn leaves, probably scarlet and yellow maple, and blue gentians and asters.

I have thought that in these days, when the tendency of life in America is to become more complicated, not only in business but in household life and amusements, it might be well to call up some pleasant pictures of the past that may have a lesson. Great pleasure may be had very simply and cheaply. Good nature, self-help, mother-wit and independence are such good ingredients that a cake baked with them is safe to turn out well. Riches must not set the pace for us all, for they are confined to a small number, and these change. We cannot all begin where our fathers left off. The family whose beautiful life I celebrate first made themselves happy in adversity by their methods, and later hundreds of others. One trait remains which I have hardly emphasized enough. I have never known a family which equaled the Alcotts in generosity, even in their poverty. Later, when better times came, mainly by Louisa's devoted work, whatever they had they gladly shared. When May at last was able to begin serious work in art her time and her materials were always at the service of others who often could well afford both better. More than this, her enthusiasm was contagious. During her last stay in Concord before her going abroad, where she married, and a year later died, two sculptors who afterward became eminent, and some painters, were helped by her advice, but more by her eager zeal, at the outset of their work.

Ladies' Home Journal 14 (December 1898): 15–16.

[Reminiscences of "Laurie"] (1901 and 1902)

Alfred Whitman

After the success of *Little Women*, readers soon learned that the work had been based upon Alcott's family. Hundreds of children wrote Alcott, asking her to reveal the identity of the real "Laurie." For a number of years afterward, Alcott said that she had conceived the character of Laurie from a young Polish man, Ladislas Wisniewski, whom she had met in Vevey, Switzerland, in 1865. Other Concord boys, most notably Julian Hawthorne, often claimed to be the basis of the character. But in a letter of 6 January 1869 to Alfred Whitman, called "Alf" by the Alcott sisters, Louisa confessed: "'Laurie' is you & my Polish boy 'jintly.' You are the sober half & my Ladislas . . . is the gay whirligig half" (*Selected Letters*, 120). But it would be almost forty years before Whitman revealed this fact in the *Ladies' Home Journal*.

Whitman, born in Cambridge in 1842, was motherless when he attended Sanborn's academy in 1857. Staying at the home of Minot Pratt, a former member of the Transcendentalist utopian experiment, Brook Farm, Whitman, despite spending only a year in Concord, became a close friend to the Alcott girls, especially Louisa. By the fall of 1858, Whitman was on his way to Lawrence, Kansas, where his father had begun a farm four years earlier. He served in the Civil War and married Mary Brown in 1867. Interestingly, her father had also been a member of Brook Farm. After spending a few years in Louisville, Kentucky, Whitman returned to Kansas in 1883, working in real estate and insurance until his death in 1907.

In the first volume of *Aunt Jo's Scrap-Bag: My Boys* (1871), Louisa described him as "proud and cold and shy to other people, . . . but so grateful for sympathy and a kind word" (15–16). In the story, she describes how she had touched the heart of this reserved youth when Whitman had played Dolphus Tetterby to her Sophy in a dramatization of Charles Dickens's *The Haunted Man*. The two corresponded in a number of letters prior to the Civil War, where she often addressed him as "Dolphus" and signed herself "Sophy." In the two articles here, Whitman, in such scenes as Louisa sewing Lizzie's death shroud or performing in the antics of the Concord Dramatic Union, portrays a youthful Louisa May, unencumbered by the trappings of fame or the demands of publishers.

"Miss Alcott's Letters to Her 'Laurie'" (1901)

In the fall of 1857, I, a motherless boy of fifteen, landed in Concord, Massachusetts (a place I knew nothing of except its Revolutionary fame), and was enrolled as a student in the school taught by Mr. Frank B. Sanborn. I became a member of the family of Mr. Minot Pratt. With John, the second son, who had just returned from the West, and with Carrie, his only sister, I formed at once an intimate and lasting friendship, and together John and I paid our first visit to the Alcott family, that had come back to Concord after its various wanderings and experiences. The Alcotts occupied half of a house near the Town Hall, where they remained until after the death of Elizabeth, when they removed for a short time into the Hawthorne cottage, and from there into their new home, Orchard House, or "Apple Slump," as it was christened by Louisa.

In the little house near the Town Hall began the acquaintance which was to bring John Pratt a loving and devoted wife, and to the writer the joy of a lifelong friendship with the Alcotts and the Pratts. So close was this friendship, and so hearty and genuine the way in which I was taken into companionship by these gifted people, that it never occurred to me that all, with the exception of Abby, were at least ten years older than myself, and although I was born and had lived all my days in Massachusetts, the last year of my life in that State seems to have included almost all that has been permanent in my memory of it, and Concord the only place that I think of as home. It is hard for me now to realize that I lived in Concord not quite one year.

It was but a few weeks after school opened when the question of having plays was talked of, and The Concord Dramatic Union was organized with Mr. Sanborn, the three Alcott girls, George B. Bartlett and his brothers Ripley and Ned, Edward and Edith Emerson, Alex. Clarke and others, as members.

The vestry of the Unitarian Church was used by Mr. Sanborn as a classroom, and here we erected a portable stage and gave a series of plays, and dramatized scenes from Dickens that were of a high order of merit, the company being composed of excellent actors. Abby Alcott, the younger sister, at this time was musical director, but later she became the leading lady of the company.

The scenes from Dickens dramatized by Louisa were among the best of the productions. Louisa and Anna Alcott as Sairy Gamp and Betsey Prig were inimitable, and Louisa was greatly given to quoting the language of these two worthies. . . . Louisa's original monologue, "Oronthy Bluggage," was not given in public, but was given occasionally at home, to the intense enjoyment of the fortunate few who were permitted to hear her. . . .

In November, 1858, I left New England for my new home in Kansas. I did not know then, and did not for many years realize fully, what an extremely fortunate boy I was in having gained the good will and affection of such loving friends as those in Concord. Letters from the various members of the Alcott family came to me. Of these letters, those from Louisa were the most inspiring. . . .

Mrs. Cheney, in her introduction to "The Life, Letters and Journal of Miss Alcott," says: "She was not a voluminous correspondent; she did not encourage many intimacies, and she seldom wrote letters except to her family, unless in reference to some purpose she had strongly at heart. Writing was her constant occupation, and she was not tempted to indulge in it as a recreation. Her letters are brief and strictly to the point, but always characteristic in feeling and expression."

. . . [J]ustice has never been done to the sweetest and most attractive side of her nature—her real love for boys, which sprang from the boy nature that was hers in so marked a degree; and how our hearts go out to her as she makes her earnest appeals for a proper recognition of this quality. She always said she ought to have been a boy, and that she could not be was one of the many crosses she had to bear. . . .

"Meg, Jo, Beth and Amy. Told by Laurie" (1902)

To the English boy or girl familiar with such schools as Rugby, Eton, Harrow and others that have existed for centuries, a school like that of Mr. F. B. Sanborn's at Concord, Massachusetts, which flourished for the brief space of eight years and numbered at no time more than from fifty to a hundred scholars, will seem to be scarcely worthy of notice. Yet in spite of its short life this school will occupy a permanent place in the history of American schools, and this for several reasons; among which may be mentioned, that it was located at Concord, which at that time was the home of the most distinguished group of American writers that ever resided in one town. It had for its head a brilliant young teacher who not only conducted the school in a most satisfactory manner, but has since its close made an enviable reputation as a public-spirited citizen, philanthropist and author.

The school was organised in 1855, and in 1857 I found myself numbered among its scholars. I did not at first appreciate the advantages of the school, for I knew absolutely nothing of the celebrated men and women who lived in and near the old town. Had I known what I now know, I could have accumulated a fund of anecdotes that would be of great interest to the literary world, but I was only a school-boy interested mostly in having a good time and entirely unconscious that fortune had smiled upon me in a wonderful way. I soon discovered, however, that in some way or other these new friends were the most companionable people I had ever known; before I knew it, I found myself transformed from a shy, bashful lad, whose relations with older people had mostly been such as to constantly remind him of his youthfulness, into a friend and companion of those who were from ten to twenty years older, but who treated him as an equal and gave him a share in all that they did.

My home at first was with Mr. Minot Pratt, the "Silent Saint" of Concord, father of John Pratt who afterwards married Anna Alcott, and has been immortalised by Louisa Alcott as "John Brooke" in "Little Women." The Pratt home was on a farm a mile or more from the village, and was an ideal home for boys, five or six of whom were members of the family. "Uncle Minot," as everybody called Mr. Pratt, was the personification of meekness and quietness, a man of wonderfully few words, but one whose influence was like the all-pervading warmth of the summer sun. No one could come near this remarkable man without feeling better and more cheerful in spirit—not because of anything he might say, but because of the wonderful power of the silent influence that went out to all who came nigh him. The following incident will illustrate this: The peach crop that year was a large one, and we boys had all we could possibly eat, but a boylike idea took possession of us that it would be a fine adventure to steal some peaches from the orchard; so, in accordance with a carefully devised plan, one morning each of the six boys made some sort of an excuse to leave the breakfast-table one at a time, and making a wide detour of a mile or more we approached the peach orchard, which was not a great way from the house, from the opposite direction. Tramping single file through a cornfield, wet with the morning dew, we came near to the stone wall which enclosed the orchard. From the rear where I was plodding along I called out to the boy leading, just as he stood on the wall ready to jump, "Ed, doesn't your conscience smite you?" and then from the other side of the wall spoke Uncle Minot in his quiet, gentle voice, "Don't you think *I* had better smite you?" He had seen through our carefully-arranged plot and gone over to the orchard to await our coming. What a sheepish lot of boys we were to be sure, as we one by one climbed over the wall! but not one word of censure, not one word of reference to the affair from that time on—there was no need. We had had our lesson, and no scolding, no abuse, no threats, could have made anything like such an impression upon us. The desire for that sort of fun had vanished.

John Pratt, although ten years my senior, took the fifteen-year-old boy into his heart, and treated him as an equal and a chum. He was a cultivated and refined man, gentle and kindly to a marked degree in his outward bearing, and full of love and sympathy for all with whom he came in contact. Together we paid our first visit to the Alcott family, which had just returned to Concord after some years of absence. Here began an acquaintance that brought to him a loving and devoted wife, and to me the rich treasure of a life-long friendship with the members of the Alcott family. Of the two families, the Pratts and the Alcotts, John's two sons—the "Little Men"—his older brother, and May Alcott's daughter, Louisa May Nieriker, are all that survive. At this time the family was complete. Mr. and Mrs. Alcott, Anna, Louisa, Elizabeth, and Abby (the four "Little Women," "Meg," "Jo," "Beth," and "Amy"). It was, with the exception of Elizabeth, a hearty and healthy family, notwithstanding their vegetarian diet. For many years the Alcott family were strict vegetarians, and I was present when Abby, the youngest (Amy), then eighteen, tasted her first meat. Beefsteak had been prescribed by the doctor, and she took it as a medicine—was not sure whether she liked it or not. Louisa wrote me an extremely amusing account of a certain rice pudding, but the letter has been lost, so I cannot give the story in her own words. Rice pudding was her special abomination, but occupied a prominent place in the simple *menu* of the family. This particular pudding, a good large one, had appeared upon the table meal after meal: in her dreams she was haunted by rice puddings of every form and size, that fell upon her from immense heights, or which appeared in all sorts of unexpected places. Finally, in carrying it from the table one day, she tripped, and the rice pudding died a sudden death, and furnished a meal for the cats.

Later the family gave up their vegetarian diet, to which they had adhered faithfully for many years under the strong influence of the father.

It took the romantic lives of Mr. and Mrs. Alcott and their pathetic experiences in trying to carry out their high ideals and at the same time to bring up a family of children, to make Louisa Alcott and "Little Women" possible.

Miss Alcott has portrayed her parents as she has herself and her sisters in "Little Women," but those who knew them both say that their lives were far more romantic than she ever pictured them. Lovers of Miss Alcott will find it a rare pleasure to read the "Life of A. Bronson Alcott," by F. B. Sanborn and W. T. Harris. In Concord, where the best years of Louisa's life were spent, she had for neighbours and friends, men and women whose names are household words in the world of Literature, Art, Science and Religion! Emerson, Thoreau, Ellery Channing, Hawthorne, Garrison, Phillips, Whittier, Lowell, Higginson, Geo. W. Curtis, Theo. Parker, Jas. Freeman Clark, and a host of others, who, while not so well known to the world at large, were fitting comrades for this distinguished company. Mr. Sanborn says: "The simple but romantic life of this village, this family, this circle of friends, gave Louisa Alcott her opportunity as an author, and for this she was indebted not so much to her own studies, or even to her own character, as to the character of her father and mother and the events of their chequered lives. No experience, great or small, elevating or humiliating, through which they passed, was lost upon her; and all went to form that attractive picture which, as drawn by her pen, has made Concord a place of deep interest to myriads of young people."

Mr. Alcott, after completing his college education, began his business life, as was the custom in the early days for Connecticut youths to do, as a peddler, and pursued his vocation in the south, mostly in Virginia and the Carolinas. His gentle bearing and his cultured mind gave him access to the homes of the very best families in those States, where he was treated as a friend and passed much of his spare time in conversation with the gifted and brilliant men and women or among the books in their extensive libraries. To a youth, bred as he had been in the narrow way of a country town in Connecticut, the comparatively elegant and courtly life of these plantations was a graceful and impressive revelation. It was the first school of fine manners (except that which he entered at his mother's knee) in which he was trained.

Mrs. Alcott, Louisa's mother, was a daughter of Col. Joseph May of Boston, and sister of Rev. Samuel J. May. She was a woman of rare talents and distinguished virtues. She was a most loyal wife and devoted mother. To all of her husband's plans for the uplifting of mankind she gave her best efforts, even when the plans must have seemed to her impracticable and visionary. In a letter to her brother, shortly after her marriage, she wrote: "My husband is the personification of modesty and moderation. I am not sure that we shall not blush into obscurity and contemplate into starvation." There were times in after life when this doubt seemed to be on the point of fulfilment; but the end was fortunate, for their gifted daughter, Louisa, had later the proud satisfaction of surrounding her loved parents with every comfort and luxury that they could possibly desire. Mrs. Alcott is said to have been the best writer in the Alcott family, although she never published a book, and perhaps never thought of writing one.

No reader of "Little Women" will ever forget the story of "Beth," told by Louisa with such exquisite sweetness, nor "Jo's" devotion to the dear sister during the long days of her fatal illness; but no written words can convey an adequate idea of the love and care which Louisa ("Jo") lavished upon Elizabeth ("Beth"). During the long evenings of that eventful winter, when John Pratt and I were to be found most of the time in the family circle, Louisa would be backwards and forwards from the upstairs room to which her sister was confined, always full of life and fun, making everybody feel happy and cheerful, yet at all times ready to answer a call from "Lizzie." What a happy group it was, happy in spite of the cloud which hung over it in the thought of the dear one who could not share in the joy and pleasure except as it came to her through others.

This room, small and bare of ornament, was a veritable enchanted palace to the motherless boy whose nature opened in that atmosphere of love and unselfishness like a flower, drinking in the aroma of peace and joy that filled the house. Here we were together, Mr. and Mrs. March, Jo, Meg and Amy, with John Brooke and Laurie — only at that time all those characters were yet to be born in the fertile brain of the noble girl who was the life of the little household. It was only the Alcott family, with its four girls, Anna, Louisa, Elizabeth and Abby, Mr. Alcott, the gentle scholar and philosopher, Mrs. Alcott, the loving, devoted wife and mother. Anna, the oldest, quiet and domestic in her tastes and habits, unselfish if ever there was an unselfish person; Louisa, the brilliant girl who had already begun her career as a writer of stories, who took hold sublimely of life's duties and did the things she least liked — the every-day drudgery of household cares — when her head was full of fancies and her brain busy weaving beautiful thoughts into shape, to some day be put on paper and bring her fame; Abby May, the youngest, the baby and pet of the family, then a young woman of eighteen, lovely in form and character, with a passion for music and drawing, full of vivacity and fond of all sorts of gaiety, destined to gain distinction as a painter, to marry a worthy man, and after a brief period of almost ideal happiness, to pass on to the new life, leaving as a legacy to her dear sister Louisa, a little girl, Louisa May Nieriker. These, with Elizabeth, the invalid sister, are "The Little Women."

How well I remember the bright Sunday morning in March when I stopped on my way to church to inquire about Lizzie. I entered the house without knocking, and as I opened the door of the little sitting-room, found Louisa there alone. She had turned her back to the door as she heard me come in. Before I could speak, she threw down the white garment upon which she was sewing, burst into tears, and with the words, "It is Lizzie's shroud," hurried out of the room. This was forty-five years ago, yet it seems as though it were but yesterday. All readers of "Little Women" remember the account of Beth's death and of Jo's devotion to her till the end came, when "On the bosom where she had drawn her first breath, she quietly drew her last, with no farewell but one loving look, one little sigh."

No account of the Concord days would be complete without some reference to "The Concord Dramatic Union." This organization sprung into being soon after the coming of the Alcott family. The Alcott girls were fond of acting, and Anna and Louisa were exceedingly clever at it. Anna was the best actor of the two, and was a capital comedienne. She would have made a name for herself had she adopted the stage for a profession, as both she and Louisa thought of doing more than once. Louisa was stately and dignified, and played leading parts with a certain dash and fervour that was very effective and pleasing. Abby acted as prompter, and looked after the musical part of the entertainments. Later she played leading parts successfully.

The Dramatic Union numbered among its members Mr. Sanborn, Mr. Geo. B. Bartlett, the Alcott girls, Edward and Edith Emerson (R. W. Emerson's children), and a number of Mr. Sanborn's scholars.

Louisa dramatised many scenes from Dickens, which were acted with great success, and many standard plays were produced. What jolly times we did have with our rehearsals and getting the stage ready, making the scenery and the necessary accessories! And what fun we got out of the numberless little accidents and incidents connected with the preparation and presentation of the plays. Of the scenes from Dickens dramatised by Louisa, the scene from "Martin Chuzzlewit," between Betsy Prig and Sairy Gamp, acted by Louisa and Anna, was one of the best. They were greatly given to quoting from it, and generally called each other *Betsy* and *Sairy*. "The Tetterby Family," from "The Haunted Man," was another that I remember well, because in that I had the honour of playing the part of "Dolphus," with Louisa as "Sophy."

Referring to this in one of her books, Louisa says: "We played Dolphus and Sophia Tetterby in 'The Haunted Man' at one of the school festivals. What fun we had to be sure, acting the droll and pathetic scenes together with a swarm of little Tetterbys skirmishing about us! From that time he has been my Dolphus and I his Sophy, and my yellow-haired laddie don't forget me though he has a younger 'Sophy' now and some small Tetterbys of his own."

In making up the cast for "The Tetterby Family," Mr. Sanborn begged Louisa to let him be one of the children. As he was six feet three inches in height, and as she did not wish to make a burlesque of the play, she very decidedly declined; but he was not to be put off so easily. When the night of the play came, in a scene where the children in their night-gowns swarmed all over the stage, who should come skipping in but Mr. Sanborn in a long white night-gown which stopped several inches short of the bottom of his trousers. As he ran across the stage he pulled the chair from under Ned Bartlett, who took the part of the newsboy and was warming himself at the fire, letting him down upon the stage in no gentle fashion. Ned was on his feet in an instant, and as Mr. Sanborn disappeared from the stage, he gave the retreating figure a realistic kick that evoked a round of applause from the audience.

"The Jacobite" was a favourite play, and in this Louisa played Mrs. Pottle, Anna, Patty Pottle, and John Pratt, John Duck. From being lovers in this play, John and Anna became "sure enough" lovers, and adopted their stage names, Patty Pottle and John Duck, as pet names. . . .

It was by means of these theatricals that I learned to know Louisa Alcott so well. She enjoyed them more than any other form of recreation, and I am sure I could in no better way have gained an insight into the sunny side of her nature. And so also in telling of her love for boys, no words other than her own are needed to show to the thoughtful reader what a wonderful influence she must have exerted over those whom she included among her "boys." She never scolded, and scarcely ever preached, but by the rare quality of her affection and love and by the wonderful power of that *silent* influence which is stronger than anything that can be put into words, the lives of these boys were strengthened and blessed. Among all of her boys no one is better fitted to pay the tribute of love and affection to Miss Alcott than Frank Edwin Elwell, the talented New York sculptor, for he has, through the influence of her noble life, been able to give to the world works of art that are not only evidences of his own genius and skill, but monuments to the woman who first gave him, as a poor boy, the right-hand of fellowship and started him on his career with an equipment of high ideals and noble motives. One of the most noted of his works is the statue of "Dickens and Little Nell," which occupied the centre of the display of statuary at the World's Fair in Chicago, and is now in Fairmont Park at Philadelphia.

He has also made the finest bust of Miss Alcott that has been given to the world, which he presented in person to the Kansas State University. In speaking of her who has been so much to him he has said: "Somehow 'Aunt Jo' was not a human being, but a celestial soul in a human body, the embodiment of virtue, strength and love. Her faults were like the dust specks on the crystal that never became a part of that perfection of light, and now that she is in the Great Beyond, all these dust specks are wiped away, and we see in that transparent soul, pictures of eternal things, great principles of light, magnificent ideas, human kindness, *the virtue of all virtues.*"

"Miss Alcott's Letters to Her 'Laurie,'" *Ladies' Home Journal* 18 (September 1901): 5 – 6; (October 1901): 5.
    "Meg, Jo, Beth and Amy. Told by Laurie," *The Girl's Realm* 5 (December 1902): 133 – 38.

From *The Alcotts in Harvard* (1902)

Annie M. L. Clark

Annie Clark's recollections focus on the brief time she knew the Alcotts while they were in Harvard and Still River. Most of the Fruitlands experiences, which Clark uses to set up her narrative, come from other works; however, the time that the Alcotts stayed in Still River after the demise of Bronson's utopian community is presented in vivid detail. Although these months must have been difficult for the family, especially Bronson Alcott, Clark remembers it as a happy time for the sisters. Here, events such as Lizzie's birthday celebration or Louisa's "hanging" of the chair out of the Brickends' upstairs window show the real Alcott girls living the type of childhood that Louisa would recapture in *Little Women*. The short volume of recollections gives readers a view of the Alcotts during a key time in the life of this family.

Early in the summer of 1843, curiosity and interest were aroused in the minds of the inhabitants of the quiet town of Harvard, Massachusetts, by the advent among them of a small colony of that class of high thinkers who had received the name of Transcendentalists. The little colony, sixteen in all, comprised Bronson Alcott and nine other men, Mrs. Alcott, Miss Anna Page, and the four Alcott children. This somewhat incongruous family located itself on a picturesque sidehill farm in the school district of Harvard known as Still River North, but often referred to by the less elegant name of Hog Street.

The founders of this little community were actuated by high and noble motives; and the story of their plans and failures cannot but be of interest to thoughtful minds. It would be pertinent to trace the mental and moral training and the early homes and environments of the various members; but, as that is not possible, we will, instead, turn a backward glance at the parentage and early lives of those who were the soul and centre of the enterprise.

Amos Bronson Alcott was born in Wolcott, Connecticut, 29 November, 1799, at the foot of Spindle Hill. The family name was originally Alcocke, and is often found in English history. Mention is made that about 1616 a coat-of-arms was granted to Thomas Alcocke, the device being three cocks, emblematic of watchfulness, with the appropriate motto, *Semper vigilans*. One writer says: "Mr. Alcott's ancestors on both sides had been substantial people of respectable position in England, and were connected with the founders and governors of the chief New England colonies."

Brought up on a farm, Alcott has given the story of his quaint, rustic life in the simple verse of "New Connecticut," while Louisa has reproduced it in "Eli's Education," one of her Spinning Wheel Stories, which is said to be a very true picture of her father's early days. His mother was a gentle, refined woman, who had strong faith in her boy, and lived to see him the accomplished scholar he had vowed in boyhood to become. In Louisa Alcott's journal occurs this mention of her grandmother:

"Grandma Alcott came to visit us. A sweet old lady. I am glad to know her and see where Father got his nature. As we sat talking over Father's boyhood, I never realised so plainly before how much he has done for himself. His early life sounded like a pretty, old romance, and Mother added the love passages."

From her conversations with her grandmother, Miss Alcott got, as she says, "a hint for a story;" and this story was to be called "The Cost of an Idea." It was to relate "the trials and triumphs of the Pathetic Family," with chapters entitled, "Spindle Hill," "Temple School," "Fruitlands," "Boston," and "Concord." I believe the fear of seeming to present her father's characteristics to ridicule kept her from fulfilling this purpose; at least, only the Fruitlands chapter—"Transcendental Wild Oats"—ever saw the light.

Mrs. Alcott—Abba May—was the twelfth and youngest child of Colonel Joseph May, of Boston, her mother being Dorothy Sewall. Miss May was visiting her brother, the Rev. Samuel J. May, minister over a Unitarian church in Brooklyn, Connecticut, when she met her future husband. They were married by her brother 23 May, 1830, in King's Chapel, where the bride had been baptised in infancy. It is said that Mrs. May was a woman of rare and charming character, and any one who ever saw Mrs. Alcott can readily believe what she herself wrote of her mother: "She never said great things, but did ten thousand generous ones."

Alcott was farmer boy, peddler, and teacher by turns. In 1832 he was teaching in Germantown, Pennsylvania, where on his thirty-third birthday was born his second daughter, Louisa, whose feet were to mount the ladder of fame higher than his own.

Louisa Alcott's character, which united many of the traits of both parents, may, I think, be aptly described in this quatrain of the great Goethe:

> "Vom Vater hab'ich die Statur,
> Des Lebens ernstes führen,
> Vom Mütterchen the Frohnatur,
> Die Lust zu fabulieren." [1]

From Germantown to Boston and the famous Temple School; and here Alcott was gradually formulating the plan which led to the settlement of Fruitlands, and also strenuously carrying out his conviction that the simplest food was alone conducive to high and lofty thinking and living. We are told that the children grew very tired of rice without sugar, and Graham meal without either butter or molasses.

He was, this high priest of high ideas, very critical in religious matters, writing thus: "I am dissatisfied with the general preaching of every sect and with the individuals of any sect." Some one has said that he seemed to have adopted what Sir William Davenant called an "ingenuous Quakerism." Soon the title of philosopher was added to that of teacher; and he became known as a bright and shining light among the visionary but earnest company of Transcendentalists.

Going to England, he found there congenial spirits, and in October, 1842, he came home, accompanied by three of these new friends, Charles Lane and his son, William, and Henry C. Wright.

Miss Alcott, in "Transcendental Wild Oats," which she further entitles a chapter from an unwritten romance, writes as follows:

"On the first day of June, 1843, a large wagon, drawn by a small horse and containing a motley load, went lumbering over certain New England hills, with the pleasing accompaniments of wind, rain and hail. A serene man with a serene child upon his knee was driving or rather being driven, for the small horse had it all his own way. Behind a small boy, embracing a bust of Socrates, was an energetic looking woman, with a benevolent brow, satirical mouth and eyes full of hope and courage. A baby reposed upon her lap, a mirror leaned against her knee, a basket of provisions danced about her feet and she struggled with a large, unruly umbrella, with which she tried to cover every one but herself. Twilight began to fall, and the rain came down in a despondent drizzle, but the calm man gazed as tranquilly into the fog as if he beheld a radiant bow of promise spanning the gray sky." Thus came this new Adam and Eve into their hoped for Eden.

One of the band who were here to make "the wilderness blossom like the rose" wrote thus of Fruitlands, which was the name they decided to give their new home: "It is very remotely situated, without a road, but surrounded by a beautiful green of fields and woods." Nothing could have been more romantic than the site chosen — a field of about a hundred acres on a hillside, sloping to the river, with the most lovely views of Wachusett and Monadnock to the West, the intervening stretches dotted with towns and villages, while in the background rose the tree-crowned summit of Prospect Hill.

Here gathered the little band, and began the work of forming "a family in harmony with the primitive instincts of man." No meat was to be eaten, nor were fish, butter, cheese, eggs, or milk allowed — nothing that in the taking would cause pain or seem like robbing any animal; besides, animal food, if only approximately animal, as milk and butter, would corrupt the body and through that the soul! Tea, coffee, molasses, and rice, were forbidden for two reasons — because they were in part foreign luxuries, and in part the product of slave labour. Water alone for drink, fruit in plenty, and some vegetables, were permitted; but in these last a distinction was made between those which grow in the air and those which grow downward, like potatoes and others which form underground. The latter were less suited for what these visionaries termed a "chaste supply" for their bodily needs. Louisa Alcott says that ten ancient apple trees were all the "chaste supply" the place afforded. Salt was another article forbidden, it is hard to see why. Maple syrup and sugar were to be abundant in time, and bayberry tallow was to furnish light, when anything but the inner light was required. All this was to elevate and purify the body and bring about a state of perfection in body, mind, and soul.

The following are some of the principles upon which their habits of life were to rest: "We must ignore laws which ignore holiness; our trust is in purity; with pure beings will come pure habits; a better being shall be built up from the orchard and the garden; the outward form shall beam with soul." "From the fountain we will slake our thirst, and our appetite shall find supply in the delicious abundance which Pomona offers. Flesh and blood we will reject as the accursed thing. A pure mind has no faith in them."

Certain ideas called "no government theories" held sway in Alcott's breast, which just before his going to Harvard led to his arrest by the deputy sheriff, Sam Staples, for refusing to pay his taxes, on the ground that he would "not support a government so false to the law of love." And here I must digress to tell what Thoreau calls a good anecdote. Miss Helen Thoreau asked Sheriff Staples what he thought Mr. Alcott's idea was; and he answered, with hearty if inelegant emphasis, "I vum, I believe it was nothing but principle, for I never heard a man talk honester." Even those who most thoroughly disbelieved in the practicability of the reformer's views were ready to concede his entire honesty of purpose. Emerson called Alcott "a nineteenth century Simon Stylites."

With these qualities, he set out for Fruitlands — the name, like everything else fine about these plans, but a prophecy. The projects of these people were, as Emerson was fond of describing them, "without feet or hands." Ordinary farming was not part of their plan of life. No ploughs were to be used because they would require the aid of cattle; the spade and the pruning-knife were to be all-sufficient. None of the company was used to the labour required, and of course blistered hands and intense weariness were common; but the All-soul disciples struggled bravely on for a few months, yielding at last so far to the inevitable as to allow a yoke of cattle to be used in performing the hardest tasks. In the half droll, half pathetic pages of "Transcendental Wild Oats," it is asserted that one of the supposititious oxen was a cow, and that the owner used to take long draughts at the milking pail in the privacy of the barn. The truth is that Joseph Palmer, a member of the community, of whom I shall have something to tell later, brought from his home in Leominster a cow and a bull, which he had trained to work together. He was the original of Moses White in Miss Alcott's story, in which, with a decorous alteration, this incident figures. It is said that some others of the family were glad to share the less frugal meals of kindly neighbours, though this was probably never true of Alcott.

Their dress was another matter held of great importance. Cotton was largely the product of slave labour, and wool came from robbing the sheep, so linen was as far as possible to form the material of their garments. One cannot help but wonder how men with any common sense could dream of living through our New England year clad in linen. While summer and summer warmth lasted, many deprivations could be overlooked, though even then Mrs. Alcott's shoulders must have found heavy burdens for their upholding.

The rest might be seeking the All-soul; but to her fell the task, often almost beyond her powers, of providing for their physical needs, which even with their high philosophy could not be wholly overlooked.

The education of the children was not neglected. Miss Page gave them music lessons; and Louisa frankly declares she hated the lady, she was "so fussy." From their father and Mr. Lane they had instruction in various branches. Louisa in her diary tells of things pleasant and the reverse; how she tried to be good, and how she failed; of a visit from Parker Pillsbury, and his talk about the poor slaves; of their dinners of bread and fruit; how they played in the woods and were fairies, and how she "flied" the highest of all; and of a corn-husking in the barn, with the somewhat unusual incident, if one may judge by its being recorded, that they had lamps. Indeed, a kinswoman of Mrs. Alcott's tells me that her occasional insistence on ordinary means of lighting (bayberry tallow not being as yet available) called forth much reproachful opposition. Louisa writes of a visit from Professor William Russell, and a Sunday's tramp in the woods for moss to adorn a bower their father was making, in which Mr. Emerson was to be honoured. Louisa wrote little poems and read and listened to various books. Mrs. Child's "Philothea" was a great favourite with the little girls, so much so that they made a dramatic version of it, which they acted under the trees. That the father encouraged his children in their innocent gayety is shown by the family habit of celebrating birthdays. Thus, when May was three years old, 28 July of the summer spent at Fruitlands, the whole family met under the trees of a neighbouring grove, and, crowning the little girl with flowers, Mr. Alcott read an ode celebrating the day in the child's honour, and as the dawn of their opening paradise.

Emerson's ideas had been an incentive in the establishment of the community; but much as he sympathised with the pure idealism of their plans, he never seemed to believe in their practical value, and, again, called Alcott "a tedious archangel," and said that Alcott and Lane were "always feeling of their shoulders to see if their wings were sprouting." Hawthorne wrote of Alcott "One might readily conceive his Orphic sayings to well up from a fountain in his breast which communicated with the infinite Abyss of thought." His English friend, Mr. Wright, soon pronounced him impractical. Thoreau, with many kindred beliefs, was sometimes vexed with him; and Lowell, as if in prophecy, wrote:

"Our nipping climate hardly suits
The ripening of ideal fruits,
His theories vanquish *us* all summer,
But winter makes him dumb and dumber."

Some of the members of the family went visiting at Brook Farm, and came home shocked at the luxury and epicureanism they found. Young Isaac Hecker came to Fruitlands from the larger community, as he wished to lead a more self-denying life. After a stay of two weeks, however, he departed, still unsatisfied, to enter at a Catholic priesthood. People of strange dress and stranger ideas came and went, largely drones in the world's workaday hive; and the Newness, the All-soul, must have been written in other words for overworked, tired Mrs. Alcott. Alcott and Lane went to New York to hold a discussion with W. H. Channing. Lydia Maria Child, who was a dear personal friend of the Alcotts, gives a somewhat amusing account of the matter. Mr. Child and John Hopper had been to hear the discussion, and Mrs. Child asked what had been talked about. Mr. Child said: "Mr. Lane divided man into three states, the disconcious, the conscious, and the unconscious; the disconscious is the state of a pig, the conscious is the baptism by water, and the unconscious is the baptism by fire. And as for myself," he added, "when I had heard them talk for a few moments, I didn't know whether I *had* any mind or not." Hopper declared that while Channing thought there was some connection between mind and body, Alcott and Lane seemed to think the body a sham.

In Louisa's diary we find what she calls a "sample of the vegetable wafers we used at Fruitlands:"

"Vegetable diet and sweet repose; animal food and nightmare."

"Apollo eats no flesh and has no beard; his voice is melody itself."

"Pluck your body from the orchard, do not snatch it from the shambles." These are a few of the oracular instructions the children received from the philosophers.

As cool weather came on, times grew harder. We find in Louisa's diary, under one date: "More people coming to live with us; I wish we could be together, and no one else. I don't see who is to feed and clothe us all, when we are so poor now. I was very dismal, and then went out to walk, and made a poem." This poem is entitled "Despondency;" it is interesting, denoting, as it does, the loving trust which showed itself in the young heart thus early learning of life's burdens, a trust, which is again shown in the record, of a little later date, when she tells of going under the forest trees and coming out into the sunshine, and of the strange and solemn feeling that came over her—that she, as she expresses it, "felt God as never before, and prayed that she might keep that happy sense of nearness all her life." This is the poem. Surely these lines are good for a girl not quite eleven years old:

"Silent and sad
When all is glad
And the earth is dressed in flowers;
When the gay birds sing
Till the forests ring
As they rest in woodland bowers.

"Oh, why these tears
And these idle fears
For what may come to-morrow?
The birds find food
From God so good,
And the flowers know no sorrow.
"If He clothes these,
And the leafy trees,
Will He not cherish thee?
Why doubt His care?
It is everywhere,
Though the way we may not see.

"Then why be sad
When all is glad
And the world is full of flowers?
With the gay birds sing,
Make life all spring,
And smile through the darkest hours."

One after another those who had composed the family departed, Lane and his son going to the Shakers for a while, and considerably later returning to England. Alcott also, I believe, was inclined to join the followers of Mother Ann Lee; but to this his wife utterly refused to agree. An old neighbour once told me that Mrs. Alcott said her hope for her daughters was that they should become wives and mothers; and life among the Shakers was apparently not likely to bring about that happy result. Alcott grew more and more discouraged. As his daughter says, he lay down upon his bed and turned his face to the wall, refusing food and drink, and there waited for death to end the struggle. For a while tears and pleading from the faithful wife were of no avail, and she could only cling to the words which expressed the belief of her devout but incapable husband, "The Lord will provide." It would seem that at last some kind angel brought the stricken man to see the selfishness of yielding to despair, when his wife and children were alike suffering and it was his duty to care for them. Some arrangements were made; and one cold December day the little family left Fruitlands—which the mother suggested might more appropriately have been called "Apple Slump"—for a home in the village of Still River, in a part of the house known as the "Brick Ends," then owned and in part occupied by J. W. Lovejoy. It is comforting to recall that, although Alcott, brave in his convictions, withstood the wintry blasts in his customary linen leggings, the broad-brimmed hats and linen tunics of the little girls gave way to warmer garments sent by friends and relatives. Still more delightful is it to know that Mrs. Alcott, like many another weary woman, found comfort in "cups that cheer but not inebriate," and now and then went to a sympathetic neighbour's to make herself a cup of tea.

Of course queer stories had come to the villagers regarding the Transcendentalists; so when one Sunday a long-haired man walked into the Still River (Baptist) church, interrupting the service to proclaim himself the Angel Gabriel, I think the incident seemed, though unfortunate, not altogether out of character. Gabriel, however, may have made Fruitlands his headquarters after the place had passed into the hands of Joseph Palmer, who, because of his immense beard, when full beards were very rarely seen, was known as the "Old Jew.". . . Mr. Palmer is buried in the large cemetery at Leominster, his monument bearing his portrait in relief, beneath which are the words: "Persecuted for wearing the beard."

With the spring the Still River little folks found their new neighbours a welcome accession. A May party, with queen and maypole, was, I think, an idea of the young Alcotts, whose knowledge of historic customs was greater than that possessed by the rest of us. A recent writer has called them "sad-faced children." That is a great mistake. Whatever they may have lacked in everyday comforts, they never could have been rightly described by such a term. As sure as the sun shone and skies were blue, just so sure was the afternoon gathering on the grass plot in front of the "Brick Ends," and all of us enjoyed jumping rope, tossing ball and rolling hoop (so it seems to me now) as never before. Mrs. Alcott was like the guardian angel of the merry company, often taking her seat in our midst and smiling benignly upon our gay pranks.

In the bright days of summer came the birthday of Lizzie, the "Beth" of "Little Women;" and never shall I forget the proud gladness which filled my childish heart as I went to the party given in honour of the day. Mrs. Lovejoy's kitchen was set about with evergreens, and otherwise rendered a fitting stage for the evening's entertainment. Her sitting-room was the dress circle, while the Alcott sitting-room was ornamented by a small tree, from the boughs of which hung gifts, not only for our small hostess, but for each little friend present. In the adjoining kitchen a table was abundantly laden with little cakes and luscious cherries, with a big birthday cake in the centre.

I cannot recall all the dramatic scenes enacted that evening, to me so memorable. There was part of an old English play by the older of the happy party, members of the Alcott and the neighbouring Gardner families. Then there were songs; and Anna Alcott appeared as a Scotch laddie, in bonnet and plaid. What she recited I have forgotten, though I remember how pretty she looked. But Louisa was the star of the evening. Her mother had stained her face, arms, neck and ankles to the ruddy hue of an Indian girl; her dress seemed made all of feathers; feathers, too, crowned her head. Three times she made her appearance. Once, according to her own recollection, she sang the then popular song, "Wild roved an Indian girl, bright Alfarata." Then erect, solemn as her merry face could become, she strode forward, bearing a large shield, and in almost blood-curdling accents—as an old schoolmate describes them—repeated the passage from Ossian beginning, "O thou that rollest above, round as the shield of my fathers;" and again, in tenderer, softer accents, a poem from one of the school readers:

> "*Geehale—An Indian Lament.*
> "The blackbird is singing on Michigan's shore
> As sweetly and gaily as ever before;
> For he knows to his mate he, at pleasure, can hie,
> And the dear little brood she is teaching to fly;
> The sun looks as ruddy, and rises as bright,
> And reflects o'er our mountains as beamy a light
> As it ever reflected, or ever expressed,
> When my skies were the bluest, my dreams were the best.

The fox and the panther, both beasts of the night,
Retire to their dens on the gleaming of light,
And they spring with a free and a sorrowless track,
For they know that their mates are expecting them back.
Each bird and each beast, it is blessed in degree;
All nature is cheerful, all happy, but me.

"I will go to my tent, and lie down in despair;
I will paint me with black, and will sever my hair;
I will sit on the shore, where the hurricane blows,
And reveal to the god of the tempest my woes;
I will weep for a season, on bitterness fed,
For my kindred are gone to the hills of the dead;
But they died not by hunger, or lingering decay;
The steel of the white man hath swept them away.

"This snake-skin, that once I so sacredly wore,
I will toss, with disdain, to the storm-beaten shore;
Its charms I no longer obey, or invoke;
Its spirit hath left me, its spell is now broke.
I will raise up my voice to the source of the light;
I will dream on the wings of the bluebird at night;
I will speak to the spirits that whisper in leaves,
And that minister balm to the bosom that grieves;
And will take a new Manito—such as shall seem
To be kind and propitious in every dream.

"Oh then I shall banish these cankering sighs,
And tears shall no longer gush salt from my eyes;
I shall wash from my face every cloud-coloured stain
Red, red shall, alone, on my visage remain!
I will dig up my hatchet, and bend my oak bow;
By night and by day I will follow the foe;
Nor lakes shall impede me, nor mountains, nor snows;—
His blood can, alone, give my spirit repose.

"They came to my cabin, when heaven was black;
I heard not their coming, I knew not their track;
But I saw, by the light of their blazing fusees,
They were people engendered beyond the big seas.
My wife, and my children,—oh spare me the tale!
For who is there left that is kin to GEEHALE?"

It was all so wonderful to us little ones; and I well remember how the next day we looked to see if any remnant of the paint was left on Louisa's pretty neck and arms.

Miss Louisa Chase, who taught the village school that summer, was fairly enshrined in the hearts of her pupils; and the rides and picnics in which Miss Chase and Mrs. Alcott watched over, and shared in, the happiness of the little people I shall never forget. Hay-carts would be provided with seats and trimmed with evergreen; and carefully stowing away our luncheon-baskets, we one by one would take our seats in the rustic omnibuses, and start away, singing and laughing, for a long day's pleasure.

Mr. Alcott was too much engaged in philosophising and gardening to share in such merry-makings; but a lady, who was in those days one of the Still River school-girls, tells me of one occasion when he did attend a picnic at the school-house. I have an impression that it was held on the Fourth of July, and very likely Mr. Alcott had been asked to speak. One can well believe that the doughnuts, cold meat, pickles, cakes, and pies, usually served on such occasions, were little to his taste; and, indeed, when there were passed to him some delicate cookies, contributed by the minister's wife, by whose side, unfortunately, he was sitting, the philosopher declined them with a wave of the hand, and the words, "Vanity, and worse than vanity!"

Of the merry Alcott group and their intimates, Louisa was the ring-leader whenever and wherever there was a chance to "have some fun." She often, as she says, "got mad;" but her anger went as quickly as it came. Still she *could* be severe. One day the neighbours were astonished to see a chair suspended from one of the "Brick Ends" windows. It appeared that Louisa, while "cleaning house" with great energy had "bumped" herself against a chair, whereupon that devoted article of furniture was arraigned, found guilty, and immediately hanged!

Another tale is related by the schoolmate who was Louisa's most intimate Still River friend. Calling on the Alcotts one day, she found Louisa in a little hall chamber, where she had been sentenced to remain till she was sorry for speaking disrespectfully to her mother; at present, she was not sorry. She confided to her friend, who remarked a peculiar odour, that, as she *must* stay there, she had thought it a good time to oil her hair, which she had been do-ing, most lavishly, with some of poor Mrs. Alcott's whale-oil! A recollection caused the prisoner shortly to declare she could stay indoors no longer. Deaf to her visitor's remonstrances, she explained that the day before she had accidentally killed a spider in the pasture, and must needs go and look at his monument, which she had erected. So the two little girls crept softly down stairs and out through the garden, successfully avoiding the notice of Mr. Alcott, who was busy hoeing. The monument proved to be a shingle fixed in the ground, bearing an epitaph appropriate to the unfortunate spider. All this seems very much like a chapter from one of Miss Alcott's stories.

Well do I remember my childish distress over an incident at school. Miss Chase, doubtless weary of the mending of some forty quills, had gladly welcomed the innovation of steel pens. I was very proud of the one she had given me; but one day, alas! Louisa in a spirit of mischief seized the quill-handle into which my pen was fitted, and threw it into the middle of the floor, spoiling the point, and filling my little heart with pain. A pleasanter recollection is of the first banana I ever tasted, one which Lizzie Alcott shared with me, and which I remember she called "bread fruit."

Sweet, clever Anna Alcott—"Meg"—used to write little stories in a blank book; and I can fancy myself now walking very slowly home from school, along the broad green sidewalk between the corner and Mr. Orasmus Willard's, with my dear playmates, Lizzie Alcott and Helen Lovejoy, while Anna read to us what seemed very wonderful tales.

Taught that the eating of meat was wrong, the Alcott children looked, of course, upon any form of butchering as a veritable crime, and many were the spirited debates which Lizzie and I had on the subject. Fruits, grains, and vegetables made up the sum of *their* home diet; but, like some of the older Fruitlanders, they were not averse from sharing more varied food, provided at picnics and other rural festivities. Kind friends and relatives, as I have mentioned, sent them, besides baskets of fruit, many articles of clothing; and it would seem as if this brief, bright summer must have been a welcome relief to Mrs. Alcott from the toil and care with which she had been burdened at Fruitlands.

An anecdote of Mrs. Alcott's Still River life well illustrates her generous nature. In the same village was a lady of ample means, and possessing true refinement, who paid little or no attention to prevailing styles. While of excellent materials, her clothes were, indeed, far enough from the fashion. Among a quantity of garments sent to Mrs. Alcott by friends were several bonnets, and great was Mrs. ——'s good-humoured astonishment when Mrs. Alcott, in the most delicate manner, offered one of them to her! Although the bonnet was not accepted, I have no doubt that these two good women were drawn closer by an incident which, if shared by less noble characters, might have ended unhappily.

We were all very sorry when our beloved playmates went back to Concord. Once, not many years later, Louisa was so anxious to see Still River again that she walked from Concord to visit the Gardners. She often thought of the summer spent in Still River, as is shown by the use in her stories of the names of people she had known there. . . .

In the chapter of "Little Men" where Dan tells the story of "Marm Webber," Miss Alcott was portraying a Still River character. On the slope of Prospect Hill there actually lived a Mrs. Webber, whose house was a hospital for homeless and unfortunate cats. Whatever were the old dame's faults, of temper, she was a true friend to her feline pets, although her putting the hopeless invalids out of their misery with ether is a touch of Miss Alcott's fancy, since, I believe, that anesthetic had not been invented in the real Marm Webber's time.

I well remember how great was the interest felt by old Still River schoolmates when, in the *Saturday Evening Gazette,* articles began to appear written by the merry girl who had left so strong an impression on our minds. Right proud were we when "Little Women" followed the pathetic pages of "Hospital Sketches;" and loyal hearts rejoiced in each later success, and mourned when the life lived so faithfully for others ended so early.

1. This well-known, untitled verse by the German poet Goethe may be translated as follows: "From my father I inherit my stature, / And an earnest disposition to life, / From my mother levity, / And a desire to spin stories."

From *The Alcotts in Harvard* (Lancaster, Massachusetts: J. C. L. Clark, 1902), pp. 9–44.

From *Bits of Gossip* (1904)

REBECCA HARDING DAVIS

Near the end of her life, Rebecca Harding Davis (1831–1910) reflected upon her first trip to Boston in 1862, during the midst of the Civil War. Her "Life in the Iron Mills" had appeared in the *Atlantic Monthly* the previous year, and her novel *Margaret Howth* (1862) had just been published. This triumphant trip to New England led her to meet Hawthorne, whom she had always admired, Emerson, and Bronson Alcott, as well as establishing a lasting relationship with Annie Adams Fields, wife of James T. Fields and cousin to Louisa May Alcott. Louisa had recently been staying at the Fields's home while she taught in a Boston kindergarten established by Elizabeth P. Peabody.

Davis, in her recollection, allows readers a brief comparison of the young Louisa May, struggling to support herself and family, and an older Alcott—wealthy, famous, but still giving and kind. Alcott herself wrote about her first meeting with Davis: "A handsome, fresh, quiet woman, who says she never had any troubles, though she writes about woes. I told her I had lots of troubles, so I write jolly tales, and we wondered why we each did so" (*Journals,* 109).

During my first visit to Boston in 1862, I saw at an evening reception a tall, thin young woman standing alone in a corner. She was plainly dressed, and had that watchful, defiant air with which the woman whose youth is slipping away is apt to face the world which has offered no place to her. Presently she came up to me.

"These people may say pleasant things to you," she said abruptly; "but not one of them would have gone to Concord and back to see you, as I did to-day. I went for this gown. It's the only decent one I have. I'm very poor;" and in the next breath she contrived to tell me that she had once taken a place as "second girl." "My name," she added, "is Louisa Alcott."

Now, although we had never met, Louisa Alcott had shown me great kindness in the winter just past, sacrificing a whole day to a tedious work which was to give me pleasure at a time when every hour counted largely to her in her desperate struggle to keep her family from want. The little act was so considerate and fine, that I am still grateful for it, now when I am an old woman, and Louisa Alcott has long been dead. It was as natural for her to do such things as for a pomegranate-tree to bear fruit.

Before I met her I had known many women and girls who were fighting with poverty and loneliness, wondering why God had sent them into a life where apparently there was no place for them, but never one so big and generous in soul as this one in her poor scant best gown, the "claret-colored merino," which she tells of with such triumph in her diary. Amid her grim surroundings, she had the gracious instincts of a queen. It was her delight to give, to feed living creatures, to make them happy in body and soul.

She would so welcome you in her home to a butterless baked potato and a glass of milk that you would never forget the delicious feast. Or, if she had no potato or milk to offer, she would take you through the woods to the river, and tell you old legends of colony times, and be so witty and kind in the doing of it that the day would stand out in your memory ever after, differing from all other days, brimful of pleasure and comfort.

With this summer, however, the darkest hour of her life passed. A few months after I saw her she went as a nurse into the war, and soon after wrote her "Hospital Sketches." Then she found her work and place in the world.

Years afterward she came to the city where I was living and I hurried to meet her. The lean, eager, defiant girl was gone, and instead, there came to greet me a large, portly, middle-aged woman, richly dressed. Everything about her, from her shrewd, calm eyes to the rustle of her satin gown told of assured success.

Yet I am sure fame and success counted for nothing with her except for the material aid which they enabled her to give to a few men and women whom she loved. She would have ground her bones to make their bread. Louisa Alcott wrote books which were true and fine, but she never imagined a life as noble as her own.

The altar for human sacrifices still stands and smokes in this Christian day of the world, and God apparently does not reject its offerings.

From *Bits of Gossip* (Boston: Houghton, Mifflin, 1904), pp. 38–41.

"A Concord Notebook: The Women of Concord— III. Louisa Alcott and Her Circle" (1906)

F. B. SANBORN

Well known to the scholars of the Transcendentalist circle, Sanborn became a friend and chronicler of the Alcott family, especially with his co-authorship, along with William Torrey Harris, of the two-volume *A. Bronson Alcott: His Life and Philosophy* (1893). A Harvard graduate, Sanborn was active on the political, philosophical, and social scene in Concord after his arrival there in the mid-1850s, where he ran a private academy from 1855 to 1863.

A fervent abolitionist, Sanborn in 1857 had helped John Brown arrange meetings in Concord with Emerson, Thoreau, and Bronson Alcott to build moral and financial support for his armed defense of free Kansas. After Brown's Harpers Ferry raid in October 1859, Sanborn was suspected of being part of the "Secret Six," which had backed Brown. Arrested in Concord, Sanborn, with the help of leading citizens such as John S. Keyes and Sen. Rockwood Hoar, was quickly released by legal maneuvering before he could be taken away. Such actions only made him more heroic in the eyes of the Alcott family.

After the initial sales of *Hospital Sketches* in 1863, Louisa Alcott suddenly and unexpectedly found her work to be in demand, and she reported that Sanborn "says 'any publisher this side of Baltimore would be glad to get a book'" (*Journals*, 121). Although Sanborn clearly shows here in this history of famous Concord women a somewhat condescending attitude toward Louisa's career as "a popular author," whose early works in the Boston periodicals do not "deserve preservation," he was one of the first to point out that while she enjoyed the opportunity to grow up as a neighbor to Emerson and Thoreau, she "still came to view the town with little satisfaction." He also astutely captures "a certain acerbity" in Alcott, caused by "the mortifications that poverty brings to a girl of high spirits." Pointing out the contrast between the real Louisa May Alcott and her cheerful books, he suggests that the hardships she endured as a child "sometimes dashed the enjoyment of the deserved good fortune that came to her."

The most famous of all the Concord women, in all parts of the earth, has long been Louisa Alcott, daughter of the philosopher Bronson Alcott, and commemorated by him in his volume of "Octogenarian Sonnets," every one of which was composed after he was eighty and printed in his eighty-third year. Remembering her enthusiasm as a hospital nurse in the second year of the Civil War, and that her experiences in the army hospital in Washington, as published by me in 1863, in the Boston *Commonwealth* newspaper, first made her known and dear to her countrymen, he thus, in 1880, addressed to her in verse:

TO MY DAUGHTER LOUISA

When I remember with what buoyant heart,
'Midst war's alarms and woes of civil strife,
In youthful eagerness thou didst depart,
At peril of thy safety, peace, and life,
To nurse the wounded soldier, swathe the dead,—
How piercêd soon by Fever's poisoned dart,
And brought unconscious home, with wildered head,
Thou ever since, 'mid langour and dull pain
(To conquer fortune, cherish kindred dear),
Hast with grave studies vexed a sprightly brain,—
In myriad households kindling love and cheer;
Ne'er from thyself by Fame's loud trump beguiled,
Sounding in this and the farther hemisphere:—
I press thee to my heart as Duty's faithful child.

The death of the father in March, 1888, was followed almost at once by that of the daughter; his funeral in Boston, which she was too ill to attend, had but a few days' space between it and hers; and they were deposited in the same Concord tomb, until the tardy coming of spring would permit their burial, side by side, on the summit of the ridge where Emerson, Hawthorne, Ellery Channing, and Thoreau repose not far off. Mrs. Alcott had died in the Thoreau-Alcott house in 1877, the next year after Sophia Thoreau's death in Bangor; and now all the members of these two friendly households have headstones in the same Sleepy Hollow Cemetery. . . .

Dressed in [her] great aunt's brocade, or the finery of her grandmother, Miss Alcott was a stately figure on the amateur stage, where I often acted in private theatricals with her and her sisters before the war. In spite of narrow means and the loss of their modest sister Elizabeth, who died soon after they returned to Concord from New Hampshire in the winter of 1857–58, the Alcotts were a cheerful family, with a fine turn for dramatic parts and for lively society. They had first appeared in Concord in the spring of 1840, when Louisa was seven years old, and took up their abode in the Hosmer cottage, at the extreme west end of the village. May Alcott, the youngest child, was there born in July, 1840, and there the English friends of Mr. Alcott, Charles Lane and Henry Wright, spent with the family the winter of 1842–43, before setting forth for Fruitlands, their little community, in May, 1843. They came back to Concord, disillusioned, late in 1844, and resided for a time with Edmund Hosmer, where about that time George William Curtis and his brother Burrill, fresh from Brook Farm, lived a few months. In 1846, Mrs. Alcott, with some family property, bought the house now known as "The Wayside," since Hawthorne bought it and renamed it in 1852. The Alcotts had called it Hillside, and had passed pleasant childish years there. Louisa's story-telling gift was developed here, and in the barn her earliest plays were acted by herself and her sisters and schoolmates. In her earlier years at Concord she had been for a short time a pupil of Henry Thoreau, and still earlier of her father's Boston school; her other education came irregularly from her parents, from a temporary governess, and sometimes from town schools; but she always missed the careful education that most of the Concord girls had, either in public or in private schools.

Miss Robie, a cousin of Mrs. Alcott, wrote from the first Alcott cottage, December 6, 1841, as follows. It was when the family were very poor but very generous.

"As it was time for me to expect a headache, I did not dare to go to Concord without carrying tea and coffee and cayenne pepper, and a small piece of cooked meat, in case my wayward stomach should crave it, which last article was a little piece of *à la mode* beef. Thus provided, I arrived at the Alcott cottage just after dark of a Friday evening. I got into the house before they heard me, and found them seated around their bread and water. I had a most cordial welcome from Mrs. Alcott and the children. She said to me: 'O you dear creature! you are the one I should have picked out of all the good people in Boston. How thankful I am to see you!' I had a comfortable cup of tea in a few minutes, for I did not dare to go without." (They then opened a bundle in which were clothes for the children, sent by Mrs. J. S. of Boston.) "Mr. Alcott sat looking on like a philosopher. 'There,' said he, 'I told you that you need not be anxious about clothing for the children; you see it has come as I said.'

"Mrs. Alcott wanted comfort and counsel; for, though cheerful and uncomplaining, things had got pretty low. Mr. Alcott was evidently not well, and she was quite anxious about him, and expressed some fears that the little sympathy and encouragement he received in regard to his views would depress him beyond what he could bear. However, after a good talk and a good crying spell, her spirits rallied, and all was bright again. She told me of a miserable poor woman in her neighborhood, who had just lost a drunken husband, and was in a poor hovel with four children, and she had been aiding her in their small way to a little meal, and encouraging her to have a good heart and keep out of the work-house, and had interested other neighbors in her behalf. She said it seemed as if this poor family had been brought to her notice to show her how much better her own situation was, and to give a change to her feelings by looking about and doing what she could to assist her.

"I went with her one day to see the family. In the course of the visit the woman mentioned Mr. Alcott. 'I did not know he had been to see you,'— 'Oh, yes, he was here yesterday and the day before and sawed up some wood that had been sent me. I had engaged that Mr. Somebody to saw it for me, and did some sewing for his wife to pay for it. Said Mrs. Alcott, 'Then Mr. A's sawing it did not do you much good?' 'Oh, yes; they said they had as lief give me the money for it, so I had it to buy some meal.'

"Whilst I was at Mrs. Alcott's, of course I saw no meat, nor butter, nor cheese; and only coarse brown sugar, bread, potatoes, apples, squash, and simple puddings; of these materials were the staples for food. I was obliged to have tea occasionally, but except that, I lived as they did, for I could not have the heart or the stomach to take out my beef. Mr. Alcott thought his wife did wrong to prepare the tea for me. The Alcotts had just begun to do with two meals a day, that the children might have the pleasure of carrying once a week a basket of something from their humble savings to the poor family. Now the saving must be made for themselves.

"Mr. Alcott said he could not live with debt burdening them in this way; that they must live simpler still. He started up and said he would go into the woods and chop for his neighbors, and in that way get his fuel. He has since entered up on this work. They said they should give up milk. I persuaded them against this, on account of the baby. Mr. A thought it would not hurt any of them."

The baby at this time was May, afterwards the artist, who was nearly 18 months old, having been born in that cottage in July, 1840. From this cottage, which still stands, though much changed, and in which the Alcotts received their three English friends in the winter of 1842–43, they removed to Fruitlands in May, 1843,—returning to Concord in 1844, and occupying the present "Wayside" house till 1850. While they were temporarily living in Boston again, the Concord estate was sold to Mr. Hawthorne.

In the summer of 1852, having prospered by the success of his "Scarlet Letter" and "House of Seven Gables," Hawthorne came back to Concord and bought the Alcott place, containing some thirty acres of land and the remodeled house on which, and on the grounds, Mr. Alcott had expended much labor and good taste in decoration, tree-planting, and arbor-building. Considering its present pecuniary value, the price paid was ridiculously low. The note in which Mrs. Alcott's cousin, Samuel Sewall, who had the care of her property and of Louisa's in after years, announced the sale to Hawthorne, is before me. He wrote:

"Dear Cousin:

"Mr. Hawthorne called on me a few days ago and offered $1500 for the place in Concord. I wrote Mr. Emerson, who called on me yesterday. I find he agrees to the sale. Mr. Brooks, to whom I also wrote, thinks we had better make the sale. I shall conclude the bargain unless I hear from you to the contrary to-day. I have not had time to call to see you, but I presume, from what you have said, that you will assent to the sale. $500 will be invested, by Mr. Emerson's orders, in trust for Mr. Alcott, and $1,000 for you.

"In haste, yours affectionately, S.E. Sewall."

Mrs. Alcott, as just mentioned, was then residing in Boston, where I called on the family for the first time, with the late Mrs. Ednah Cheney, then Miss Littlehale, in the autumn of that year, 1852. I had entered Harvard College in the July preceding, while Hawthorne was settling himself at the newly purchased "Wayside.". . .

Louisa Alcott, when I first knew her in 1852, was a serious, bashful girl, sensitive and industrious, who had not then found her vocation, and suffered from the mortifications that poverty brings to girls of high spirit. Traces of a certain acerbity due to this cause, and heightened by her ill health in later years, remained with her through life. It sometimes dashed the enjoyment of the deserved good-fortune that finally came to her, and was so dutifully and generously shared with others. But the warm fancy that shines in all her books kept her usually cheerful, and often gay; so that the rather sad impression given by Mrs. Cheney's biography is not quite just to her life as a whole. Her literary success was long in arriving, but was very complete at last, and promises to be permanent. It began with her recognition by a keen-eyed publisher, Thomas Niles (of Roberts Brothers), who saw in the MS. of "Little Women" the promise of a good writer, and so published it under favorable conditions in 1868. From that time forward she was a popular author, and has been far more widely read than any other of the Concord writers, though, of course, not ranking with most of them in genius.

Long before I knew Louisa Alcott she had begun her career as a story-teller,—orally at first,—but she was a lively (if not very correct) writer in 1845, at the age of twelve. In 1851, when her first story was printed in W. W. Clapp's *Saturday Evening Gazette* of Boston, she had twice come and gone as a Concord resident, following the migrations of her family; but was then a Bostonian. She wrote rapidly then, at nineteen, and, as she said, easily turned off a dozen a month. Those accepted for the *Gazette* were printed and paid for by Mr. Clapp, under the impression they were written by a man; when it appeared a girl had sent them, it was proposed to reduce the price. But, as she said long afterward: "The girl had learned the worth of her wares, and would not write for less, and so continued to earn her fair wages, in spite of sex." Very few of these tales have been reprinted, or deserve preservation. It was only when she began to relate her own experiences, or those of her family and dear friends, that she interested the wider public which has continued to read her, one generation after another.

Concord, although a place very dear to her father, and attractive to her by the presence of Emerson and Thoreau, whom she greatly admired from girl-hood, was never otherwise a pleasant home to her. It had been associated with the mortifications that poverty and the unpopularity of her father and his friends brought to a sensitive girl; and though she afterwards received and gave much happiness by her joyous relations with the boys and girls who lived near her, or were pupils of my Concord school, she still came to view the town with little satisfaction. She had small talent for general society, and could not well accommodate herself to customs and formalities which she could throw off in the company of her juniors.

To this picture of Miss Alcott in the family circle at Concord may be added another of ten years later (October 1, 1873), drawn by her own humorous pen. Mrs. Lucy Stone, head of the Woman Suffrage Society of Massachusetts, of which the Alcotts were members, as they had been of the earlier Anti-Slavery Societies, had written to Miss Alcott for some service to be rendered in that cause. She replied as follows:

"I am so busy proving 'woman's right to labor' that I have no time to help prove 'woman's right to vote.' When I read your note to the family, asking, 'What shall I say to Mrs. Stone?' a voice from the Transcendental mist which usually surrounds my honored father instantly replied: 'Tell her you are ready to follow her as a leader, sure that you could not have a better one.' My brave old mother, with the ardor of many unquenchable Mays shining in her face, cried out: 'Tell her I am seventy-three, but I mean to go to the polls before I die,— even if my three daughters have to carry me.' And two Little Men, already mustered in, added the cheering words: 'Go ahead, Aunt Weedy, we will let you vote as much as ever you like.' Such being the temper of the small convention of which I am now President, I cannot hesitate to say that, though I may not be with you in body, I shall be in spirit, and am as ever,

"Hopefully and heartily yours, Louisa May Alcott."

Four years later Mrs. Alcott died without having had the opportunity to vote; and the family then left the Orchard House, to reside in the Thoreau-Alcott house, nearer the railroad station, wherein I had preceded them as a four-years' tenant of Sophia Thoreau. Louisa bought the house for her sister, Mrs. Pratt, mother of the "Little Men," one of whom now occupies it with his four children. May Alcott died two years after her mother, and is buried in France, near Paris, where she died, leaving her only child, a girl named for Louisa, whose Swiss father took her to his own home in Zurich, after Miss Alcott's death in 1888. Mrs. Pratt died a few years later, at Concord, and is buried beside her husband in the cemetery there, not far from the graves of her father, mother, and sisters, and near the graves of Thoreau, Channing, Hawthorne, and Emerson.

The Critic 48 (April 1906): 338–50.

From *The Alcotts as I Knew Them* (1909)

CLARA GOWING

Published in 1909, Clara Gowing's remembrances of the Alcotts in Concord focus primarily on the 1840s and 1850s, when she grew up with the two older Alcott sisters. She was the same age as Louisa, having been born in 1832 in Charlestown, Massachusetts, the daughter of Jabez and Hitty Eames Gowing. Her connection to Concord was a strong one; both of her grandfathers had been at the Concord fight in April 1775. Gowing, educated in Concord, grew up to be a teacher and occasional writer. She taught at schools for black children in Lynchburg and Alexandria, Virginia, and in Nashville, Tennessee. Employed for a time by the State Primary School in Massachusetts, Gowing was, for over a decade, president of the Women's Christian Temperance Union in Reading, Massachusetts, where she lived. Clearly, the arrival of the Alcotts to Gowing's "East Quarter" neighborhood of Concord in spring 1845 was something to remember. As she recalls, Bronson had been in the village "long enough to acquire the reputation of being a fanatic in belief and habit"; he was "supposed to be something entirely unorthodox." While Gowing notes how different the Alcott girls were from others in their beliefs and education, she also portrays them as ordinary and easily accepted into the Concord children's daily life. She gives us vivid scenes of Louisa before writing became her focus, a rare glimpse into a life filled with frolic and games, despite little money. The account of the "postoffice," where the girls left messages for each other, provides the autobiographical foundation for the "P.O." in *Little Women,* and her description of Louisa instantly calls to mind the fictional Jo March: "She was . . . in character a strange combination of kindness and perseverance, full of fun, with a keen sense of the ludicrous, apt speech and ready wit; a subject of moods, than whom no one could be jollier and more entertaining when geniality was in ascendency, but if the opposite, let her best friend beware."

In the spring of 1845 the usually tranquil neighborhood in Concord, Massachusetts, known as the "East Quarter," was somewhat agitated by learning that Mr. A. Bronson Alcott had purchased a place in that part of the town, which he would occupy with his family.

Previous to this he had been a citizen of the town long enough to acquire the reputation of being a fanatic in belief and habit, and he had recently come from a community of Transcendentalists in Harvard, Massachusetts. (What the term Transcendentalist really meant was not generally understood, but it was supposed to be something entirely unorthodox.) He attended no church, had been arrested for not paying his taxes because he would not support a government so false to the law of love as that which was advocated in the Boston papers, eschewed all animal food, and had attempted to do without everything the use of which cost the life of the creature, such as leather for boots and shoes, and oil for burning; and he carried his anti-slavery principles so far as to give up sugar and molasses made at the South, also cotton, or anything produced by slave labor. In a family of restricted means it was found rather impracticable to carry out all these ideas, and when they came to the "East Quarter" they used oil for light, cotton goods and sugar, and yielding to the wife's and children's requirement, milk.

The place he purchased, about a mile from the village, consisted of several acres of land and a two-story house standing quite near the main road, with the front door in the middle, on which was an old-fashioned knocker. A wheelwright's shop was on one side of the house, and a barn on the opposite side of the road, with a high hill covered with trees for a background. Over this hill a part of the British troops marched when they entered and left Concord on the memorable 19th of April, 1775, the hill being on the north side of the road from Lexington to Concord and extending for a mile, ending just beyond the old church.

To use Mrs. Alcott's own words, "we moved the barn across the road, cut the shop in two and put a half on each end of the house." On each L so formed was a piazza with a door opening into the front room as well as one into the L. There were no less than eight outside doors to the house. Mrs. Alcott used to say, when a rap was heard, each one started for one of the doors. In the west L each of the two older girls, Anna and Louisa, had a little room for a studio all her own, in which she reigned supreme. Louisa loved to be alone when reading or writing, and a door from her room opening toward the hill gave her opportunity to slip out into the woods at her pleasure.

On the opposite side of the road their land extended to a brook where Mr. Alcott built a rustic bathhouse with a thatched roof, which they used daily in warm weather; the girls scampering across the road and field, plunging into the brook and back again as quickly as possible. In winter time a shower bath in the house was used instead, for bathing and outdoor exercise were important elements to the Alcotts. On the hill back of the buildings Mr. Alcott made a rustic summer house and laid out walks and terraces. With a high picket fence and shrubbery in front, the lower rooms were quite screened from the passers-by, and this gave a feeling of retirement which was congenial to them.

The family consisted of Mr. and Mrs. Alcott and four daughters—Anna Bronson, Louisa May, Elizabeth Sewell and Abby May. On account of the peculiar views held by Mr. Alcott, in many of which his wife felt no sympathy, the neighbors were not forward in calling, and though all summer and fall I passed the house in going to the village to school, my acquaintance with the girls did not progress much beyond our peeping at each other through the fence, and a mutual desire for companionship, each hesitating to make the advance. But the next winter, 1845–46, by dint of much teasing, Anna and Louisa persuaded their mother to allow them to attend the district public school, something they had never done before. As the teacher was a young man, John Hosmer, who had recently come from the Brook Farm Community School and was in some degree in sympathy with the Alcotts, their desire was more readily granted than it would otherwise have been.

Louisa was thirteen years old, tall and slim; in fact, limbs predominated and were used freely, so that she was the fleetest runner in school, and could walk, run and climb like a boy. At one time she trundled her hoop from her home to the foot of Hardy's Hill, the distance of a mile, turned and came back without stopping. She had dark brown hair, pleasant gray eyes with a peculiar twinkle in them, and a sallow complexion. She was not prepossessing in personal appearance, and in character a strange combination of kindness and perseverance, shyness and daring; a creature loving and spiteful, full of energy and perseverance, full of fun, with a keen sense of the ludicrous, apt speech and ready wit; a subject of moods, than whom no one could be jollier and more entertaining when geniality was in ascendency, but if the opposite, let her best friend beware.

That she was not a boy was one of her great afflictions; her impulsive disposition was fretted by the restraint and restrictions which were deemed essential to the proper girl. Most of her books have some one character in which her own traits are more or less conspicuous. In "Hospital Sketches" and "Little Women" they are very prominent; the latter, in fact, as is well known, is a family book, the traits of character, except those of Mr. Alcott, being true to life, and many, though not all of the incidents. The opening chapter of "Hospital Sketches" is a good sample of family conversation, and as the following chapters were letters written home, they are really part and parcel of herself, and through them one sees Louisa in maturity in her true self, impulsive, warm-hearted, self-reliant, earnest to do good, self-sacrificing, gentle and tender to the suffering, indignant at wrong, cheerful under difficulties, sympathetic and grateful for kindness, with a quick sense of the comical under all circumstances.

In regard to the studies of the sisters that winter (for one sister cannot be considered without the other, so closely united were the two) I have only faint recollection, but I am inclined to think they did not join classes in general. Mr. Alcott did not believe in the use of text-books and the usual method of imparting knowledge, and he had taught them at home by his own method, that of conversation. Grammar they never studied from books. Of the jolly good times during that winter, both at school and at their home, and in the years that followed, I have most pleasant remembrance. It was a new life to the sisters, who for the first time associated with those of their own age in a promiscuous school, and the friendship then formed between Anna and myself, though interrupted by seasons of separation, was never broken.

Louisa, though younger than Anna, was the controlling spirit, and often shocked her sensitive sister by some daring speech or deed. Thus, one morning on their way to school, seeing the horse and sleigh of a neighbor at a house they were passing, Louisa, much to the chagrin of her sister, took possession of it and, coming along as I was starting for school, took me for a short drive, then returned the team to the place where she found it. Years after, when the white mingled with the brown on our heads, reference was made, in our reminiscences, to this schoolgirl episode; she laughing, said, "and Bart kissed me when I got out." (Promiscuous kissing was under a ban in their family.)

The three months of school being over, we could not of course be together every day, and the plan of having a postoffice was originated; so on the hillside about midway between our homes, a hollow stump was cleared out and a box duly installed to receive our missives, and much sentiment and much fun passed through this repository. It was visited daily or oftener, and cruelly abused did we feel if on going there we did not find something for ourselves. Each had a fictitious signature. In looking over these little notes, which have been carefully treasured for more than half a century, I do not find

[136]

one commencing in the usual schoolgirl style of that time, "I now take my pen in hand" nor ending with "My pen is poor, my ink is pale," etc. I do not think they ever used such a form; formality in all respects was distasteful to them; but Louisa now and then sent a rhyme. The following accompanied a bouquet:

> "Clara, my dear, your birthday is here
> Before I had time to prepare,
> Yet take these flowers, fresh from Nature's bower,
> All bright and fair."

In winter evenings whist was a favorite diversion, Mrs. Alcott thinking a game of cards much more enjoyable and less harmful than the kissing games usually resorted to among the young. When a little party was invited for the girls, she was always present to suggest and assist in the games, selecting those in which this feature was not admissible. At one time a boy in some game ventured to kiss Anna, much to the indignation of all, and Louisa especially stormed about it. He was ever after known in the family as "Mr. Smack." They were in the habit among themselves of using nicknames for some of their mates, chosen for some incident connected with the person; thus, a boy at school who would one day wear a pair of mittens, leave one or both on the window seat, and come the next day with another pair, or odd ones, as the case might be, was dubbed "Mr. Mitten." Louisa was very fond of whist and was the life of the party, yet, if she was deeply interested in a book when her presence was desired, no persuasion could lure her from her den till she chose to come,—then all was sunshine.

After the winter at school, the girls studied at home, reading French and German, and reciting to George Bradford or Henry Thoreau. They spent much time together over their books, one often reading aloud while the others sewed, and Mrs. Alcott was one with her daughters, entering with sympathetic heartiness into all that concerned them, and telling stories of her family and past life, many of which Louisa wove into her writings to give them the charm of naturalness. If there were any schoolgirl secrets, it was only for a time, to end in a happy surprise.

They were very fond of fairy tales in those days, and writing them was one of Louisa's first attempts at composition. Their library contained all Miss Edgeworth's novels, Scott's, Miss Bremer's and Dickens' works, and other standard books of the day. Dickens was a great favorite; they never tired of his comic scenes and characters from real life, and frequent peals of laughter were always heard when "Boz" was the entertainer. Having a good memory, Louisa stowed away the funny parts for future diversion, recalling them at opportune times for her own amusement and that of others.

Birthdays were always noticed by the family as well as all holidays; tableaux and plays were then brought out, as they were in fact at any other time when the spirit moved. By enclosing a piazza at the end of the house with draperies, they improvised a stage very easily, and in their attic was a quantity of ancestral finery, brocaded silks, satin slippers, old laces, shawls, wigs, etc., which did duty on these occasions. Louisa usually took a comic or tragic part, or that of an old woman. If memory failed, she never hesitated, but extemporized from her own brains and often put the other actors to their wits' end by some unexpected originality. If an impromptu play was desired, the mother and sisters could do their part by just knowing the spirit of the subject.

The Alcotts lived and dressed plainly at this time, ignoring fashion, and thus had much time for outdoor exercise, even while doing their own work. Although they lived a mile from the village, the distance was thought nothing of. I have known the girls to walk three miles after dinner, make a good social call, and return to supper. A walk of five or six miles was just good exercise for them. In later years Louisa walked from Boston home one Sunday, a distance of twenty miles, having missed the train Saturday night, and arrived in Concord about 1 p.m.; and as there were callers that evening, she walked part way to the village with them, "for exercise," she said.

Mrs. Alcott was in the habit of joining her children and a few of their mates in long walks; and days or half-days were spent at Walden Pond, Fairy Land, Fair-haven and other quiet resorts in the woods. Mr. Alcott sometimes accompanied us and mingled some of his wise thoughts with our pleasure. One day at Walden he wrote on the sand with a stick, much to our amusement, to show how he learned to write when a boy. The sand and his mother's kitchen floor were his copy-book, which he was allowed to use just before it was to be washed.

A favorite resort with us girls near our homes, where we could go with safety by ourselves, was to a pool which F. B. Sanborn in his "Reminiscences of Seventy Years" calls "Gowing's Swamp"; it was a walk to which he and his group did not invite everyone, he says, but one day Channing took Hawthorne there; the latter was not an observer or lover of nature, and after giving a glance around he desired to "get out of this dreadful hole."

We girls approached the pool by a narrow path at the foot of a wooded hill which skirted a blueberry swamp and led out to a knoll, and there jumping across a narrow stream, we were at the pool which was bordered by flowering shrubs in their season, and in the vicinity were to be found the pyrola with its exquisite waxen blossom, foxberry, or eye-bright whose dainty delicate white bloom changed to the bright red berry, half hidden among the leaves, sweet-fern, Solomon's seal, checkerberry leaves, ferns, and in fact all the rich treasures of nature found in the wild woods and of which we girls plucked abundantly. We named the place Paradise, and spent many happy hours there.

At the end of three years, in 1848, the family moved to Boston, and Louisa taught a few pupils, had the care of little children or sewed, and wrote fairy tales and stories for papers and magazines as she had time. Writing and enacting dramas engaged her leisure hours, for she had a natural taste for the stage.

In 1857 the Alcotts returned to Concord and purchased, with money left to the girls by a relative, the place adjoining their old home, which was then owned and occupied by Nathaniel Hawthorne. Here Louisa soon found an agreeable circle of young people and entered into their social functions with the energy and zeal which was characteristic of her; in fact she soon became a leader in their amusements, masquerades, tableaux, charades, etc., which were her special delight. Her mirth and good humor made her a favorite everywhere.

An amateur artist of Woburn (C. W. Reed), accepted an invitation from a friend to attend a masquerade in Concord and there met Louisa Alcott; again he met her at a small social party where the entertainment was chatting, telling stories and music. During the evening Louisa asked him to sketch their house at "The Orchard" or as she sometimes called it, "Apple Slump." Accordingly next morning he took his stand in the field across the road opposite the house and with sketch book and pencil began his work. Louisa, her sister, May, and their friend, Miss Barrett, were sitting on the porch under Louisa's den at the end of the house. When Louisa spied him, she bounded down the path across the road and at a hand vault cleared the bars of the gateway and entered the field where he stood and asked if he minded her looking on while he drew. "Certainly not," replied Reed. Presently she asked where his line of sight was, his point of sight, his vanishing points, etc. All of which Reed knew nothing about and so informed her. "Then how do you draw your lines?" she inquired. He replied, "I make my lines where I see they are." Whereupon she called to the girls, "Oh, goody, come quick and see an artist who doesn't bother about making points of sight, lines of sight, or vanishing points." So the two girls ran across the road, jumped the fence in the same way Reed had done when he entered the field, and Louisa, also, and all three watched the sketching.

When finished, Louisa said she would like her father to meet Reed and see the picture, so they all went to the house. After Mr. Reed had been presented to Mr. Alcott and the latter had examined the sketch, he placed his hand on the artist's head and said, "Young man, you are a child of light, a child of God." Reed replied he thought he did not quite understand what Mr. Alcott meant by that. Mr. Alcott took him around the house, and, pointing to some bright flowers, said, "These are God-like; they represent all that is good, but the nightshade, belladonna and others of like nature are of darkness, of evil." Reed, being but a youth, was about to express his lack of conception of the idea, when Louisa gave him a poke with her toe as a hint for him to keep silent and let her father ramble on in his own deep faraway manner, which he did for a time while the young people listened with due respect, then Mr. Alcott retired to his study and the young people chatted after their own manner. Louisa drew a hand in the artist's sketch book on the page opposite the house; it represented a hand, with all but the index finger closed, and showed that the pencil was not her forte. Then she wanted Reed to draw one. He took the book and said, "Hold out your hand, please." "Oh, is that the way you do it?" she said. The old sketch book of more than fifty years ago now bears evidence of this little episode in Louisa's girlhood.

When the war broke out, Louisa was among the first to go to Washington as nurse in 1862. Her letters written home during her stay of about two months there were published in the Boston Commonwealth and copied by other papers all over the North. On her recovery from the fever which had made her stay in Washington so brief, these letters, which had been revised, were published in book form with one or two chapters added, under the title of "Hospital Sketches." As every one at that time was deeply interested in anything that pertained to the soldiers, the book made a stir and sold rapidly.

Thus encouraged, she took to her pen again, writing stories for papers and magazines, and after a while ventured to have "Moods" published. In her "Life, Letters and Journals," edited by Mrs. Ednah D. Cheney, is a graphic description of her trials and discouragements in getting this, her first novel, before the public. It was severely criticised by some on account of its views of marriage, yet when republished after fame had been acquired from "Little Women," the same persons said "it was not so bad, after all."

In 1865 she accompanied an invalid lady to Europe, and during her travels she met a Polish youth from whom she conceived the character of Laurie in "Little Women." More than one young man on this side of the water has claimed the distinction, but the Pole in Vevey was the real original. Two years later, in 1867, "Little Women" was written. Its lifelike incidents made it very attractive to both young and old; the children were wild over it, and like Oliver Twist, "asked for more." The financial success of the book made the family independent, and "An Old-Fashioned Girl" followed.

Another trip was taken to Europe, the incidents of which are given in "Shawl Straps" in her own amusing style; but, on account of nerves shattered by overwork, she did not find the enjoyment or improvement she had expected. One reason may have been that she continued to use the pen, for while she was in Rome news was received of the death of her sister Anna's husband, and she immediately wrote "Little Men," the proceeds of which were devoted to the education of the two little boys left fatherless.

At one time Scribner wanted her to write a serial for his magazine, and she declined on account of her mother, who was not well, while her own health was also not good. He asked her to set her price; she replied "three thousand dollars," thinking he would not give it, but he told her to go on, and "Under the Lilacs" was produced. Other books of hers are "Work," "Eight Cousins," "Rose in Bloom," "Jack and Jill," "A Garland for Girls," "My Boys," "Transcendental Wild Oats," "A Modern Mephistopheles," etc., etc. One of her last books was "Lu Lu's Library," a series of short stories written for her little niece, the daughter of her artist sister.

In the autumn of 1877 Mrs. Alcott, after much suffering, passed away. Louisa had been able to be with her during most of her sickness and wrote while caring for her. Her death was a severe blow to Louisa, as the tie between them was most tender and sweet. Their dispositions were much alike. Her sister May, who was in Paris at this time, was married the next spring, and the acquisition of a brother, together with May's happiness, served to distract attention from her grief, but the memory of her dear mother was held sacred through life.

She looked forward to a visit to May, in the near future, her health not permitting it then, but two years later the dear petted sister May followed the mother. Anna writes of Louisa at that time: "I have never seen her brave heart so broken; so many hopes are shattered, and so much to which she has looked forward so long has now vanished forever." Her little namesake, the child of May, became Louisa's, the last bequest of the mother. Of her coming to them, Anna wrote, "a healthy, happy little soul, she comes like sunshine to our sad hearts, and takes us all captive by her winning ways and lovely traits."

To this child Louisa devoted her time and love until, broken in health, she was obliged to leave her home and cares for a quiet place to rest and recuperate. But she had ventured too much in writing so incessantly in the past. Her nervous system never rallied from the strain and for several years she was an invalid. Though not able to write, her brain still thought stories for the children.

The last fifteen months of her life she made her home with Dr. Lawrence of Roxbury, who attended her wherever she went for a change. A day or two before her father passed away, she drove to Boston to see him, and as she stood by his bedside, just before leaving, she said, "As you lie here, father, what do you think about?" Pointing his finger upward, he said, "I think of the loved ones up there, and I am going to them soon." Louisa replied, "I wish I was going, too." And her wish was gratified; the next day she was taken very ill with meningitis and on the 6th of March, 1888, just two days after her father left this life, she followed, not knowing he had gone before. The last service of love which friends give to the departed was paid to her in the same rooms at Louisburg Square so recently left by her father. Her poem, "In Memoriam," to her mother, and a poem from her father to herself formed part of the sacred tribute friends rendered to her life; and the body which had been the dwelling place for the soul of Louisa May Alcott for fifty-six years was taken to Sleepy Hollow Cemetery in Concord and buried with her parents and her sister Elizabeth.

Louisa had a fine figure and a well-formed head, covered with an abundance of brown hair, which she wore in a simple, becoming style, rather than follow the fashion, if not pleasing to her taste. An easy dignity of bearing, a face beaming with intelligence and good nature, and a twinkling of the gray eye when something pleased her, made her an attractive woman, if not what would be called handsome. An hour spent with her when she was feeling well, in listening to some recital of her experience, either pathetic or humorous, was like a refreshing cordial to the spirits.

Knowing from her own experience the benefit of a little help to a struggling aspirant, she delighted, in her quiet way, in assisting young persons who were thus striving.

While appreciating with pleasure the honest interest and respect which her talent duly received from those she esteemed, she instinctively shrank from the rude and obtrusive curiosity of the mere sight-seers. She once said to some young boys, "Whatever you do, don't do anything to get fame." The many callers which the School of Philosophy brought to Concord, and their curiosity, which drew them to the home of the Alcotts, were truly distasteful to her, and when circumstances favored, she avoided them.

She advocated "woman suffrage," and when the opportunity to vote for school committee was given to the women, she was the first to register in Concord, and she endeavored to interest the women of the town to do so. She was much tried by their apathy on the subject, but was herself one of the twenty to vote.

She enjoyed writing and felt she had a special gift for that, which no one will deny, but she was also ever ready to adapt herself to the circumstances of her checkered life. Often in the midst of writing a book she would need to leave it for days or months, while she attended to the work of the family, cheerfully doing the cooking, washing dishes, cleaning house, nursing, or sweeping, as the case required, for she could turn her hand to anything. At one time she wished for a hat to match a new dress, and failing to find one to her mind in Boston, she bought a white straw and painted it to suit her taste; and that was after money was plenty. The desire to write one book at leisure and uninterrupted was never gratified, for when leisure came, ill health prevented her writing more than an hour or two at a time, and at last it was only half an hour.

Going West with her father in the fall of 1875, she began to realize how famed she was. At Oberlin College the young ladies wished to hear her speak; but as public speaking was not in her line, though she was delightful in conversation, she said she would stand and turn round, so all could see her, and so she did turn round three times. On the return she stopped in New York City, intending to remain there the rest of the winter, but a sudden return home disclosed a singular fact. Finding herself greatly lionized and having worn her one party dress, a black silk, till "Mrs. Grundy" demanded a new one, she thought best to fly to the home nest before she was led into extravagance and become vain through flattery.

Of the effect of this popularity on her character her sister testifies that she was not made proud by it, but was still the same loving, self-sacrificing, devoted Louisa as of old. Thus her good sense and warm heart kept her soul pure and made her worthy of the love and esteem which she received in life and which makes her memory dear.

From *The Alcotts as I Knew Them* (Boston: C. M. Clark, 1909), pp. 1–30.

"Reminiscences of Louisa M. Alcott" (1912)

F. B. Sanborn

Sanborn (1831–1917), who has long been seen as helping to mythologize the Transcendentalists and especially his connection with them, worked hard to keep their ideas alive for the early-twentieth-century reader. Many of his personal encounters with the New England authors and poets can be found in his two-volume autobiography, *Recollections of Seventy Years* (Boston: Richard G. Badger, 1909). With Moncure Daniel Conway, he was co-editor of the *Boston Commonwealth* and also a co-editor of the Massachusetts *Springfield Republican*, where he often reported on the famous authors of Concord. Louisa, after reading one of his notices in the "Gossipy old Republican" telling about her personal adventures during her 1870 European grand tour, wrote her family: "I should like to knock their heads off for meddling with what dont concern them old tattle tails!" (*Selected Letters*, 148).

Sanborn had also just published one of the first in-depth profiles of Louisa in his "The Author of Little Women," in the 16 July 1870 *Hearth and Home*. Upon receiving a copy in Italy, Alcott crossed out his description of *Moods* (1865) as "embodying but incompletely her idea of love and marriage and failing, for that reason, perhaps, to take the position in literature which the author's talent justified." Here, however, Sanborn recounts his own involvement with the family, including his first meeting with Louisa in 1852, where he was impressed by her "expressive face and earnest, almost melancholy eyes." This first meeting, almost a decade after the debacle at Fruitlands, also captures the lack of interest by Louisa in her father's philosophical talk, a fact biographers and critics would focus upon during the next century. In this recollection, occasioned by the success of a *Little Women* play in theaters around the country, Sanborn reflects upon Alcott's own dramatic talents as a teenager and young adult, noting that she possessed the quality of an effective actress—"A serious and profound vein of feeling."

The representation of Miss Alcott's "Little Women" as a drama, in theaters from Buffalo westward, amid applause and appreciation, is a long-deferred tribute to the dramatic element in her gifted nature. This tendency to the melodramatic, which she began to manifest as a child, and which almost placed her on the stage as an actress in the mimic scenes that had attracted her so forcibly in the plain country landscape amid which she grew up, is worth dwelling on for a moment, altho it never took effect so as to make of her a prima donna of the exalted and attractive class. For that role she was qualified by nature, had the circumstances been a little more propitious.

The actual qualification by nature for an effective actress is varied and diverse. Beauty is an element, but a superficial one; except for light comedy, mere beauty is insufficient in an actress; tragedy, and even melodrama, demand a serious and profound vein of feeling. This Louisa Alcott, as I first saw her at her father's Boston house in Pinckney street, in the autumn of 1852, seemed to have in her a well-endowed nature; and it was exprest in her energetic but represt manner. I made a half hour's call while I was in Harvard College, for the purpose of being introduced to her father, Bronson Alcott, whose attached friend and final biographer I became. Mrs. Ednah Littlehale Cheney was my introducer, while she still bore her maiden name, tho affianced to Seth Cheney, the graceful artist, whom she married the next year. All thru that ceremonious call Louisa sat silent in the background of the family circle, her expressive face and earnest, almost melancholy eyes were fixt on the visitors; but slight appeal was made to her interest in the conversation, which turned on the philosophic themes that Alcott had made his own long before 1852. He had been one of the leaders in the spiritual movement that began twenty years before, about the time of Louisa's birth—November 29, 1832—the very day of the month and year with her father, who was thirty-three years old the day this daughter was born. She saw the light in Germantown, not then a component part of Philadelphia, in a house which Mr. Reuben Haines, a wealthy friend of education, had bought for the school that Mr. Alcott had been invited to conduct at Germantown for children up to the age of nine. Mrs. Alcott, a daughter of Col. Joseph May, of Boston, writing to her father in May, 1831, said of it:

"It is a fine house on the main street, the grounds and garden standing back, including an acre or more, all beautifully laid out. Our garden is planted, our house neatly furnished. The garden is lined with raspberries, currants and gooseberry bushes, in a large ground, with a beautiful serpentine walk, shaded with pines, firs, cedars, apple, pear, peach and plum trees; and a long cedar hedge extends from the back to the front. Mr. Haines presented us with busts of Newton and Locke, and our rooms are tastefully fitted up."

In such surroundings was the future dramatist and storyteller born, altho she was brought back to her mother's Boston of 1834 too early to have received many pictures of that charming scenery on her childish retina of a very appreciative eye. The city life did not agree with her early constitution, and in the summer of 1835 her father wrote in his diary:

"Both my children (Anna and Louisa) are suffering for the want of purer air, renovating imagery and spiritual inspiration. They are morbid in sensibility, dimmed in intellectual vision, and require the benefits of natural and spiritual sympathy to raise them from their depression. The city does not give their young natures room; they are fettered, and fall back to prey on sentiments, instinct, ideas, that have not been allowed to flow forth."

Concerning girls of three and five years old this may sound like strange comment from a father. But Alcott had been, from the first, doing what the Italian educator, Maria Montessori, has been doing for a few years in Rome—watching carefully all the indications of mental and spiritual development in children. He kept elaborate journals of his observations thus made, which, at the invitation of his friend, Mrs. Edith Talbot, of Boston, he submitted to the American Social Science Association at Saratoga in 1880.

I suppose Louisa's first dramatic appearance was on her third birthday (November 28, 1835), when Mr. Alcott's pupils in his Boston school, at the Temple, on Tremont street, celebrated the joint advent of father and daughter the day before, because it was Saturday, and it would not have been decorous to have the ceremony on Sunday, the actual anniversary. In his diary Alcott gave this account of the festival:

"This morning my pupils celebrated my birthday at the schoolroom. They assembled at the usual hour, nine. At ten o'clock they crowned me with laurel, and also Louisa, my little girl being three years old. An address was then given in the name of the school by one of the pupils, and they presented me with a fine edition of 'Paradise Lost.' I then gave them a short account of my life, and an ode was pronounced by one of the little girls. We then partook of some refreshment."

The beginning of the ode was this:

> This hour in love we come
> With hearts of happy mirth,—
> We've sallied forth from home
> To celebrate a birth.
> *Chorus.*
> A time for joy,—for joy!
> Let joy then swell around!
> From every girl and boy
> Let joy's full tones resound.

The laurel was prophetic on Louisa's head, and the tones of joy were those which naturally she used. But the gift of "Paradise Lost" to the father was no less prophetic, since from that day forward he was exiled from one Eden after another, till this laurel-crowned daughter restored him to the "Paradise Regained" of Concord, as he reached the age of three score and ten. The town was no paradise to Louisa; she had experienced many disappointments and mortification there; but to Bronson Alcott and to his artist daughter, May, it was a delightful abode. Alcott, but a few months before Emerson's death and his own paralysis in the same year (1882), wrote and published this sonnet of praise and description:

CONCORD IN MASSACHUSETTS

> Calm vale of comfort, peace and industry,
> Well doth thy name they home-bred traits express!
> Considerate people, neighborly and free,
> Proud of their monuments, their ancestry,
> Their circling river's quiet loveliness,
> Their noble townsmen's fame and history.
> Nor less I glory in each goodly trait,
> Child of another creed, a stricter State:
> I chose thee for my haunt in troublous time,
> My home in days of late prosperity,
> And laud thee now in this familiar rhyme:
> Here on thy bosom the last summons wait:
> To scenes, if lovelier, still reflecting thee,
> Resplendent both in hope and memory.

It was the loss of his Boston Eden of infant education that finally drove the Alcott pair, with their "Little Women," to Concord in 1840. At first supported by a section of the old families of Boston, the Quincys, Savages, Mays, Channings, etc., his school, in excellent rooms at the Masonic Temple, flourished and grew. But presently his views of theologic truth began to be suspected, and it was found that he was also friendly with the despised Abolitionists. When he went so far as to admit a colored girl named Robinson to the same classes with his own three girls, his wealthy patrons withdrew their children, and left him with only five pupils in all — three Alcotts, a child of the Scotch scholar and elocutionist, William Russell, and the Robinson child. This was in 1839, and his income was so reduced that he could no longer live in Boston. Emerson made the way easy for the Alcotts to rent the Hosmer Cottage, a mile or so from his own house and garden; a small house on the lands of the Hosmer farm, near the river, and with outbuildings and an acre or two of land for an Alcott garden, and an opportunity to work as a hireling in the neighboring farms, which he did.

The cottage and its surroundings were picturesque when, late in March, 1840, the five fugitives from Boston took up residence there, and began a life of poverty and neglect, most of the friends who had hoped much from this reformer of education being ready to give him up after his hope had so completely failed. He then took to manual labor and to parlor conversations, by which he gained a small revenue, but could not keep his children from pinching poverty, really more severe than that in which the opening of the story of "Little Women" finds the four girls of the March household in the early months of our Civil War. The name March is a substitute for May, their mother's maiden name, and there are many changes of time and place; but the substance of the drama is the family romance of plain living, high thinking and generous giving and receiving. Meg is Anna, sixteen; Jo is Louisa, fifteen; Beth is Elizabeth, thirteen, and Amy is Abby May, really but seven, yet actually represented as nearly twelve. She was, in fact, born July 28, 1840, in the Hosmer Cottage, and the assumed date, governed by these ages, would be 1847–48, but is in truth that period of the war when Louisa, at the age of twenty-nine, was going to Washington as a hospital nurse. The scene of the action is not exactly Concord, on the Lexington road, a quarter mile east of Emerson's corner, but an imaginary place, now here, now there, yet never far from Boston, from which the Orchard House is eighteen miles distant.

I had known the family (chiefly Mr. Alcott, Louisa and May) for some five years before they occupied the old Orchard House in April, 1858, and fifteen years after they had left the Hosmer Cottage for their next planted Eden, at

Fruitlands in Harvard, on the Nashua River, thirteen miles to the southwest, in constant view of the New Hampshire mountains. In that brief residence the four little women first appeared dramatically together, in a family festival, repeating, on a larger field, the laurel crowning of father and second daughter. The day was June 24, 1843 (birthday of Beth, then eight, and within four days of the birthday of May, then three). The narrator is Meg (Anna), in her journal of a twelve-year-old diarist; and into it is copied her father's ode and Charles Lane's brief and pleasing verse:

A FRUITLANDS IDYLL

"This was Lizzie's birthday. I rose before 5 o'clock, and went with Louisa and Willy Lane to the Grove, where we fixed a little pine tree in the ground, and hung all our presents on it. Mother gave her a silk thread case, Louisa a pincushion, I a fan, Willy a book, and Abby a little pitcher. I made for each of us an oak-leaf wreath. After breakfast, we all, except Wood Abraham, marched to the wood. Mr. Lane carried his violin and played, and we all sung first. Then father read a parable and an ode which he wrote himself. Here are some verses of it:

> Here in the Grove, with those we love.
> In the cool shade, near mead and glade.
> The trees among, with leaves o'erhung,
> On sylvan plat, on forest mat.
>> Hither we all repair.
>> Our hope and love to bear:
>> In rustic state to celebrate
>> Mid this refulgent Whole,
> The joyful advent of an angel Soul
> That twice four years ago, our mundane life to know,
>> A presence to our eyes
>> Descended from the upper skies;
>> Before us stands, arrayed
>> In garments of a maid.
> *(To the Child.)*
>> And close that treasure keep
>> That in thy heart doth sleep!
>> Mind what the Spirit saith.
>> And plight thereto thy faith.
>> My very dear Elizabeth!

To Elizabeth.
Of all the year the sunniest day
   Appointed for thy birth,
Is emblem of thy longest stay
   With us upon the earth;
Now drest in flowers
The merry hours
Fill up the day and night;
   May thy whole life,
   Exempt from strife,
Shine forth as calm and bright.

"Father then asked us what flowers we would give Lizzie? I said, 'A rose, the emblem of love.' Father chose the rose also. Louisa said 'A lily of the valley for innocence.' Mother said she should give a forget-me-not, for remembrance. Christy Greene said 'An arbutus, for perseverance'; and Mr. Lane gave her a piece of moss, meaning humility. Lizzie looked at her presents and seemed much pleased."

These festivals were common and natural in this family, where in many simple ways imagination and generosity were cultivated or quickened. When in 1845, after the departure from the Fruit-lands paradise, and the return to house and garden, garret and barn, under the long range of hills in the East Quarter of Concord, facilities for the dramas of children were afforded without leaving their own grounds (which then covered thirty acres, with a woodland behind and a rippling trout brook in front), the imaginative instinct had full play. Its product (in part) were those amazing "Comic Tragedies" which Meg (then Mrs. John Pratt) published in 1893. They show imitation, invention, impossibility and an unaptness of language that indicated, as did the "Flower Fables" of about the same period (which were published in a small volume in December, 1854, with poorly drawn illustrations by "Amy"—the artist May), that many trials must be made and much mortification endured, before Louisa could find her true field in literature.

The attempt of Louisa to go on stage as actress was made after the Wayside House was given over to the Hawthornes, or at least was abandoned about 1849, by the Alcotts, who removed to Boston in the hope of finding occupations and incomes for so much talent that was yet unrecognized. Louisa studied and rehearsed for the stage, and even made a contract for appearing in minor parts, and had the dream of writing plays in which she should act her own creations. But the time had not arrived, and when in 1857 the whole family came down from New Hampshire and presently bought the Orchard House, with its old apple trees in front and its pine wood on the hill top, she was still in her long apprenticeship to the weekly newspapers, wherein her stories found many readers and but few dollars for the family purse, so she tried kindergartening, lady's companioning and other respectable arts, and still kept on writing. The war came on; she volunteered as a nurse, tended the wounded faithfully, but nearly died of the fever thus caught; and thru that gateway of pain and sorrow came at last into the golden harvest-field of pathetic fiction for which all her multiplied experiences had fitted her to touch the heart of youth, as none of her sex in America has done, before or since.

The houses in which serious stages in her life were passed—the Hosmer Cottage, the Hillside (now Wayside) House, and the Orchard House—are here represented. In the last, her best work was done and her most serious experiences endured. It has now become a memorial of her genius, and is to contain the souvenirs of her family, who were joint authors with her of those ever-pleasing books.

The Independent 72 (7 March 1912): 496–502.

Caroline Hildreth's crayon portrait of Bronson Alcott, 1857. From a copy in the Joel Myerson Collection of Nineteenth-Century American Literature, University of South Carolina.

Engraving of Abigail May Alcott.

Abigail May Alcott. Louisa May Alcott Memorial Association.

Elizabeth Sewall Alcott. Louisa May
Alcott Memorial Association.

Early daguerreotype of Anna Alcott Pratt.
Louisa May Alcott Memorial Association.

Early daguerreotype of Louisa May
Alcott. Louisa May Alcott Memorial
Association.

May Alcott Nieriker. From a copy in
the Joel Myerson Collection of
Nineteenth-Century American
Literature, University of South Carolina.

Dove Cottage (the Hosmer Cottage), where the Alcotts
moved in 1840. From a copy in the Joel Myerson Collection
of Nineteenth-Century American Literature, University of
South Carolina.

Main building at Fruitlands, where the Alcotts lived in 1843. From a copy
in the Joel Myerson Collection of Nineteenth-Century American Literature,
University of South Carolina.

Hillside (Hawthorne's Wayside), where the Alcotts lived from 1845 to 1848. From a copy in the Joel Myerson Collection of Nineteenth-Century American Literature, University of South Carolina.

Bronson Alcott's sketch of Hillside (1845).

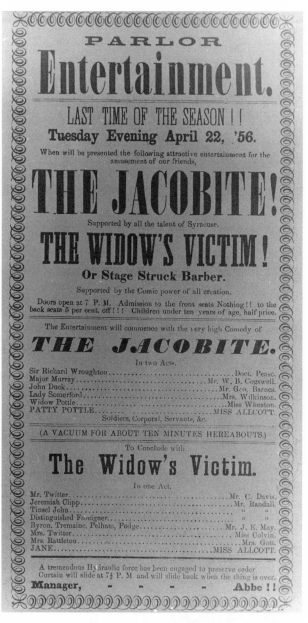

Playbill for *The Jacobite* and *The Widow's Victim* (1856),
performed by the Walpole Amateur Dramatic Company.
Louisa May Alcott Memorial Association.

John Bridge Pratt. Louisa May Alcott
Memorial Association.

John Bridge Pratt in theatrical costume.
Louisa May Alcott Memorial Association.

Engraving of Franklin
Benjamin Sanborn.

Central Concord in the mid-1860s. Concord Free Public Library.

Orchard House in the mid-1860s, with the Alcott family before it. Louisa May Alcott Memorial Association.

May Alcott's frontispiece illustration to *Little Women, Part One* (1868). Louisa May Alcott Memorial Association.

Thomas Niles, editor at Roberts
Brothers Publishers. From a
copy in the Joel Myerson Collection
of Nineteenth-Century American
Literature, University of South
Carolina.

Louisa May Alcott. From a copy
in the Joel Myerson Collection of
Nineteenth-Century American
Literature, University of South
Carolina.

Engraving of Bronson Alcott.

Orchard House. From *The Cottage Hearth*, May 1888.

Alfred Whitman.

The Hawthorne children in the early 1860s (from the left, Una, Julian, Rose). Peabody Essex Museum.

Orchard House and the Concord
School of Philosophy. From a
copy in the Joel Myerson
Collection of Nineteenth-Century
American Literature, University
of South Carolina.

Fred and John Pratt. Louisa May
Alcott Memorial Association.

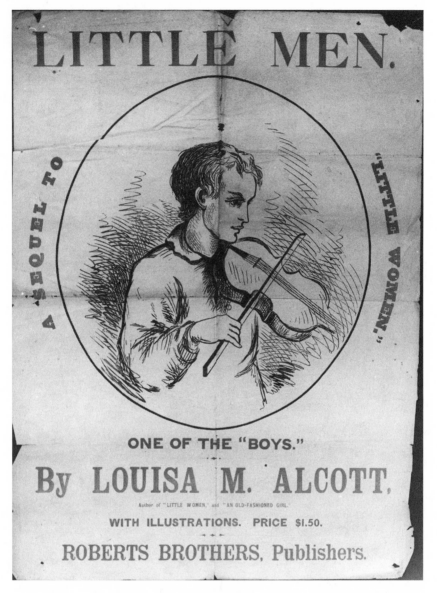

Advertising poster for *Little Men* (1871). Louisa May Alcott Memorial Association.

May Alcott Nieriker's drawing of Bronson Alcott in his study. Louisa May Alcott Memorial Association.

May Alcott Nieriker's drawing of Hillside. From *Concord Sketches* (1869).

Bronson Alcott on the steps of the
Concord School of Philosophy.

Bronson Alcott, ca. 1870s.

Advertising poster for Bronson Alcott's Conversations (1875).
Louisa May Alcott Memorial Association.

Louisa May Alcott. From a copy in the Joel Myerson Collection of Nineteenth-Century American Literature, University of South Carolina.

May Alcott Nieriker's drawing of Louisa May as "The Golden Goose" (1871). Louisa May Alcott Memorial Association.

The Thoreau House on Main Street in Concord, where the Alcotts moved in 1877. From a copy in the Joel Myerson Collection of Nineteenth-Century American Literature, University of South Carolina.

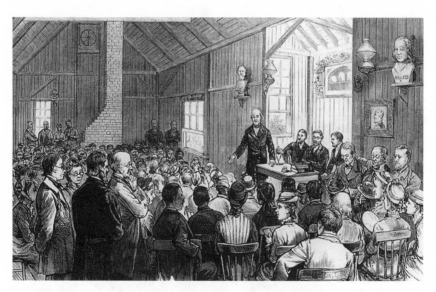

Drawing of a Bronson Alcott lecture at the Concord School of Philosophy. From *Frank Leslie's Illustrated Newspaper* (14 August 1880).

Ernest Nieriker. Louisa May Alcott
Memorial Association.

Louisa May "Lulu" Nieriker. Louisa May
Alcott Memorial Association.

Louisa May "Lulu" Nieriker. Louisa May Alcott Memorial Association.

Anna Alcott Pratt.
Louisa May Alcott
Memorial Association.

Fred Pratt. Louisa May Alcott Memorial Association.

Louisa May Alcott.
Louisa May Alcott
Memorial Association.

Drawing of No. 10, Louisburg
Square in Boston.

George Healy's portrait of Louisa May Alcott (1871).
Louisa May Alcott Memorial Association.

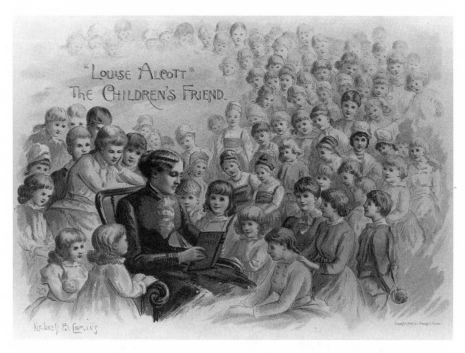

Frontispiece to Ednah Dow Cheney's *Louisa May Alcott: The Children's Friend* (1888).

"The 'Little Women' of Long Ago" (1913)

John S. P. Alcott

Written upon the appearance of the first officially sanctioned production of *Little Women*, adapted to the stage by Jessie Bonstelle and Marian de Forest, these recollections by John Sewall Pratt Alcott, Anna's younger son, recall his own childhood growing up among the Alcotts. Here, the second generation of "Brookes," the children of Meg and John, act out dramas and scenes from Charles Dickens, with some help from their stage director, Aunt Jo herself, or they play at *Pilgrims' Progress*, just as the March sisters did with their own "bosom enemies." John Pratt was officially adopted by Louisa May shortly before her death in order to ensure that he could renew the copyrights for her works, thus providing for the family in death even as she done in life. She also left her two nephews each a trust of $25,000 and helped them to get a start in the business world by securing them positions at Roberts Brothers publishers. He notes Louisa's role in the family as "Duty's faithful child" and emphasizes: "No matter what interfered with her work, if it belonged to the family, if it was anything connected with the family, it didn't matter. . . . No sacrifice she could make for them was too great."

Although the librarians and the publishers tell us that the popularity of "Little Women" has never been on the wane, since the days when it was brought out, I find that the personal interest of its readers in the author has had a revival since the book has been dramatized and its characters have been brought to life upon the stage. As the only living descendant of Miss Alcott in America who can claim a personal acquaintance with her, I find myself in the peculiar position of answering the same questions and queries in regard to "Little Women" that deluged my aunt, ever after the book was published.

She hated publicity, reporters, lionizing, autograph-hunters and all the other concomitants of fame, but always tried to send a personal answer to the little tots who wrote her a nice note about one of her books and asked her sensible questions about its characters. To be sure, she once did plan to publish "Aunt Jo's Funny Budget," a collection of funny letters which she had received from her readers, as a warning to her own nephews and nieces not to go and do likewise, and "to nip a new generation of innocent bores in the bud," but I know, also, that nothing pleased her more than spontaneous praise from a youngster, and that she was always willing and eager to give of herself to others if she thought it of any help or benefit to them. Therefore, it is in the spirit of her generosity and with no fear of violating a trust that I am going to try to share some of my memories and recollections of a wonderful woman with the countless numbers who have felt the influence of her strong and beautiful personality through her books.

Judging from the queries, it doesn't seem to be known generally, even yet, that the March family is the Alcott family in a very thin disguise. "Meg" was Anna, the oldest of the four girls, who married John Bridge Pratt; "Jo" was Louisa, of course, who never married anybody, because, as she said, "Somebody has to be the old maid in the family;" "Beth" was Elizabeth, who died when she was a little over twenty years old; and "Amy" was May, the artistic one of the quartette, who studied art abroad and later married a Swiss by the name of Ernest Nieriker, with whom she lived in Paris only two short years before her death. And I? I am "Daisy." You see, I was more carefully disguised, for I am neither a twin, nor a girl— only Meg's youngest boy.

Because it is all about our own dear relatives,— my brother, Amy's daughter and I—hesitated for eight years or more before we would sanction the dramatization of "Little Women." It wasn't that we thought that our Aunt Louisa wouldn't like it— on the contrary, we had every reason to believe that she would, since she was always keenly interested in the stage, even to the extent of wanting to make it her own profession at one time—but because we feared that no dramatist could or would make a play of the book that would preserve its atmosphere of sweet wholesomeness; we feared that the taint of theatricality might make a sacrilege of our home. To us "Little Women" was the story of our home and our family, a theme too intimate for the publicity to which the stage might subject it.

But when we grew to appreciate the reverence and the love which Miss Jessie Bonstelle,— one of the first and *the* most persistent applicant for the stage rights of the book—harbored for Jo and for "Little Women," and when she agreed to submit everything to us for approval before making it final, we gave in. And we have not once had cause to regret it— not even I when I saw myself brought on the stage as a papier-mâché baby in swaddling clothes. It has meant much work to Mrs. Alcott and myself, but it has meant

[154]

more joy and pleasure. We have come to realize, too, that instead of hurting the book, as we had feared it would do, the dramatization is helping it by bringing its story into the lives of people who have never read it, but who would go to see the play. How many men and boys, who scorn to read what they regard as a girl's book, will refuse to escort their wives or sisters or friends or sweethearts to the theater?

If the play seems real, that is because it tells a story that was real, in the midst of a stage-setting that is as real as we could make it, with the help of history and memory and family chronicles. What I did not remember—I was twenty-three years old when my Aunt Louisa died,—I was able to read up in the diaries and journals of the Alcotts. Fortunately, for us, the keeping of a daily record of deeds and thoughts was more important to them than eating, and, thanks to the economy they had to practice and the sentiment they attached to all family things, they saved everything of big or little or no importance, so that we could, when the play was to be produced, dig up all the information, the pictures, descriptions, or the things themselves that were necessary to restore the March household.

When Miss Bonstelle had finally succeeded in finding William A. Brady, a manager who had the courage to produce this simple, narrative play, so unlike the Broadway successes, a play without a big thrill, without a gripping climax, without a star and without a problem, she and the scenic artist, Mr. Law, also Mr. Luce, the representative of the Shuberts in Boston, Mrs. Alcott and I went out to Concord one day to get the atmosphere, the correct background, the "local color," if you will, for the production.

Three houses in this historic village, the home of New England philosophers, harbored the Alcott family at different times. The first, which was afterward bought by the Hawthornes and called "The Wayside," is now owned by Mrs. Daniel Lothrop (Margaret Sidney, the author of "The Five Little Peppers"), the second is "Orchard House," where "Little Women" was lived and written, and the third is the house on Main Street, once owned by Thoreau, in which my sister-in-law, Mrs. F. Alcott Pratt, still lives. But it is only the second that really concerns us here. For many years it stood empty, rotting away in its little hollow by the roadside. It was a very damp sort of place, as I remember it; I don't know how they kept it warm, for they used only wood in the grate fires for many years for all their heating. Only a few days ago, Mr. Edward Gaylord, who knew the Alcotts earlier, probably, than anyone living today, told me how he had come upon the girls fetching in wood from the pile outside and how he twitted them about the small quantity that they could carry, to which Louisa, being then but a tiny little bit of a mite, replied, "Pwetty good for wegetables, though."

They were vegetarians, not from economy but from principle, for Grandfather Alcott believed that any food obtained by hurting or robbing an animal, would corrupt the body and, through it, the soul. It was not until they were quite grown up that any of his children ever tasted meat. That was only one of his many ideas that seem strange to us now; they were certainly all more ideal than practical. He could develop a new system of philosophy and evolve ideas that were far ahead of his times, but he could not make money.

Money meant nothing to him and so, of course, he never cared whether or not he had five cents in his pocket, and when he had, he was certain to give them to the first one who asked him for them. He was one of the most loveable, one of the most ideally inclined men that ever lived, and just because he was so gentle and high-minded and guileless, everyone forgave him for what he was not—a financial success, a "good provider." "Marmee,"—that is, my grandmother, Mrs. Alcott,—suffered the most through this, but she never complained, for had she not been willing to give up much besides her social prestige in marrying this impecunious school teacher only because of the love she bore him? She was indeed a wonderful woman, strong and patient, gentle and practical. Judging from the quality of her letters, her children inherited as much of their mentality and their talents from her as they did from their father. Do you remember what Miss Alcott wrote in her diary, "All the philosophy in our house is not in the study; a good deal is in the kitchen, where a fine old lady thinks high thoughts and does kind deeds while she cooks and scrubs."

Many of the educational ideas they held in common may seen odd to us today. For example, they never admonished the children openly or reproved them in one another's presence. If one of them did anything reprehensible, she wouldn't know that it had displeased her parents until she went to bed and found under her pillow a little note from mother or father, discussing the fault committed and hinting at more desirable methods of behavior. The children thought these things over at leisure and then sent back their replies and conclusions in the same quiet, unobserved way. There was no chance for a flare of temper here, no opportunity to answer back; only a little silent contemplation of one's wrongdoings and then an endeavor to express contriteness and apology in writing. What a chastening of the spirit! One of these periods of meditation brought the following note from Louisa to her mother:

> "I'll be contented
> With what I've got;
> Of folly repented,
> Then sweet is my lot.
> From your trying daughter,
> "Louy."

To which her mother replied:

"My dear Louisa:

"Your note gave me so much delight that I cannot close my eyes without first thanking you, dear, for making me so happy, and blessing God who gave you this tender love for your mother. I have observed all day your patience with baby, your obedience to me and your kindness to all.

"Go on 'trying,' my child; God will give you strength and courage, and help you fill each day with words and deeds of love. I shall lay this on your pillow, put a warm kiss on your lips and say a little prayer over you in your sleep.

"Mother."

I think it has been rightly said that the Alcott girls put their hearts into their mother's keeping; their souls they intrusted to their father.

How far afield from Orchard House I have strayed! It was the dampness of the house and the poverty of the inhabitants that led me to digress. Neither of these factors, however, prevented the happiest sort of a home life; on the contrary, they only served to knit the ties closer, to develop the resourcefulness of the girls and to bring to the fore the strength and the force in Louisa, who felt herself called upon to assume the responsibilities "of the man in the family." This house is associated with the jolliest and the saddest things in their lives; here they acted "Pilgrim's Progress," here Beth died, and Meg was married; and it was here, up in the attic at the base of the chimneys, that Louisa sat "when genius burned." "With my papers 'round me and a pile of apples to eat while I write my journal, plan stories and enjoy the patter of rain on the roof, in peace and quiet," as she said.

I suppose it was because it was right in their midst the people of Concord forgot the existence of Orchard House. We tried many times to buy it, but it was not until the club women of the town brought their united efforts to bear that the price was put within reasonable limits. Two years ago they bought it, and when they had collected enough money they set right at work, making the necessary repairs and putting on the needed patches. The house was in such bad condition that one of the carpenters called into consultation advised Mrs. Henry Rolfe, the president of the Louisa Alcott Memorial Association, "to tear it all down and build a new one." The house has been restored, practically, through little self-denials. Just as soon as it became known that it had been bought, the contributions came pouring in. One of the first was from a little girl who wrote: "I have an allowance of one cent a week. I have saved it for five weeks. Please, I want to buy Miss Alcott's home." Another wrote that she hadn't eaten any candy for ten days and here were the ten cents she had saved—how much of the house would it buy? One poor old woman to whom the cost of living was almost unattainable, sent in a quarter of a dollar, saying that she had denied herself little things here and there for a year that she might add her contribution to the fund, and another one who had read "Little Women" in the edition for the blind, got up an entertainment in her own home out West somewhere to make money for the fund. So the stories go—from East and West, from over the seas, even; women and children, and here and there a man or two, have sent in their mickles that go to make the muckle that will make the home of the "Little Women" live forever. I do not know where nor how they hear of it, but they do, and pilgrims come from far and near to visit at this shrine. Since the nineteenth of last April, I believe, there have been over seven-thousand visitors in the house, who have left over one-thousand dollars in the free contribution box at the door. The work of restoring is slow, but although there isn't so very much to see as yet, the visitors all tell Miss Moore and Miss Freeman, the two young Concord girls who are guides and custodians of Orchard House, that there was plenty of atmosphere there already; that one could fairly see the March girls revelling in its cosy corners, its commodious closets and its comfortable little nooks. I know that Miss Bonstelle and Miss Marian de Forest, who dramatized the book, felt this way about it. I almost feared that they had taken all the atmosphere home with them and put it on the stage!

It is a homey looking place, that yellowish-brown house tucked away under the shade of kindly elms. What fun we used to have in that old grove behind the house! There was never a jollier party than the one Aunt Louisa gave me on my sixteenth birthday. We played games and charades under the direction of the inimitable Aunt Louisa, and as a glorious climax, there was a wonderful cake with all the sixteen candles and this little verse of dedication:

> "A sunshiny cake
> For a sunshiny boy,
> For him and his friends
> To eat and enjoy;
> Sixteen years hence
> When he is thirty-two
> May his friends be as many
> And his sorrows be as few."

The big tree on the right, which was a favorite hiding place of my youthful days and the haunt of Aunt Louisa's friend, the owl,—which Amy perpetuated over her mantelpiece, as you will remember,—has just been plumbed up by the tree-doctor, so that no more little boys and no more owls can find refuge in it. It is the same tree under which Grandfather Alcott used to sit as he discussed transcendentalism with his friends. The bench around it, as so many little odds and ends in and about the house, like the bookcase that he made out of a melodeon, the clothes dryer, the garden fence and the arbor, he built himself. I remember him best as he was tinkering with his tools in the "summer kitchen" or woodshed, and when he was teaching us our alphabet. Here, he had a novel method. Instead of using a book alphabet he invented one of his own, which he illustrated with anything he happened to have on hand,—even if it was only himself, as, when, lying on his back, with his legs straddled in the air, he personified a "Y," to our intense enjoyment and edification—for I have never forgotten how a "Y" looks from that day to this.

The living room was our real joy. The carpet was threadbare, perhaps, and the furniture worn, but it was full of books piled up on shelves which our grandfather-carpenter had built into every available bit of space and the scene of all our glorious charade parties and story-telling bees. When we had our theatricals, it was the auditorium, and the dining room was the stage. It seems to me that we were always having theatricals, my mother and Aunt Louisa were an everflowing source of plots. One of their chief diversions, as I remember, was to play that they were Sairey Gamp and Betsy Prig and act out long scenes from the Dickens' book. Aunt Louisa could really act and mimic very well, and sometimes even put this ability to practical use, as, for instance, when she went to the door herself, dressed as the maid, to tell a troublesome reporter that she was out of town. We played "Pilgrim's Progress" just as they did in "Little Women," and to this day, I remember my entire part in "Box and Cox," which had been drilled into me until I could say it backward. I was Cox, my brother Fred was Box, and my mother, Mrs. Bouncer; Aunt Louisa was the stage-director. We kept the audience in an uproar of laughter, but I don't believe anyone enjoyed the performance more than we children did. People were always laughing when Aunt Louisa was around, for without trying to be entertaining she could keep her guests and callers in a roar. Even her every-day talk to us in the household was bright and witty. But while she was talking with people, she was always making a study of them, too, drawing them out, watching them,—you never could be sure that you weren't going to get into some story of hers, some day! When May,—that is "Amy"—died and left her a little baby-girl as a legacy, she dreaded the responsibility of taking care of so precious a thing and was probably a little worried lest a baby interfere with her work, but consoled herself with the thought that "she may have a literary turn and be my assistant, by offering hints and giving studies of character for my work."

No matter what interfered with her work, if it belonged to the family, if it was anything connected with the family, it didn't matter. Many a time she gave up whole months to minister to someone who was ill, to visit someone in the family who was lonely, to do the cleaning or the sewing or the cooking to the neglect of her literary work, which was much more to her liking, of course, and her real work. There wasn't a thing she couldn't do, from trimming hats to discussing philosophy, and if it would make any member of the family happy, she would do any and all of them at once. No sacrifice she could make for them could be too great.

Had she not been so generous with her time she would doubtless have written more novels; as it was, she was always waiting for an opportunity to write another book like "Moods," which I believe to have been her own favorite. When her publishers first asked her to write a girl's book, she protested, saying that if she must write for children, she would rather write for boys. She always wanted to be a boy, you know, and somehow she felt that she understood boy-nature better. I don't think the fact that we two youngsters were boys had anything to do with it. I doubt whether she ever got more enjoyment out of anything than the writing of her first "penny-dreadfuls," her melodramas, full of romance and adventure. Only the other day I noticed in looking over the manuscript of "The Witch's Curse," the play which they act in "Little Women," which shows with what fervor it was written, that the love passages are penned in a flowing hand and the parts dealing with the villain, with a fierce, defiant looking back-hand.

She wrote very little in Concord, but usually escaped to the quiet of some hotel in Boston. This she did to free herself from an environment that meant much sorrow and worry to her. Once or twice, in the earlier years, she walked the eighteen miles into town (which she did in five hours, according to her diary) and whenever Amy was at home, she took her along for company.

Miss Alcott was keenly in sympathy with every movement which would tend to increase woman's educational and political opportunities. From the very beginning, one might almost say, she was a firm believer in woman suffrage, and although she was certainly not in sympathy with militant methods, she was always willing and glad to do what she could to help the cause. At one time she wrote in her diary: "Saw my townswomen about voting, etc. Hard work to stir them up; cake and servants are more interesting." But later, in writing to her publisher about a book which a friend of hers had written on suffrage, she took a more confident view of the success of the cause, for here she wrote: "Will you look at the manuscript, by and by, or do you scorn the whole thing? Better not; for we are going to win in time, and the friend of literary ladies ought to be also the friend of women generally."

None of her pictures do this fine woman justice, for her chief charm lay in her coloring and in the spirituality of her expression. As she said herself, "my pictures are never successes. When I don't look like a tragic muse, I look like a smoky relic of the great Boston fire."

"The 'Little Women' of Long Ago: Stories of Louisa M. Alcott, and the Old Days in Concord, Apropos the Highly Successful Play Based on the Book," *Good Housekeeping* 53 (February 1913): 182–89.

"Beth Alcott's Playmate:
A Glimpse of Concord Town in the
Days of *Little Women*" (1913)

Lydia Hosmer Wood

The family of Cyrus and Lydia Parkman Wheeler Hosmer must have been per-fect neighbors for the Alcotts when they moved to Concord in 1840, the year of May's birth. Settling into what was known as the "Hosmer house," the Alcott girls found immediate friends in their neighbors, the five Hosmer children: Sarah Parkman (b. 1824), Martha (b. 1829), Henry Joseph (b. 1832), and twins Cyrus and Lydia (b. 1833). Lydia's father, Cyrus Hosmer, grandson of Major Jo-seph Hosmer, a leader at the battle of Concord in 1775, was head of the acad-emy in Northfield, Massachusetts, but he had died almost a month after her birth. His widow, who had a number of relatives in the village, returned to Con-cord with the children. Since they were contemporaries, the Alcott and Hosmer children formed close friendships that would last through the years. Lydia's older brother, Henry Joseph, married Laura Whiting in 1874, when both were in their early forties. After marriage, Laura practiced medicine in Concord and corresponded regularly with Louisa May.

Wood's reminiscences show the Alcotts as a poor but happy family. Her de-scriptions give many details that only someone on intimate terms with the family could provide. For instance, her recollection of Louisa's account of Eliz-abeth Alcott's death ("As her spirit left her body I saw it rise, and, floating in the air, leave the room") foreshadows how "Beth's death" would become one of the lasting images of *Little Women*.

When my grandchildren see the tears roll down my cheeks, as I read *Little Women,* they think I am just a little foolish and sentimental, because they don't understand what it meant to me to follow my own old playmates, the Alcotts, and to experience again the sorrow and the grief that came to me with the death of the dearest of them, "Beth." The children laugh and cry, too, but they don't take every word to heart as I do, because they are not living the past over again as I am, nor are they being flooded with memories of people and times long past recall. To them it is an interesting book—to me it is some of my girlhood brought back with all its sad and its merry memories.

For I was Lydia Hosmer, one of the little girls of Concord town who played beneath its famous old elms in the days when it was building the foundations for the literary shrine it has become to-day. My mother's house where my childhood was spent was built by Major Hosmer, my great-grandfather, who took part in the Concord fight of 1775.

The cottage next door, where the Alcotts lived for one year and where Amy was born, was originally owned and occupied by some of the Hosmer family. It was the first of the five houses in which they lived in Concord, and the one which is described in *Little Women* as "Meg's dove-cote." It has been said that they moved twenty-one times within twenty-two years, but just how much foundation there is for that statement I do not know. I do know, however, that they were very poor.

The Spirit of Neighborliness

As my father had died when he was still a very young man and had left his wife and five children with but a little money for their support, my mother was having her difficulties to meet her own needs and to bring us up properly; but even so, she was able to give help of one kind or another to the Alcotts. She couldn't loan money on their furniture, as some of the neighbors did, but she frequently sent over such food as her cows and her chickens permitted.

It was quite easy to find something which might be regarded as a bit of a delicacy for the children, who sometimes—and quite naturally—tired of a diet of boiled rice or graham meal without even the addition of sugar or butter or molasses to make it more palatable. In the summer-time, as Louisa wrote in her journal, "We lived much as the birds did, on our fruit and bread and milk; the sun was our fire, the sky our roof, and nature's plenty made us forget that such a thing as poverty existed."

It was not only necessity, but principle, that prescribed this diet for the Alcott children. Their father, Bronson Alcott, was a strict vegetarian who believed that any food obtained by hurting or taking the life of an animal would defile the body and, through it, the soul. This was a belief that was quite common among the philosophers of that time; I was too young to be affected by it, but my older sister, Sarah, who, like Louisa Alcott, often went to the Emerson house to talk with "the sage of Concord" and to borrow books of him, adopted these ideas and adhered to them for a great many years.

Mrs. Alcott, who came from two of the oldest families in Boston—the Sewalls and the Mays—had to learn through bitter experience to conquer her pride and to accept gifts from friends who understood her needs as the wife of an impractical idealist. Her husband, Bronson Alcott, was one of the most lovable men one could ever hope to meet, so kind and so wise, but he did not know how to make money, and as a consequence, when his dear wife's dowry was all gone there was no further source of income. Money meant nothing to him and he never seemed to understand why they didn't have any. He did teach school at different times, but never with any financial success. One time, I know, he brought home $1,000 dollars after a tour out West during which he had given a series of "conversations" in philosophy.

The Trip Abroad

When they lived in the cottage near our home and when the children were very young, Amy a baby, some friends offered to take him abroad with them. He accepted with alacrity and the whole family seemed delighted at the op-portunity; if they thought about their means of subsistence at all, it was prob-ably with the conclusion that "Heaven would provide," and surely it was with that thought, if with any, that the father ordered a new suit at a Boston tailor's shortly before sailing. When it was sent home he turned to his wife and said in his delightful, absent-minded way: "I don't believe that I paid for that suit, but if I didn't you will attend to it, will you not, my dear?"

In answer, she only smiled in her quiet, patient way, never mentioning the fact that all they had in the world to live upon was a box of oatmeal standing upon the pantry shelf.

In spite of the poverty, theirs was one of the most hospitable households I ever knew. We always felt welcome and happy in this home which fairly radi-ated sweetness and wholesomeness. The house may have been scantily fur-nished, but it was always neat, and whatever they had was good and pretty. As the mother and the girls had to do all the housework themselves (the Han-nah of the March household was a myth in the Alcott home), they were al-ways very busy about the house, but never too busy to romp and play.

Louisa, of course, was always the leader in the fun; it seems to me that she was always romping and racing down the street, usually with a hoople[1] higher than her head. That was the best way in which she could give vent to the exuberance of her spirits, I suppose.

She was continually shocking people, just as Jo does in the book, by her tomboyish, natural, and independent ways. Somewhere, in one of her earlier books, little read to-day, she tells the story of how she went down to the fields one day, to talk to some men who were hoeing potatoes. As they were chewing tobacco, Louisa, always curious and never afraid, wanted to know what it was they were chewing, and asked for a quid. When they gave it to her, she chewed it so vigorously that she had to be carried home in a wheelbarrow. The boy who was there when it happened, who helped to get her home, and afterward told me all about it, was my brother Cyrus, the "Cy" of the book.

A Novel Bath

While we are on the subject of their frugality and their natural ways, which to others might have seemed shocking, let me tell you of the novel method of taking a bath adopted by the Alcott girls. As water is commonly known to be a great beautifier and as systems of plumbing such as we have to-day were practically unknown then, what did they do but take a shower out on the little back piazza, facing the grove and completely hidden from the gaze of the passer-by, in nature's most approved fashion, whenever it rained.

One of the first things little girls ask me when they hear that I used to play with the Alcotts is whether I ever took part in their theatricals, so fascinatingly described in *Little Women.* No, "Beth" (Lizzie we always called her) and I were more quiet and preferred to be the audience, but I remember well some of the performances in which Louisa was the stage-manager and Anna (she is Meg in the book) was the servant-girl.

They were such a dear, conscientious family, so harmonious and so lovable. The atmosphere of their house was almost sanctified, so much better did you feel for having been in it. There was so much love in their make-up, and love was the only medium through which the parents ruled and disciplined their children.

Louisa and May (Amy) were the unruly ones; Anna and Lizzie were by nature more quiet and subdued. Whenever they did anything distasteful or naughty, instead of rebuking them with words, Mr. or Mrs. Alcott would write them little notes which they tucked under their pillows at night. After due deliberation over their sins, the children then sent their answers. It was a lesson in humility, self-chastisement, and self-expression, and it always seems to have had the desired effect.

Another method of punishment which Mr. Alcott sometimes used was to serve a meal, and then, without eating anything himself, he would rise and leave the table. Naturally the child with a conscience guilty with the thought of having caused her father sufficient unhappiness to make him lose his appetite would lose hers too, and until a reconciliation could be effected felt thoroughly ashamed and disgraced.

"Remembering to Be Good"

The "Bon-box" was another device the Alcotts had for remembering to be good. Inside the front door of their house stood a box which served as the symbol of an honor system, for into it, at the end of each day, the child who had been good and hadn't disregarded a single rule of conduct dropped a little slip bearing her name and the code-word "Bon" with three crosses after it, like this: X X X. It was such a distinction to be a depositor at the end of the day, that I asked whether I might be allowed to work for it, too. I do not remember how often my name went into that box attached to a Bon-slip, but I do know that I used to examine my stock of virtues very carefully in those days.

I think that I may safely say that no one now living knew the Alcott family as well as I did, because I was practically brought up with them for a while, as you see, and even though I was away from Concord quite a bit later on, I always saw a good deal of them whenever I returned for a visit. As they learned all their lessons at home with their father, we didn't go to the same school, but together with Ellen Emerson we did attend the same Sunday-school class conducted by Mrs. Ralph Waldo Emerson. Later, when I taught school in Concord myself, Mr. Alcott, who was then chairman of the school board, used to come and preside for a whole session, once a month.

In those days we had school from 9 to 12 in the morning and then again from 1:30 to 4:30 in the afternoon, and on Saturdays too. Vacations amounted to nothing, save for a few days during the berrying season in the summer and at Thanksgiving and Christmas time. The children's heads, consequently, were so crammed with facts that they hadn't the time to acquire much knowledge. You can imagine, then, what a treat a nice, leisurely talk from Mr. Alcott was for them. He would call their attention to the beauties of the world that had been lost to sight in the search for dry learning, would talk to them

[166]

of big and wonderful things, and divert their thoughts into channels quite different from those in which they generally flowed.

What the Alcott Girls Looked Like

Whenever people have asked me what the Alcott girls really looked like, I have always said, "Quite a little like the March girls in the book," and now I add, "and like the March girls in the play." I don't remember the details of their coloring—you see, it was over sixty years ago that I used to play with them—but I think that Anna was the darkest, Louisa had the chestnut-colored hair of "Jo," May was blond, and Elizabeth, with light brown hair, was between these two.

Amy was really the only one in the family whom one might call pretty, and, as is often the case with the prettiest, she was the least likable. She was, as I remember her, a little haughty, but an extraordinary young person, highly gifted and strong-willed. Sometimes, indeed, she was so independent that one marveled she should be the child of those sweet and gentle parents. Each of the girls had a distinguishing characteristic—Anna was the most domestic one, the real "mother's helper," Louisa, of course, the literary one (though it was Anna, and not she, who published the first story in a penny-dreadful); Amy was the artistic one in the family and Beth the most musical. The latter was always a little frail, especially after the illness from which she never recovered until the angels came to release her from her mortal suffering in her twenty-first year. So she was always more passive than active, more appreciative of the achievements of the others than creative herself. She had not as keen a sense of humor as her sisters, but a serener temper and a very lovely, quiet manner.

Amy and Beth

Perhaps the incidents I remember best of all are Amy's birth and Beth's death. I can see Beth now running across from her house to ours on that bright sunny morning on which Amy was born, to bring me the glad tidings that a new little sister had arrived at their house. I was nine then, and Lizzie (you know her best as Beth) was about a year and a half younger.

I remember equally well the day the sad news was brought to us that that same sunny little Beth had been taken from us. I had just returned to Concord, and though I had known for some time that she was very ill, the news came as a great shock to me. When I went to the Alcott house—they were then living on Bedford Street—I saw Louisa, who was almost overcome with grief. I remember so well how she said to me, "As her spirit left her body I saw it rise and, floating in air, leave the room," and she said it with such firm conviction that no one could dream of doubting her.

After Beth had been laid away, they found among her treasures a number of little keepsakes which she had made for her family and her friends as a last remembrance. She must have known that her end was near, because for months before she died she was always busy sewing, but she would never say what she was sewing for, and it wasn't until she was silenced forever that any one knew. Each little thing, so perfectly made, was carefully wrapped and labeled with the name of the person to whom it was to go. For my brother Henry she had made a penwiper of two leather disks with twelve little leaves of black taffeta between, all tied together with a cerise ribbon; for Cyrus a pin-block covered with green checked silk on one side and a purplish brown on the other; for my sister Sarah, a blue needle-book lined with white silk; and for me one of purple silk with a yellow lining. These I count among my most precious possessions.

1. A hoople, a child's toy, is a large wooden hoop rolled along the ground.

Harper's Bazaar 47 (May 1913): 213, 246.

From *Alcott Memoirs* (1915)

FREDERICK L. H. WILLIS

Frederick Llewellyn Willis (1830–1914) was raised by his grandparents in Cambridge in a devout Baptist household. When he publicly expressed his disbelief in foreordination at the age of twelve, he was expelled from the church as a heretic. While boarding at the Bowles Willard farm in Harvard, Massachusetts, in the summer of 1843, he heard numerous stories about the "strange" people at the Fruitlands community. However, not until the following summer of 1844 did he actually meet the Alcotts, who were then staying at Still River. As one of the few male playmates to the Alcott girls, Willis formed a strong relationship with the family for approximately the next decade.

Llewellyn, as he was known to the Alcotts, went on to study at the Harvard Divinity School, and in 1858, he became a minister in Coldwater, Michigan, for some six years. After the outbreak of the Civil War, he began to study medicine in New York City and later became professor of materia-medica at the New York Homoeopathic Medical College for Women, one of the first women's medical colleges in the country. He ended his career in private practice in Massachusetts and New York.

Many people who knew of his relationship to the Alcotts often believed he was the model for "Laurie," although he never publicly acknowledged that connection, only smiling when the topic came up. His recollections of the Alcott family were published in 1915 and were an important source for early-twentieth-century biographers of Louisa May. Willis does present one piece of incorrect information when he claims Abigail May was descended from the "Jewett" family. Perhaps this may have even been an early printer's error, with someone reading the word "Jewett" for the correct "Sewall." Although his memories of the Alcotts were written late in Willis's life, they are key in giving an insider's view of the family, especially Louisa May, during an important decade of financial struggle for the family.

How I Met the Alcott Family

A delicate boy of fourteen, I was journeying in early June, 1844, from Boston to Still River Village in the town of Harvard, in one of the lumbering stage-coaches which at that time had not been displaced by the steam railway, save upon a few important thoroughfares, to spend my long summer vacation as boarder in the home of a relative.

It chanced after one of the stops made by the stage, that upon starting again, the fingers of my right hand were caught in the closing door. I fainted from the intense pain and upon my consciousness returning, I opened my eyes upon what seemed the dearest, kindest, most motherly face I had ever beheld, looking into mine, as a lady held me in an embrace as tender and as pitying as if I had been one of her own bantlings, rather than a little orphan stranger traveling alone of whom she knew nothing.

It was Mrs. Alcott, who was returning from Boston, where she had been to solicit aid in her then constant extremity from wealthy relatives and friends. With ready tact, to divert my mind from my suffering fingers, she began to describe to me in lovable manner her four girls at home; and she told me stories of their juvenile pranks until the pain was a forgotten thing and the remaining hours of the journey had been delightfully whiled away.

When the stage drew up at her door there burst out four merry-hearted, bright-eyed, laughing girls—Anna, Louisa, Lizzie and May—my first sight of the Meg, Jo, Beth and Amy, immortalized afterwards in "Little Women." Then ensued the prettiest possible struggle, while the driver was taking down the old haircloth trunk, for "Marmee's" first kiss. The next day, as I had promised, I called upon the "Little Women." School had just closed in Still River and the long summer vacation had begun. I shall never forget the awkwardness of this first call. The mother was absent, only the children were at home. I was a city boy—a new genus to the young ladies—widely different in dress and manner from the boys of the village school, and as I stood, a focus of concentrated gaze from four pairs of bright mischievous eyes, not a syllable being uttered meanwhile by any one of their owners, I felt as if I were being weighed in the balance. I could feel the hot blood mounting to my cheek and brow. At length Louisa, who suddenly seemed to realize the embarrassment of the situation for me, proposed an adjournment to the garden. There the ice was broken, relieving seemingly strained relations, and we were comrades from that time forth. This first interview was ever after the subject of laughing comment with us. Within a week I had secured my grand-mother's permission to change my boarding place, and thus live at Mrs. Al-cott's house.

There was a beautiful sheet of water in among the hills about a mile from the village, unprosaically called Bare Hill Pond. Here was our favorite resort. Thither we went, Anna, Louisa and myself, the other two girls being deemed too young; passing day after day, carrying our luncheon and whatever Mrs. Alcott thought wise in the way of wraps, and story books, in a little four-wheeled cart. And here, through all the bright days of July and August, we lived in the fairy land of imagination, a life of childish romance. We chris-tened a favorite nook, a beautiful rocky glen carpeted with moss and adorned with ferns opening upon the water's edge, "Spiderland." I was the King of the realm, Anna was the Queen, and Louisa, the Princess Royal; we never laid these characters aside as long as we were in the "Royal Realm." Louisa had even then begun to string her rhymes and weave her little romances, though but twelve years old. For years afterwards we talked of that summer as the golden era of our lives.

I was then too young to realize the financial struggle Mrs. Alcott was pass-ing through to keep her little family together; but after they removed to Con-cord I spent the vacations of several successive summers with them, when I realized the whole situation most forcibly; and as much as I reverenced and admired Mr. Alcott—he had a peculiar charm for the young—I remember feeling a burning sense of indignation at his seeming indifference to the do-mestic burden that was resting upon his devoted wife and the actual poverty that enshrouded the little family. Mrs. Alcott became very fond of me and truly looked upon me as a son. As I look back I can think of but one other woman with whom I came in contact during my entire life who so fully rep-resented sympathy, love, and tenderness.

During the times when burdens pressed heavily upon Mrs. Alcott through the poverty and frequent actual want that was ever at the door, she had al-ways a word of counsel, encouragement and cheer. She never turned a deaf ear to an appeal from whomsoever it might have been and frequently shared her own scanty store with others aside from her own.

I think I was the only person, apart from her family, in whom she confided, a confidence years alone did not warrant. I remember one occasion while she was talking to me she suddenly burst into tears, which was a thing quite un-usual. Just then Anna came in announcing a caller. A most kindly looking and motherly woman entered, garbed simply as a Quakeress. Seeing the tears upon Mrs. Alcott's cheeks, she said:

"Abba Alcott, what is the matter with thee?"

"Oh, nothing much. But much or little, this dear boy is my little comforter."

It was thus that I met for the first time Lydia Maria Child, whose brother, Dr. Convers Francis, was afterwards my instructor at Harvard. He and Mrs. Child were my warm friends the remainder of their lives.

Family Life

Through continued and dire poverty Mrs. Alcott was sunshine itself to her children and to me, whom she looked upon as a son. No matter how weary she might be with the washing and ironing, the baking and cleaning, it was all hidden from the group of girls with whom she was always ready to enter into fun and frolic, as though she never had a care. Afternoons we usually gathered in the quaint, simple, charming, old-fashioned parlor at Hillside—Hawthorne's old home—bought by Mrs. Alcott with the pittance she received from her father's estate made sufficient for the purpose by a donation of $500 from Ralph Waldo Emerson. To this day, over all the years, that simple Concord room with its pretty chintz curtains, its cool matting, its few fine engravings, its Parian busts of Clytie and Pestalozzi, and of Una and the Lion (the latter given Mrs. Alcott by Una Hawthorne), its books and cut flowers, and its indescribable atmosphere of refinement, is deeply engraved within my memory as an expression of inherent simplicity and charm.

One of our number, usually myself, would read aloud while the mother and the two elder daughters engaged in the family sewing. Thus we read Scott, Dickens, Cooper, Hawthorne, Shakespeare and the British poets, and George Sand's "Consuelo." Mrs. Alcott's comments upon and explanations of our reading, when we questioned, were most instructive to us in beauty of expression, and revealed the wealth of her own richly stored mind. Mr. Alcott's table talks were constantly delightful. It was particularly at these times he took especial care to so discourse that the youngest listener might comprehend and fully understand. I have seen him take an apple upon his fork, and while preparing it for eating, give a fascinating little lecture as to its growth and development from germ to matured fruit, his language quaintly beautiful and charmingly poetical.

A child in speaking of him in my hearing said: "I love to hear him talk. He is so plain and tells me much I didn't know, fastening it on to what I know."

He rarely talked of else at table but nature's wonderful and benevolent processes in preparing food for the maintenance of man and in ministering to his taste through her countless presentations of the beautiful. Indeed his great love of nature, his keen, close observation of all her processes and his power of expression, all combined to make him charmingly instructive and entertaining.

Even in my youth Mr. Alcott seemed to me always strangely out of place in the midst of the practical utilitarianism of the 19th century, and out of place, too, clad in modern broadcloth. He should have been of the days of Socrates or Seneca and worn the flowing robes of classic Greece or the toga of ancient Rome. He was possessed of a captivating yet almost childlike simplicity of manner and bore about with him an air of serene repose, contrasting sharply with the bustling, business-like manner of most of the literary men of those days.

In person he was tall and spare, his fine head crowned with silvery locks, his complexion remarkable for its clearness and purity, the flesh tints being as clearly white and red as those of an infant. I have fancied this was due, in large measure, to the simplicity of his diet, which was principally fruit and cereals. He was fond of some varieties of vegetables, giving preference to those that matured above the ground, saying, "Man, like the gods, should pluck his food from on high." Meat he positively abhorred. Morally and physically he was the cleanest and sweetest of men. His entire sphere radiated purity. He was exceedingly tender towards all animals, having that reverence for life, even in its most insignificant forms, that characterizes the followers of Buddha. He would not crush a worm.

He was endowed with rich intellect and a broad humanitarian spirit; but he was also *sui generis*; a rare and elevating model of a man, not to be measured by ordinary standards. His sublime indifference to the practical affairs of life and apparently to the heroic struggles of his devoted wife was not indicative of his lack of affection for her or for his children. For no man loved his family better, and although at times he sorely tried them by his utter lack of practicability their affection and reverence for him never faltered. Mrs. Alcott struck the keynote of his character when I heard her say: "He carries his head in the clouds."

Mrs. Alcott was Abba May, daughter of Col. Joseph May, for many years one of the wardens of Kings Chapel, Boston. He was a strikingly handsome old gentleman and I well remember him as a conspicuous figure in the streets of Boston in my early boyhood, not only because of his fine carriage, but because he wore until his death the picturesque Continental costume which, at that time, was practically obsolete. The "small clothes," with knee and shoe buckles set with brilliants, made a fine setting for his shapely limbs. He stood as a model for the body of Stuart's portrait of Washington, a picture, for aught I know, still hanging in Faneuil Hall. It has been said he was the figure O. W. Holmes refers to in his poem, "The Last Leaf."

By descent Mrs. Alcott was a Jewett, one of the most ancient of Boston families. She was one of the noblest and most practical women I ever knew, large-brained and whole-souled, with the manners of a queen; a head like Harriet Martineau, but a heart incomparably larger, and endowed with fascinating powers of conversation. She bore Mr. Alcott's utter impracticability with wonderful patience; equal to any emergency in any direction, no matter how exceedingly tried. I can remember but two or three instances where she manifested impatience. Once, at some outrageously impractical thing her husband had done, she exclaimed impetuously: "I do wish people who carry their heads in the clouds would occasionally take their bodies with them." And I recall her saying upon another occasion: "If I should send my husband for a quart of milk, I should fully expect to have him drive home a cow." . . .

It was in Concord in 1846, that Mrs. Alcott told me the story of the failure of Mr. Alcott's "Tremont Street" school conducted in the Masonic Temple, a failure she largely attributed to the merciless ridiculing of Harriet Martineau, saying, I well remember, "Thus Harriet Martineau took the bread from the mouths of my family," and then spoke of Fruitlands. In substance her story, told me with smiling emotion, was as follows: After the failure of the school, Mr. Alcott, upon visiting England, became acquainted with an Englishman of some means, Charles Lane, a man who was thoroughly imbued with his own transcendentalism, and was also a believer in Robert Owen's Communistic ideas. Together, after returning to America, Mr. Alcott and Mr. Lane attempted to found an Utopian community in the town of Harvard. They bought a land-worn farm of about ninety acres with an old house and barn upon it, which they repaired and christened Fruitlands, Mrs. Alcott said in subtle irony, since there was no fruit upon the place save what little might be looked for from a few venerable apple trees, less than a dozen in number, and Mr. Alcott, his family, Mr. Lane and his young son, with at the outset five others, took up their abode there. With the single exception of Mrs. Alcott, no adult among them possessed a modicum of common sense, there was but one practical agriculturist among them and he an old man, and to any thinking person the experiment was doomed to failure. Under the ideals forecast but one ending could be possible.

Indeed in any age the scheme of Fruitlands would have been impossible since it was eminently impractical of application to the simple principles of common sense. The original plan, which for obvious reason to even these visionaries could not be adhered to verbatim, was a remarkable one. All labor was to be manual, man to supersede ox or horse, and the spade to entirely replace the plow. The pastures were to be transformed into bearing orchards as if by the magic touch of the gods and naught was to be raised save fruit, grains, and vegetables. These were not to be "cultivated," but would, it was firmly believed, mature and ripen in substance for the needs of the community through Nature's processes alone, unaided by any fertilization or even any labor saving the sowing and reaping. No living thing upon the ninety acres of Fruitlands was to be destroyed, neither weed nor worm, since all living things were God's creatures entitled to their natural or preferred sustenance.

Water was to be the only beverage, tea and coffee tabooed since their production in the lands from whence they came involved the use of slave labor. For the same reason sugar or even salt were not to be used. Milk, butter, and cheese were considered as polluting as the flesh which was their source, and eggs condemned for the same reason. The day was to begin with the dawn, when every one, young or old, should arise. Every day was planned upon the lines of its predecessor; beginning by bathing the body, this to be followed by music prior to the breakfast of fruit, bread made from unbolted flour, and water. From breakfast to the midday meal every one was to find an useful and congenial occupation, not essentially one that urgently needed to be done but rather to the daily taste and pleasure of the worker. After the midday meal rest for the body from the labor of the morning was to be found in serious conversation that would, too, develop the mind. From thence to the evening meal the same congenial labor of the morning was to be engaged in, the company then assembling for exchange of thought and conversation until sundown, when every one was to retire. No candles or oil were to be allowed since they were of animal source. Despite this edict, Mrs. Alcott told me, she kept a sperm oil lamp which she used only after all had retired for light upon needed mending of clothing or for the single pleasure of reading. Covering for the body was to be of linen only, since cotton, wool, and silk were not only the product of slave labor, but securable only through the murder of worms and sheep.

With the coming autumn the bubble burst. The community of Fruitlands decreased person by person until but the Lanes and Alcotts remained. Towards early winter Mr. Lane and his son took their departure, there remaining but Mr. Alcott, his wife and the four girls, the philosopher still steadfast and faithful to his dream. Mr. Lane as owner of the property permitted the Alcotts to remain until a tenant could be found, but denied them the privilege of cutting wood or grinding any more grain. It was then Mr. Alcott's health gave way under the strain. He had firmly believed he was to found in Fruitlands the Kingdom of Heaven upon earth, and so solve for all time the life problem for struggling humanity. His principles were ever a religion to him, and unable to admit defeat even in the face of it, he took to his bed to die. Turning his face to the wall, he refused food and water and silently, with the resignation of a philosopher, waited for death. Mrs. Alcott ministered to him in devotion, silence, and suffering. For weeks, taking but little food at her urgent supplications, his life hovered in the balance; but when death seemed close at hand, with all else within him faltering, his quality of love for his wife and offspring sustained him as a bird upon a fluttering wing; and with all else within him weary and worn, death even beckoning, through the very quality of his tender passion for his own, he rallied. Thus he struggled back to life again. His heroic wife encouraged and comforted him, sold everything she could spare from their slender stock of household goods, and rented four rooms from a neighbor who owned a house in a village near by. Thither they moved upon a December day and there Mrs. Alcott sewed and Mr. Alcott chopped wood, together making meager ends meet.

It was thus the family left Fruitlands in poverty to reside in the half of the humble but homelike house in the lovely little village of Still River, still in the town of Harvard, where I made their acquaintance the year following in the manner I have described and through which there came to me the most beautiful friendship of my early life, a friendship lasting through many years. As I write it all comes back to me like a golden halo resting upon the fields of memory.

Louisa and Her Sisters

Louisa May, the Author, the "Jo" of "Little Women," had a clear olive-brown complexion with brown hair and eyes. She answered perfectly an ideal of the "Nut Brown Maid"; she was full of spirit and life; impulsive and moody, and at times irritable and nervous. She could run like a gazelle. She was the most beautiful girl runner I ever saw. She could leap a fence or climb a tree as well as any boy and dearly loved a good romp. We have many times clambered together into the topmost branches of the tall trees at Hillside. She was passionately fond of Nature, loved the fields and the forests and was in special harmony with animal life. Her brief and racy description of herself in the opening chapter of "Little Women" is most accurately true: "Fifteen-year-old Jo was very tall, thin and brown and reminded one of a colt, for she never seemed to know what to do with her long limbs which were very much in her way. She had a decided mouth, a comical nose, and sharp gray eyes which appeared to see everything and were by turn fierce, funny, or thoughtful. Her long thick hair was her one beauty, but it was usually bundled into a net out of the way. Round shoulders had Joe, big hands and feet, a fly-away look to her clothes and the uncomfortable appearance of a girl who was rapidly shooting up into a woman, and didn't like it."

Louisa had great love of personal beauty and wide open eyes were her especial admiration. Her own were rather small and, as mine were also, we heartily sympathized with each other on this point. One day after the family had moved to Boston she was walking upon Washington Street. The thought came to her: "Now if I keep my eyes open people will think that I have beautiful large eyes"; so she fixed her eyes in the manner she thought would impart the most captivating expression to her face and continued her promenade. She began to notice that many looked at her intently, and thought as a child might, they were admiring her beautiful eyes, mentally congratulating herself upon the success of her efforts. I had called during her absence and upon her return sat chatting with Anna and her mother. As she entered the room I exclaimed, "Why, Louisa, what on earth ails you?" She made no reply, but walked directly to the mirror, giving, the instant she looked into it, a shriek of horror. She had retained the expression upon her face that she had imagined so enhanced its beauty until she could get to a mirror and observe for herself its effect, discovering, to her dismay, that she had been parading

Washington Street with an insane stare upon her face. Her effort to keep her eyelids open to their widest possible extent had contracted the skin of her forehead into wrinkles and the effect produced was as of an insane person. As she explained to us we burst into shouts of laughter and for a long time afterwards we chaffed her unmercifully upon the "well open eyes."

Louisa was an enthusiastic admirer of Dickens. She reveled in his works and could recite many chapters from memory. His literary style made an indelible impression upon hers and the effect of his humor is very perceptible in all her works. His characters were living beings to her and she was on terms of remarkably close intimacy with all of them. She and her sister Anna often acted in costume, inimitably, the quarrel scene between Sairy Gamp and Betsey Prigg over the imaginary Mrs. Harris, with all the accessories of the "tea podge," and the pickled salmon, Anna taking the part of Betsey Prigg and Louisa of Sairy Gamp. I have rarely seen anything better in comedy by professionals and I recall many instances of Mrs. Alcott laughing until tears came to her eyes over the girls' performances.

I carried the first manuscript to press that Louisa ever offered for publication, a story entitled "The Prince and the Fairy." I took this story to the "Boston Olive Branch," a paper published for many years under the auspices of the Methodist denominations. Rev. and Mrs. C. W. Dennison, at that time well known in the literary circles of Boston, were the editors. Mrs. Dennison read the story in my presence, accepted it, and paid me, for the young author, the munificent sum of $5.00. I remember well how I bore it to her with as much exultation as if it had been $5,000. This story filled about one and a half columns of the paper. In comparatively a few years the lowest price received for any article of equal length, she told me, was $100.

Louisa always lamented she was not born a boy. With the exception of rope skipping, at which she excelled all of us in power of endurance, she preferred boys' games to those of her sex. But nothing gave her more pleasure than plays and tableaux. She would conceive an idea and write a little drama about it, cast all of us in well-chosen parts and direct, with her sister Anna, a fairly creditable children's performance.

One evening during the first summer at Concord Mrs. Alcott mentioned Hamilton Willis of Boston, whom her sister married. I knew well the story of my father's family and from what I said Mrs. Alcott discovered he was a distant cousin of Hamilton Willis and, that consequently, I was remotely related in law but not in blood. This last decision of "Marmee's" was a source of regret to the two elder sisters, but they decided very seriously that I was a "real cousin" notwithstanding, and that a play should be written telling the story. Louisa forthwith spent two days upon a play she entitled "The Long Lost Cousin," which we performed before Mr. and Mrs. Alcott and Mr. Emerson under the trees about Hillside and in which, under my own name, I was given the principal part. At its end we were to raise our flag upon the cupola of the house. But as we did not have a flag, nor know where we could borrow one, Louisa and Anna, with an old red flannel skirt and some strips of muslin, together with an old blue flannel cape upon which were sewn white muslin stars, made a very creditable looking National banner which was raised with enthusiasm and flew for many days afterwards, to our childish joy and admiration.

Louisa M. Alcott left to the young people of her own and coming generations the legacy of her clean, sweet, and pure books. One might look in vain for any great art in them, but their ethics cannot be questioned nor the brilliancy and sparkling quality of her style. All her books should live. But, as is often the case, the fame of an author flatly rests enshrined within a certain work. Louisa's is "Little Women." Its immense popularity and steadily continued sale through all the years, as well as the wonderful success of the play recently adapted from it, is due directly to its truth and fidelity to real life. But the very slenderest thread of fiction runs through it. And truth, genuine truth sincerely stated, will live within or without the covers of a book. In most of the scenes portrayed in "Little Women" up to the time of Lizzie's death, I enacted a part. Just after this book was published, and when the first edition was selling rapidly, I met Louisa's proud and happy father in the Fitchburg Station in Boston. He came up to me, beaming, and rubbing his hands together in a manner quite peculiar to himself when well pleased, saying: "Well, my boy, did you recognize yourself as Laurie in Louisa's book?" I had just returned from abroad, the book having been issued while I was away, and I had to confess I had not read it. I immediately procured a copy and absorbed with delight its realistic descriptions of familiar, well remembered scenes.

Louisa M. Alcott was noble and true in her impulses. She had a tender and beautiful side to her nature. This quality was charmingly expressed in her hospital experiences during the Civil War, and in her pathetic "Hospital Sketches" there are very true glimpses of it. She made a brave, heroic, winning struggle through adversity to success and fame, lifting, through this success, the entire family from poverty and deprivation to comfort and affluence. She had a naturally vivacious, keen-witted view of life and was extraordinarily quick at repartee. From my matriculative year at Harvard, until shortly before my marriage, I maintained a correspondence with Louisa. It is a matter of deep regret to me that, together with many papers of value, her letters, which were among my most valued treasures, were stolen. They were full of a sparkling wit and humor, particularly the series written to me during my college life, wherein she was "Mrs. Propriety Coreander" and I was her only son, "Thomas Propriety Coreander." They were full of frolicsome and serious advice and admonition suitable for every occasion of my college experience and daily conduct.

If I were asked to designate two words best describing Louisa I should say wit and tenderness. Her witticisms were sparkling as a brook and as continuous as its flow. Once when asked a definition of a philosopher she instantly replied, "A man up in a balloon with his family at the strings tugging to pull him down." Her big heart ached at the burden of poverty under which her family rested and it was due to the element of tenderness in her nature that she persisted in her literary work through all sorts of failures and disappointments until success crowned her efforts with "Little Women." It has been said that genius is the capacity of taking infinite pains. If so, it is also the capacity of indomitable perseverance. Louisa owed her great success as much to these qualities as to any talent or natural endowment. The "blood and thunder" stories written by her and sold to inferior magazines and newspapers brought a pittance for the family exchequer, but were of more value as practice in the art of story writing. To these she owed her ready style when it came to the writing of her masterpiece. She was ashamed of these stories in later years, but she need not have been, for while they catered to a crude taste they were never unclean or unworthy, or in violation of any canon of propriety or morality.

Her muse was dramatic and had she lived in these days and formulated her talent along dramatic lines her success would have been a marked one.

Elizabeth Sewall, the third daughter, the "Beth" of "Little Women," was aptly named by her father "Little Tranquillity." Pages would not better describe her. She was possessed of an even, lovable disposition, a temperament akin to Mr. Alcott, indeed more than akin, since it was a very counterpart. Under any and all conditions she was as sunny and serene as a morning in June. Her appearance was that of a typical Puritan maid. In her book Louisa calls her "a rosy, smooth-haired, bright-eyed girl with a shy manner, a timid voice, and a peaceful expression which was seldom disturbed; she seemed to live in a world of her own, only venturing out to meet the few whom she loved and trusted." She loved music, played the piano with more ease than any of her sisters and with something of real appreciation.

She was possessed of her mother's practicality and housewifely qualities, and at a very early age aided in the preparation of the simple family repasts; later, and particularly while the family lived in Boston and Mrs. Alcott was directing her Intelligence Offices, taking full charge of the family kitchen. She died upon the threshold of womanhood. Her fame rests in the purity and innocent charm of memory she bequeathed to those who knew her and, in the broader sense, the perpetuation of these same qualities to the thousands who have read "Little Women," and hence know her as a wholesome character in a sweet and wholesome story.

Anna Bronson, the eldest of the four girls and the "Meg" of "Little Women," had a clematis and wild rose complexion, wide open blue eyes, and a wealth of golden hair. The Still River summer, I had nicknamed her "The Ox-eyed Juno" and for years after so called her. She had the calm poise of her father, a more amiable disposition than any of her sisters, was possessed of a quiet, keen sense of humor, and while taking full part in our play enjoyed the fun and frolic with a certain dignified zest that was in no sense a pose but rather a part of her.

She was possessed of genuine dramatic ability and would, as Louisa, have brought honor and credit to the stage had she adopted it as a profession. She married John Pratt, son of Minot Pratt of Concord, and was early left a widow with two sons whom Louisa educated. I had not seen her for many years when shortly after the death of Louisa and Mr. Alcott I called upon her at her home in Boston. She was then the sole surviving member of the family. We spent a pleasant afternoon together talking over the halcyon days of our youth and early friendship. As she bade me good-by she said: "You know you always were our Laurie."

Abba May, the youngest, and the "Amy" of "Little Women," was a slender girl with the clear complexion of her father and had blue eyes and golden hair. Being the baby of the family and much petted she was inclined to be childishly tyrannical at times. "Abby" May, as she was called by all, was very active and, after Louisa, the biggest romp among her sisters. She was fond of sketching and her little drawings were a source of admiration to all of us. That she had genuine talent as an artist was evidenced in her studies abroad after the success of Louisa's book, where it was said she won honors at her chosen profession. She died young, never returning to America, after her marriage, I think in Switzerland, to Ernest Nieriker, an artist, by whom she had one child. I never saw or heard from her after she crossed the Atlantic.

From *Alcott Memoirs: Posthumously Compiled from the Papers, Journals, and Memoranda of the Late Dr. Frederick L. H. Willis,* ed. Edith Willis Linn and Henri Bazin (Boston: Richard C. Badger, 1915), pp. 19–45.

From *Across My Path: Memories of People I Have Known* (1916)

LaSalle Corbell Pickett

LaSalle Corbell Pickett (1848–1931) was the third wife of Confederate general George Edward Pickett, leader of the famous "Pickett's Charge" at the battle of Gettysburg in 1863. At only fifteen years old, she departed her family's home behind Union lines to wed the thirty-eight-year-old military leader in Petersburg, Virginia. In order to support herself and her young son after the general's death in 1875, LaSalle wrote and toured the country as a speaker, telling stories of the Civil War and of the famous people she had met. The conversation that Pickett recalls here focuses on Alcott's "natural ambition . . . for the lurid style" and the restrictions she felt that "the proper grayness of old Concord" put upon her literary imagination.

Alcott's novel *A Modern Mephistopheles* was published anonymously in April 1877 by Roberts Brothers as part of its No Name series. This series, presented as a publisher's contest, issued a number of titles and asked readers to guess the authors. The public was surprised at the contest's conclusion to discover that the author of *Little Women* had penned this dark, Hawthorne-like novel. It was not until 1889, a year after Louisa May's death, that Roberts Brothers issued *A Modern Mephistopheles and A Whisper in the Dark* with Louisa's name on the title page. "A Whisper in the Dark," which had originally appeared in *Frank Leslie's Illustrated Newspaper* on 6 and 13 June 1863, was offered as an example of Jo March's "necessity stories." Pickett, of course, was unaware both at the time of her conversation with Alcott and when she wrote the book chapter in 1916 that the famous author had written dozens of anonymous "blood and thunder" tales for the penny dreadfuls.

In 1869 "Little Women" came into the world and took by storm all young people and all people who had once been young.

Miss Alcott had been known as a writer of fairy tales, had published a volume of "Flower Fables" and had contributed a number of stories to Boston journals. In 1863 she published her experiences in a war hospital, under the title of "Hospital Sketches," having been compelled by the failure of her health to give up the work into which she had put her strength and patriotic enthusiasm. To comfort herself for the disappointment she recorded her war memories, putting into the volume so much of the earnestness and sympathy that had formerly gone into her hospital work that her story reached the hearts of the readers and became a popular book. Some years later her novel of "Moods" was published.

It was not until "Little Women" had been added to the ever-increasing list of Miss Alcott's works that her public became acquainted with the home life and inner thought of the author. It was soon discovered that the "Little Women" were the author and her sisters in the old home at Concord and the interest was as great as that of watching a group of young lives expanding before the eyes of the readers. There was a heart knowledge and a heart interest in the book not to be found in fiction.

Miss Alcott's friends were not only surprised but incredulous when it was discovered that she was the author of the volume in "No Name Series," called "A Modern Mephistopheles." I could scarcely accept the statement when first presented, but it recalled to me a conversation I once had with her in Boston. Speaking of "Little Women" I said:

"The story is so natural and lifelike that it shows your true style of writing,—the pure and gentle type, with innocent young lives and the events that would inevitably befall bright girls and boys with the thoughts and feelings befitting a quiet loving home circle."

"Not exactly that," she replied. "I think my natural ambition is for the lurid style. I indulge in gorgeous fancies and wish that I dared inscribe them upon my pages and set them before the public."

"Why not?" I asked. "There seems to be no reason why you should not be gorgeous if you like."

"How should I dare to interfere with the proper grayness of old Concord? The dear old town has never known a startling hue since the redcoats were there. Far be it from me to inject an inharmonious color into the neutral tint. And my favorite characters! Suppose they went to cavorting at their own sweet will, to the infinite horror of dear Mr. Emerson, who never imagined a Concord person as walking off a plumb line stretched between two pearly clouds in the empyrean. To have had Mr. Emerson for an intellectual god all one's life is to be invested with a chain armor of propriety."

"The privilege of having such a Titan of intellect to worship is worth being subjected to some trammels of propriety."

"And what would my own good father think of me," she asked, "if I set folks to doing the things that I have a longing to see my people do? No, my dear, I shall always be a wretched victim to the respectable traditions of Concord."

The "No Name" gave poor Louisa an opportunity to escape for a moment from the Concord traditions, and I think she enjoyed the writing of every sentence in the "Mephistopheles."

Perhaps the Seer of Concord never had a more devout worshipper than Louisa Alcott who, when a child, wrote him adoring letters which were never sent. When she was a mature woman with her well-earned honors thick upon her a great sorrow, the death of her best loved sister, May, the "Amy" of "Little Women," was announced first to Mr. Emerson that he might break the tidings gently to her and comfort her with his tender, loving sympathy.

As the home circle narrowed by the passing of its members the tender bond of affection between Louisa Alcott and her father drew yet closer and the feeling of interdependence grew still deeper till death came and the old house was left desolate. At the funeral of Mr. Alcott the mourners were yet more deeply saddened by the message that Louisa had just passed from earth.

From *Across My Path: Memories of People I Have Known* (New York: Brentano's, 1916), pp. 105–10.

[A Visit to Louisa May Alcott] (1917)

[RUSSELL H. CONWELL]

Russell Herman Conwell (1843–1925), born in South Worthington, Massachusetts, worked as a schoolteacher in Minnesota before joining the Union army in 1862. After the Civil War, he practiced law in Massachusetts, but later decided to join the ministry. He served as an assistant pastor at the Baptist church in Lexington, Massachusetts, from 1872 to 1879. When he was ordained as a Baptist minister in 1880, he accepted the position as pastor of Grace Baptist Church in Philadelphia, where he remained for the rest of his life. During his lifetime, he was best known as a lecturer and motivational speaker and was part of the Chautauqua circuit. He believed that wealth and power were possible for anyone and that nobody had the "right to be poor." He also professed that "love is the grandest thing on God's earth, but fortunate is the lover who has plenty of money." Conwell, whose most famous speech (which he delivered over six thousand times) was entitled "Acres of Diamonds" (1887), used the fortune he made primarily to finance philanthropic enterprises. He founded Temple College, now Temple University, and Conwell School of Theology, now part of Gordon-Conwell Theological Seminary, as well as establishing three hospitals in Philadelphia. Edmund Franklin Merriam (1847–1930), who wrote about Conwell's meeting with Alcott, was an author most noted for his books on the American Baptist missions. Conwell, who was both a lawyer and newspaper reporter in Boston for a time after the war, had the opportunity to meet many New England authors, including Longfellow, Emerson, Lowell, Whittier, and Alcott. Conwell's brief description of meeting Louisa May and her father, which most likely took place in the 1870s, concisely illustrates how unpretentious the author was and how little she let fame enter into her everyday life.

In the course of his newspaper work Mr. [Russell H.] Conwell went out to Concord to interview Louisa M. Alcott. He rapped at the front door of the old-fashioned house, and someone, whom he took for the maid, came to the door.

"I'd like to see Miss Alcott," he said.

"Come right in," she said.

"But please take my card to Miss Alcott. Perhaps she will not care to see a newspaper man, and I do not wish to intrude unless I am welcome."

Throwing a dish towel over her shoulder, she said:

"Oh, come in. I am Miss Alcott."

So he went in, and had a cordial and pleasant interview with the writer who has so perfectly interpreted the spirit of girlhood. As they were talking Miss Alcott's father, the originator of the Concord School of Philosophy, came in the door. Miss Alcott handed him the dish towel and said:

"Here, father, you go and finish wiping the dishes. I was not half through, but I want to talk to this newspaper man."

All really great people are simple, commented Dr. Conwell.

E. F. Merriam, "Memories of Longfellow and Others," *Magazine of History* 25 (September–October 1917): 104–10.

[Memories of the Alcott Family] (1922 and 1932)

JULIAN HAWTHORNE

Providing a portrait of Louisa May Alcott prior to *Little Women,* Julian
Hawthorne, in his in-depth recollections, shows an Alcott seldom seen by her
countless admirers during her lifetime. Hawthorne concentrates on the Concord days when he knew the family well—as only a next-door neighbor can.
Born in Boston in 1846, Julian, the son of Nathaniel and Sophia Hawthorne,
grew up like Louisa, in a world filled with literati. In 1852, the Hawthornes purchased "Hillside" from the Alcotts and renamed it "Wayside." They lived there
only a short time before Nathaniel assumed the U.S. consulship to Liverpool,
a position he had gained by writing the campaign biography of Franklin Pierce,
his old Bowdoin College classmate and now president of the United States.
Thus, Julian spent much of his formative childhood traveling abroad, living primarily in England and Italy. The family returned to Concord in 1860 and once
again settled in their "Wayside" home on Lexington Road. Louisa wrote to her
cousin about the family's auspicious arrival: "We are all blooming and just
now full of the Hawthornes whose arrival gives us something to talk about. . . .
Mr. H. is as queer as ever and we catch glimpses of a dark mysterious looking
man in a big hat and red slippers darting over the hills or skimming by as if he
expected the house of Alcott were about to rush out and clutch him. Mrs. H. is
as sentimental and muffin as of old, wears crimson silk jackets, a rosary from
Jerusalem, fire-flies in her hair and dirty white skirts with the sacred mud of
London still extant thereon. Una is a stout English looking sixteen year older
with the most ardent hair and eyebrows, Monte Bene airs and graces and no
accomplishments but riding which was put an end to this morning by a som-
erset from her horse in the grand square of this vast town. . . . Julian is a worthy boy full of pictures, fishing rods and fun and Rose a little bud of a child with
scarlet hair and no particular raiment, which is cool and artistic but somewhat
startling to the common herd" (*Selected Letters,* 57).

The children of the two families became close friends, especially May and
Julian. Julian attended Sanborn's academy and entered Harvard in 1863; however, he proved a desultory student and was asked to leave at the beginning of
his senior year. Of course, some of his poor performance may have been re-

lated to the unexpected death of his father in 1864. He then went on to study engineering in Germany, returning to America in 1870, when he married and took a job in New York as a hydrographic engineer. He soon started writing, publishing stories and articles and eventually, in 1873, his first novel, *Bressant*. For the next twenty years, Julian published two or three novels a year as well as histories, biographies, short-story collections, and essays. Despite his enormous creative output, his most lasting works are those about his famous father: *Nathaniel Hawthorne and His Wife*, two volumes (1884–85), and *Nathaniel Hawthorne and His Circle* (1903). He died in 1934.

His recollections of the Alcotts were published late in his life, long after all of the immediate members of the Alcott family were dead, yet he recaptures an important time in the life of Louisa May, from her performances in the town dramatics to her activities during the Civil War. Julian's accounts are not always trustworthy. He liked attention, as his claim to being "Laurie" demonstrates, and his memory was sometimes obviously faulty, as shown when he calls Anna Alcott "Anne" and says May married an artist. Despite these flaws, Julian's intimate stories of May's offer to go swimming in Walden Pond and of a disguised Louisa May pretending to be a romantic suitor for her sister display the creativity and imagination of the Alcott sisters. As Julian admits, "The Alcott girls were society in themselves, and Concord would have been crippled without them." One of the strangest images in his reminiscences, however, does not involve the real Alcott sisters, but instead their celluloid counterparts. The thought of Julian Hawthorne watching a film version of *Little Women*—a work that extols the idyllic childhood of Concord—shows that time was quickly moving onward and the last of the people who actually knew Louisa May Alcott in a real sense would soon be gone and their memories, except those committed to paper, like Julian's here, lost forever.

"The Woman Who Wrote *Little Women*" (1922)

When in the 1860's you thought of the Alcotts you thought of Louisa; and some malign wit said that she was her father's best contribution to literature. Even before she wrote *Little Women*, she was eminent in her family, though none of the other members of it was negligible. She was a big, lovable, tender-hearted, generous girl, with black hair, thick and long, and flashing, humorous black eyes. Humor she had, and wit too, and dramatic talent; and in spite of what Henry James once told her—I shall tell that story by and by—she did have genius.

All these good qualities and gifts finally assembled themselves in the great gift of story writing—of stories about girls and boys, and addressed to them. *Little Women* was published in the late sixties, and a few months ago I saw a moving picture based upon it; the picture was not so good as the book, but it drew big audiences all over the country, and paid more money to the producers, no doubt, than Louisa herself ever made out of the book. These audiences, which laughed and were tearful by turns, were composed mainly of persons who either in their childhood or in maturity had read the book; and of the residue who had not read it, few, I imagine, failed to get it out of the local lending library immediately afterward. There is a popularity of more than fifty years, a Victorian success lasting over to our revolutionary and sophisticated twentieth century, and still vigorous and unafraid. A book written just after our Civil War, and keeping sweet and good all through the World War, and likely to survive the next cataclysm, whatever that may be. Nothing short of genius could achieve such a result; yet it is the simplest, most naïve thing imaginable.

Why *Little Women* Is Still Popular

That, indeed, may partly explain it. The story is made not only of the very stuff of human nature but of the nature of boys and girls, fresh and fragrant, comical and pathetic. The style is as unpretending as family gossip round the fireside, and its material is such as was—and I hope and believe still is—intimately familiar to simple American families from north to south and from east to west. Yes, that kind of families still abounds, in spite of flappers of both sexes, jazz, divorce, curved space, undulating morals, and all the rest of our up-to-date improvements. There is no doubt a new type of Little Women who seem to be neither women nor girls, but an amalgam of the least admirable qualities of both, rotten before they are ripe, and pithless before they are rotten; and there are boys to match them. But they are an artificial spawn of the times, with which our current fiction and magazine covers have had a good deal to do, not to mention the movies. The dissemination of them is wider, one inclines to think, than their numbers are large, or, at any rate, than their survival will be long. This is an age of advertisement, and advertisement can always create interest; the flapper is because she or he is talked of, and will vanish when the talk is talked out. Whether they read Louisa Alcott I don't know; perhaps they prefer Elinor Glyn; but tens of thousands do read Louisa, only we don't hear about it, because newspapers and magazines don't mention them, and the popular illustrators of the day don't select them as models for their magazine covers and toilet advertisement pictures.

However, I am not here to write literary criticism, or to discuss New Thought or Fourth Dimension, or to scourge the present generation, or to moralize upon the data of transition. We have people enough and to spare to do all those things. But the number of persons who knew Louisa and all her tribe intimately and long, and who are still alive to tell of it, is now so small that an ordinary five-fingered hand could enumerate them twice over; in fact, it is not improbable that I am the only one of them left. So I feel myself under a certain obligation to hand over my memoranda on the subject. It is as interesting as the "inside history" of the League of Nations, and more edifying; and for me it is a labor of love.

There were in those days three dwellings within a few minutes' walk of one another on the old Boston highway—that road by which the British marched to Concord by way of Lexington, and at Concord Bridge met the embattled farmers, who fired the shot heard round the world. You will find mention of that episode in Emerson's verses, read by him at the dedication of the monument erected on the spot, eighty-six years ago, and when Emerson himself was thirty-three years old.

Those eight hundred British lobster-backs—as we called them in those pre-khaki times—passed by these three dwellings, one after the other, little thinking what a famous adventure they were taking part in. The first of the houses was a small frame building close beside the road, at that time occupied—is the tradition—by a man experimenting in quest of the elixir of life. Long afterward it was occupied, and somewhat enlarged, by the apostle of peace and love, Amos Bronson Alcott, begetter of Louisa and of her charming sisters, May and Anne—the other sister, Elizabeth, had died before I knew them. But in 1853 the place was bought from Alcott by my father, Nathaniel Hawthorne, and he named it Wayside. In the same year he took his family to Europe, and did not return until 1860. He built on additions, and lived and wrote there till his death in 1864.

As for the Alcotts, they moved on to the next house on the road, a picturesque old shanty even then, which Louisa christened Apple Slump, though I believe historians have picked a more dignified name for it. It still stands, and looks less weatherworn than it did sixty years ago, in my time. In fact, they have transmogrified it into a sort of museum or monument, and a little building in the background was erected some time in the seventies, I think, for the accommodation of the Concord School of Philosophy. Little battalions of late Victorian highbrows used to assemble there to deliver lectures and to listen to them; I was invited there once myself, and discoursed to the audience on the theme of Emerson as an American. The last time I visited Concord, about six years back, we were expected to step softly around the place, with hushed voices and reverent looks. This sort of piety is very American and funny; we are the only sentimental people left on earth.

THREE FAMOUS NEIGHBOR FAMILIES

To finish these preliminaries, Emerson's house was half a mile farther along the highway, a four-square, two-storied edifice, painted white, and shadowed by pines and other trees. When Emerson made his last visit to England this house, during the absence of the family, caught fire and burned down, only some books and furniture being saved. Thereupon the Concord folks, in a spirit of local patriotism and affection, got together and rebuilt the house exactly as it had been before, and presented it to Emerson, with their compliments, on his return. It was a good idea, and to him a pleasant surprise.

Our place and the Alcotts' adjoined, the houses themselves being less than two hundred yards apart; and when we came back from Europe, in June of 1860, we naturally fraternized with our neighbors, and my two sisters and myself and the Alcott girls were in and out of one another's houses all the time, almost forming one family. And the three Emerson children, Ellen, Edith and Edward, being but ten minutes' distant in space and even nearer in amity, were not long in getting into the game — nine of us in all, while our elders looked on approvingly. It was a fine nucleus for good society, and it is surprising, in the retrospect, that so little romance evolved from such a situation. But there were only two males in the combination, and as a matter of fact, the love-making, such as it was, and it was very mild, was restricted to Abby and myself. We kept it secret, and it is now for the first time disclosed.

Anne Alcott married a fellow altogether admirable, whom we called John, and if I ever knew his other name I have forgotten it. Abby became the wife of an artist, I believe, long afterward. Edith Emerson married a fine young gentleman, Forbes by name, whose father was rich; Ellen never married, but devoted her life to taking care of her father. My sister Una died unmarried; Rose, in 1860, was less than ten years old. Edward Emerson, after graduating from Harvard, married a Concord girl, Annie Keyes, and he may, for what I know and hope, be living yet, a veteran approaching eighty. That leaves only Louisa and myself to be accounted for; I found a wife in 1870, and Louisa lived and died a maid in 1888. Like Ellen Emerson, she devoted herself to her father and mother—and to the myriad Little Women and men who read and loved her books.

In no young woman that ever I knew was strength of character more manifest than in Louisa Alcott. Ellen Emerson, of the Concord girls, was nearest her in that respect; but Ellen was aristocratic, while Louisa was a true democrat. Ellen was deep, but narrow; Louisa was both deep and broad; her sympathies were world-wide. Ellen, for all her noble self-dedication to her father, was always conscious of herself; Louisa—aside from her dignity of womanhood—never considered herself at all. Nobody ever ventured to take liberties with the woman, but as Louisa she was hand in glove with us all. Her spirit was high and courageous. She was great in comedy, laughed and inspired laughter, but for a heart so tender as hers tragedy was always near, though she was resolute to smile her tears down for others' sake. Did she ever have a love affair? We never knew; yet how could a nature so imaginative, romantic and passionate escape it? But her control was greater than her passion, and she could put aside personal felicity for what she deemed just cause. The Alcott girls were society in themselves, and Concord would have been crippled without them. Anne, when she could be spared from her own married sphere, was a precious element; Abby's enjoyment gave joy to others; and Louisa was the hub of the little universe and kept the wheel in constant activity.

Abby Alcott's Startling Question

My first interview with Abby Alcott was on a June day just after our return from Europe. She and I stood on the path skirting the base of the hill between our abodes; we had lately been introduced and she was helping me along, I being a bashful nondescript of fourteen, seven or eight years her junior, and ignorant of American civilization. Abby began by asking me whether I didn't think it was nice for "ladies and gentlemen to go bathing together."

Those were her words. Dear, honest girl, she never suspected the voluptuous shock that her inquiry produced upon my innocent but not unimaginative nature. My conceptions of bathing had till then been confined to the severe isolation of bathrooms, or to hardly less unsocial English sea beaches,

where the sexes were rigorously segregated, boxed up in bathing ma-
chines—tiny huts on wheels—and clad from neck to heel in shapeless, dark
flannel robes; bobbing up and down, thus, in chilly splashings of gray waves,
solitary and miserable. To me, thus barbarously unprepared, were conjured
up by her question rosy suggestions of Arcadian Freedom in sparkling wa-
ters of American midsummer; ladies and gentlemen together and no mention
of flannels! I glanced at Abby's well-turned figure, her clustered yellow
ringlets, her cheerful and inviting expression; she was older than I and must
know best; one must follow the customs of the country. I stammered, I
blushed. . . .

Fortunately, she continued: "We and the Emersons often go over to
Walden this hot weather—to the cove where Thoreau used to live; there's a
tent for the girls. We're going next Thursday and you could have John's
bathing dress; it would be awfully nice!"

I felt guilty, as if I had been caught smuggling a faun of the Prime into a
Beacon Street afternoon tea. I have no recollection of the rest of the conversation, but I have no doubt that the Hawthorne children were splashing
in Thoreau's cove that Thursday, with other tritons and naiads, properly
draped.

The "tent" proved to be a strip of canvas thirty feet long by eight wide, carried round the boles of four pine trees standing at the corners of a square. In
this bower the naiads performed their Eleusinian rites, issuing thence in due
time in the irreproachable blue flannels of their British sisters, with their hair
hanging down their backs, we men, on the other hand, having withdrawn to
a suitable solitude beside the pond to swaddle ourselves in similar mummy
wrappings. There were a leaky old punt to dive from, June sunshine, blue di-
amond water and much jollity.

It was not with the tall, dark-flashing Louisa, however, that I fell in love;
she must have been close upon thirty by that time, and besides I had seen
Abby first; I was content with an adoring younger-brother attitude toward
Louisa. Adoration is not too strong a word; she always equaled and often surpassed anticipation. The Civil War so kindled her that no one was astonished, or ventured to remonstrate, when she took the almost unheard-of decision to volunteer as nurse behind the lines. But it brought the war home to
Concord as even the departure of the Concord volunteers for the front, a year
before, had hardly done.

After she had gone, our thoughts and love followed her, and almost every

[194]

week a letter came from her. Wonderful letters they were; they were published afterward, but not in the same form in which we had listened to them as Mrs. Alcott, in a voice tremulous sometimes with laughter, sometimes with tears, read them out to us, grouped around the porch of Apple Slump in those fierce, emotional first passages of the war.

Louisa put her heart and soul into them, as she was putting heart and soul into her work in the hospitals. The pathos and the humor both were there; she felt them to her marrow, and in her homely narratives she made us feel them. And this devoted and heroic figure was our Louisa! She seemed enlarged into something greater than we had suspected. What a dauntless temper, what tenderness and sympathy! Into what scenes of horror and tragedy had she entered, after the ancient peace and amenity of Concord!

Louisa Alcott as a War Nurse

One week the customary letter did not arrive, and a hush of suspense fell upon us. Then came an official dispatch from the front: Miss Louisa Alcott had caught the fever, and was being invalided home. The homeward journey was long, and to our misgivings it was almost like a funeral, with the pain of uncertainty to boot. On my way home from school I would call at the house for news, and go away heavy hearted. Mrs. Alcott would shake her head, pale and sad, and Abby's eyelids were red and her smiles gone.

She came at last, a white, tragic mask of what she had been, but with a glimmer of a smile in the depths of her sunken eyes. Her spirit was indomitable, and it pulled her through. After some weeks she could be carried out of the house to sit in the sunshine; she got well, and her cheeriness and social animation returned, but there were occasional tones in her voice and expressions of eyes and mouth that indicated depths of which she could not speak.

Various little festivals and fairs were got up for the benefit of the soldiers, and Louisa was a natural protagonist. Her histrionic ability was marked, and she and her sisters would play scenes from Dickens; Mrs. Gamp was Louisa's favorite impersonation, and Anne was inimitable as Betsey Prig. Louisa organized the fairs and gatherings, and the "bees" for the making of socks and shirts for the army. Once it was learned that a company of soldiers were to come down the Boston highway — I forget for what reason — and would pass Apple Slump. It was decided that Concord should give them another sort of welcome than that stern one that met the British in 1775.

All households in the neighborhood contributed lemons and sugar, pitchers, bowls and glasses; we all set to work, and before the appointed hour lemonade enough had been made to flavor Walden Pond, almost, had it been emptied into it. Long boards resting on sawbucks served as tables and were placed alongside the road; lumps of ice of all sizes were brought, carefully protected; Star-Spangled banners filled the air. The Alcott girls and a score more of the prettiest in the village stood in white frocks to serve out the drinks. Louisa, in her hospital costume, conducted the ceremonies.

After anxious waiting outposts reported the appearance of a cloud of dust down the road. The boys in blue were coming! There was a gleam of gun barrels above ranks of bronzed visages and uniforms thick with dust, and the rhythmic undulation of marching men. They came on at a round pace, without music, and silent save for the serried tramp of their feet. As the commanding officers passed in the lead we waved our flags and shouted, the girls held up the brimming glasses; I saw a tear run down Louisa's cheek. But the little column kept on without pausing; every man had his eyes to the front, for after two or three years of war, discipline was in the marrow of every Yankee soldier. There was a moment of consternation in our little group. Could it be that the rigidity of army rule would not permit the acceptance of our offering?

The Center and Soul of the Scene

Suddenly, when the central file of the company was opposite Apple Slump gate, the captain swung round on his heel and drew his sword; he uttered a command, the ranks halted, and out burst the beat and scream of drum and fife. The butts of sixty rifles thumped the ground as one: "Parade rest!" The men-at-arms relaxed into human beings, stretched their shoulders, tipped back their caps, wiped the sweat from their faces, and allowed their thirsty glances to rest upon the ice-tinkling refreshment awaiting them. A pretty sight it was, those shy, excited, spotless girls fluttering up and down the line, back to the tables and forward again, fetching and carrying the dripping cups to and from the tanned and grimy fellows, who were part of those who stood between our pastoral tranquillity and hell! Occasionally, while a man drank, a soft girl hand would venture to stroke the shining shaft of a rifle, or touch the hilt of the belted bayonet, with a caress that the man must have felt was meant for him.

But Louisa was the center and soul of the scene. Her greeting to the officer was cordial but brief; her chosen place was with the rank and file; she mingled and talked with them; those great black eyes of hers dimmed and brightened by turns; she knew the soldiers' language and was sister and mother to them all. When one of our young Hebes would seek orders from her for a moment, the look she would turn upon her was unseeing and her words were mechanical; she was far away on the battlefields and in the hospitals, amid the wounded and the dying. Deep tremors passed through her; her smiles had the pathos of remembered pain. A kind of grandeur and remoteness invested her simple, familiar figure; scarlet flushes alternated with pallor in her cheeks. During that ten minutes' halt she lived a lifetime.

The commands came sharp and short; the lines reformed instantly, rifles on shoulders, and fife and drum spoke again. The clump of men receded rapidly down the road, the afternoon sun making a vaporous veil of the dust that hung upon their steps. The bevy of girls, boys and old folks gazed after them, waving flags and handkerchiefs, till the soldiers had passed on to their destiny and the throb of music was stilled in the distance. But today, after sixty years, I can hear it, and see the little column turn the bend of the road past Moore's barn.

THE INSUFFERABLE ENGLISH VISITOR

Louisa had been standing a little apart from the rest, one hand resting on a post of her father's rustic fence. After the column had vanished she didn't stir for several moments, while we busied ourselves with stripping the tables and removing the half-empty bowls and buckets. At last her old mother went up to her and put an arm gently round her waist. Then the tall girl faltered and drooped, and rested her forehead on her mother's shoulder; but she recovered herself quickly and passed hurriedly up the pathway to the porch of the old house and disappeared within. We saw no more of her that day.

Pilgrims occasionally came from foreign parts to taste the transcendental springs at their source—Anthony Trollope and others; but they couldn't divert the attention of us young folks from one another. One episode, however, touched me nearly.

For some days Abby and Louisa had been letting fall obscure allusions to the anticipated visit at Apple Slump of some relative of theirs, a young Englishman of rank, as I gathered, and distinguished in the London fashionable set. They seemed quite excited about it, Abby especially; he was said to be handsome and fascinating, and what was termed in those days "a sad dog."

As has been stated, I was in love with Abby myself, and I didn't like her hardly disguised interest in the expected visitor; but I tried to calm myself with the reflection that he would be more apt to admire Louisa.

The date of his arrival was not fixed; March came and went and there was no news of him. I began to hope that his plans might have been changed. On the first day of the next month the school had to play an important match game of hockey; it was not decided till near sunset, and by the time I came abreast of Apple Slump on my way home it was dusk. At the gate, chatting with Abby, I descried a figure who could be no other than the Englishman. Abby beckoned me to approach.

Much as my jealousy bristled against this person, I couldn't deny his grace, charm and high-society bearing. He was slender and dark, and wore a black broad-cloth suit and soft black felt hat. His waistcoat and cravat, however, were rather too decorative for my taste; he twirled an absurd switch cane and occasionally caressed the points of a tiny black mustache; and as I came up, rough and disheveled in my hockey rig, he inserted a monocle in his right eye and fixed me with what Tennyson would have called "a stony British stare."

I didn't like him, the rather that in putting up the monocle he relinquished Abby's hand, which he couldn't have been holding without her consent.

On being introduced, however, he greeted me with insufferable condescension, and spoke in an airy, smiling tone, with marked English intonations. Meanwhile, by a quick contraction of the eye, he projected the monocle from its place, and with the easiest air imaginable slipped his arm round Abby's waist. Nor did she flinch from him; on the contrary! I asked her where Louisa was. She said Louisa had to change her dress.

I felt sure I could thrash this fellow—he wasn't so big as I; but my tenderness for Abby had been kept secret from the world, and one cannot protect the girl he cares for if she obviously does not want to be protected. I stepped back, and haughtily said that I guessed I'd be going home.

"Oh, I say, don't be in a hurry, my dear child," drawled this intolerable creature, flirting his cane with an effeminate gesture. "Do you know, I find you quite amusing."

I stepped up to him again with my fists clenched; my wrath must have been visible in my crimson and distorted countenance. "Child" indeed!

He snatched off his hat and tossed it up in the air, thereby letting a thick mass of black hair fall down to his waist. He and Abby burst into shouts of laughter, and with arms around each other performed a wild saraband.

[198]

Then, enchanted with the success of her masquerade, and perhaps embarrassed at her pantaloons, Louisa fled up the path and into the house, "April fool!" coming back to me over her shoulder. Abby leaned against the gate, breathless and giggling; my own emotions were mingled and indescribable. There was not even anybody to be thrashed!

Inside Louisa Alcott's Home

Hitherto I have portrayed the Alcott family outdoors only, where indeed they were very much addicted to being; but their indoor aspects were not less attractive, and readers of *Little Women* were not denied such more intimate views.

The passage from the front door opened on the right into a large room, or two rooms in one, with the kitchen in the rear. On the left as you entered there was a fireplace of the ancient New England type, round which the family and their friends would gather on winter evenings. This room was also the dining room, and there was a big square table in the center. On the other side of the hallway were the Sage's apartments, where he thought up and wrote down his orphic wisdom, but into which we never ventured to penetrate.

It was not until the war was over that Louisa could detach herself from that great preoccupation sufficiently to make any sustained attempt at writing in this beloved home of hers. In her girlhood, to be sure, she had competed for and won a hundred-dollar prize offered by Robert Bonner's *New York Ledger*, for the best short story; and afterward she had composed a novel, *Moods*, highly romantic and emotional, which never made a stir, and I suspect I am the only surviving reader of it. She herself abhorred recollection of it, but it probably cleared some cobwebs out of her mind. About 1867, however, she began to seclude herself more than usual, and would laughingly reply to our remonstrances that she was "scribbling some rubbish."

The rubbish was later to be known to the world as *Little Women*. In its first conception it was a fanciful, informal drama of New England domestic life, with her sisters, herself and a few of her friends as *dramatis personæ*. I forget the distribution of parts, but I am sure Abby was the heroine, and probably for that reason she felt obliged to select me for Laurie—an amiable idealization of course, she herself being Jo. But of these details we knew nothing until the book was done, and Louisa read parts of it to us. We all thought it wonderful; she had grave doubts, and was inclined to throw the silly stuff, as she called it, into the fire. She was overruled, with the less difficulty in that the family was sorely in need of money; and she was ready to sell her manuscript outright for a hundred dollars, or even for half that if a publisher could be persuaded.

HER STORY OF *LITTLE WOMEN*'S SUCCESS

So one day she took the train to Boston with her package under her arm, wondering whether the outcome of her journey would repay the sixty cents it cost. After some rebuffs she found her way into the den of the lion and escaped unmaimed; he would look over the stuff when he found leisure; couldn't think of advancing anything on it; novels were a drug on the market. She returned soberly to Apple Slump, convinced that she had heard the last of *Little Women*. The sixty cents remained uncovered.

Louisa waited three months for news from her lion's den, got none, and resolved to visit him once more and know the worst. She was back late that afternoon, and The Wayside received a message to come over to Apple Slump that evening and hear her adventures. Louisa could make even a tragedy amusing in the telling, and over we came.

I can't reproduce the dash and sparkle of a mountain torrent, or the kaleidoscope of a Roman carnival; still less the words and manner of Louisa's narration. Mrs. Alcott sat paring apples for a pie; Abby was on the piano stool with her back to the keyboard, but once in a while whirling round to evoke a crash or a crescendo, and at other moments, when attention was focused on the teller, letting her hand slip into mine. The Sage appeared at intervals in the doorway, vaguely suspicious.

Louisa began by saying that the sidewalk in front of the publisher's shop was cluttered up with packing cases, which truckmen were loading onto drays, and clerks hurrying in and out of the entrance; it was difficult to force her way in. Inside it was worse; she had to edge her way along narrow crevices, colliding with impatient shopmen and porters; she feared the establishment was being seized for debt; probably her manuscript would be in the rubbish heap in the back yard. But her blood was up and she kept on.

Upstairs she found the little office in which her enemy sat curved like a capital G over his desk, his eyes through his spectacles shining with, excitement, buttressed behind bills and books, his hand shaking as he dipped a pen in the inkstand to sign a check. Like the Duke of Marlborough, he was riding the whirlwind and directing the storm; something tremendous was evidently going on. Having crossed Her Rubicon, however, Louisa had the courage of desperation. "I've come to ask you—"

Without looking up he waved her away. "Go away. I've given orders—most important. How did you get in here?"

Louisa's ire rose. "I want my manuscript!"

He finished signing the check and looked up. "I told you to get out—" He stopped, petrified as at a Gorgon. Then an exclamation burst from him.

Louisa's impression was that he vaulted over the desk and landed at her feet, leaving his spectacles in mid-air. He grasped her frenziedly by both elbows; she thought he was going to bite her, and recoiled; the man was plainly mad.

Noises spluttered from him, but to no intelligible purport.

At last her astounded ears caught this: "My dear—dearest Miss Alcott! At such a juncture! You got my letter? No? No matter! Nothing to parallel it has occurred in my experience! All else put aside—street blocked—country aroused—overwhelmed—paralyzed! *Uncle Tom's Cabin* backed off the stage! Two thousand more copies ordered this very day from Chicago alone! But that's a fleabite—tens of thousands—why, dearest girl, it's the triumph of the century! A great day indeed, Miss Alcott, for us—for you! At this very moment I was writing you a check; but you are here! You prefer cash? Would a thousand dollars—two thousand—name your own figure! Here, boy! Run to the cashier and bring me bank notes and gold; look sharp now!"

So the packing cases and the bustle had been about Louisa's book!

In spite of all the amusing exaggeration of her spirited account, we realized that *Little Women* had made a staggering hit, and we were informed that Louisa had come back to Apple Slump with the pockets of her gingham skirt bulging with specie—skirts had pockets in the sixties. Hard times for the Alcott family were over forever. We that evening saw the first flowing of the liberating tide.

The book has charmed the Anglo-Saxon race. It has been translated into all varieties of languages; it has become endemic. Wherever it has gone it has softened human hearts and sweetened human thoughts.

Its victory was followed, as years went by, by other victories, none perhaps quite so renowned, but none unworthy. They were books that begot personal love for the woman who wrote them, and assurances of this came to her in many thousands of letters, which gave her happiness during her life.

She endowed her family with comfort, gave Abby the art schooling that she aspired to, and supplied the Sage with black suits and white, tailor made. She never recovered the strength lost in the war, and she died in 1888, when she was but fifty-six years old; her father had died two days before at the age of eighty-nine.

Her Meeting with Henry James

I said I would tell the story of her meeting with Henry James. It was in the winter after the publication of *Little Women,* and Louisa was running the gantlet of receptions and dinners given her by important people in Boston and elsewhere, and her wit and charm won her great popularity, which, however, never turned her head; she kept her own very modest estimate of her achievement.

At one of the first dinners she attended, Henry James was present, and his seat was beside her.

Henry was born in 1843, and was therefore eleven years younger than Louisa, but his gravity and reserve were portentous and amply bridged the gap; in fact, he was one of those who get younger and more approachable as their years increase. He was already a reviewer for the New York *Nation,* and his first novel, entitled *Watch and Ward,* had either been published or was running serially in *The Atlantic.*

He took his literature seriously, almost prayerfully, and felt the obligation laid upon him to warn and to command, more than to comfort, his contemporaries in the venerated craft.

The literary fashions of Boston fifty years ago do not appear to our generation frivolous, but to James they were so, and he strove by example and precept to stem and divert the shallow, glittering stream. I doubt whether he had found it possible actually to read *Little Women,* but he had, as it were, scented it, and his conscience compelled him to let Louisa know that he was unable to join in the vulgar chorus of approval.

He was silent during the opening stages of the dinner, and his gravity deepened as he overheard the compliments which Louisa was absorbing with her wonted humorous discrimination; the ego in her cosmos, as I have intimated, having been long ago licked into modesty by the bufferings of chance, success to her was a happy accident, and laudation nine-tenths whipsillabub. She laughed and smiled, hoped her good luck might continue, and was resolved to do her best to be not undeserving of it.

At length Henry, from the height of his five-and-twenty winters, felt that it was time to act. He bent toward her and spoke thus: "Louisa—m-my dear girl—er—when you hear people—ah—telling you you're a genius you mustn't believe them; er—what I mean is, it isn't true!"

Then he relapsed, spoke no more, and—er—declined the pudding.

THE LAST TALK WITH HER

Louisa's mimetic faculty enabled us to see and hear the judge in Apple Slump sitting room, as he handed down his decision. Years afterward, as he and I walked on Hastings Esplanade, in England, I told him the anecdote. He made inarticulate murmurs and smiled thoughtfully, and looked up at the gray sky and along the populous promenade, and he observed, after due consideration, that he couldn't fix the episode.

"But—well," he added, rubbing his chin through his clipped dark beard, conscientious to the last, "you know, after all, dear Louisa isn't."

But at any rate, Louisa had a delightful talent, and the greater part of human nature, as of the pyramids at Gizeh, is on the lower levels. Those vast underlying courses support the apex and exist for that purpose, though knowing and caring little about it. Moreover, the apex, sublime though it appears, is the first part of the structure to wear away, and when it is cast down it has no honor. Henry James has written exquisite books of which the man in the street knows nothing; but something of whatever is good and sound in the man in the street he owes to influences such as Louisa's stories bring him.

A dozen years and more after *Little Women* had become part of American household furniture, I had returned from Europe to New England and was spending a summer at Nonquitt on Buzzards Bay. Louisa came to visit a friend there, and I walked over to the cottage and sat an hour with her on the veranda.

She was the same tall, rather rustic looking woman, dressed in black silk, her shoulders a little bent, her cheeks somewhat thin, her big black eyes sparkling now and then with humor or irony. The contours of her face had begun to sag a trifle, making her powerful chin more noticeable than of old. She seemed to be happy; she had lived a hard-working, generous life, returning good measure for all she had received. But it seemed to me that I discerned beneath her cheerfulness some veiled sadness; the bright and lively pattern that she showed the world did not wholly hide the pensive background.

"There has never been anything else like our nights at Apple Slump," I said.

After her smile the corners of her mouth drooped. "Everything belonging to us, that can be seen and touched, drops away," she said, "till nothing is left. But maybe the things we wanted and never got are more real than the others and the rest is just padding."

"And perhaps the things we never got are waiting for us somewhere?"

"I'll ask father about that someday—he ought to know!"

I thought of the blameless Sage, blinking blandly round at his little circle [of acolytes]—he ought to know; but would he? I let the subject drop.

"By One Who Knew Her" (1932)

I began to know and like the Alcotts about seventy-two years ago, and Louisa of that ilk in particular—though she was born just a hundred years ago and was even in 1860 fourteen years my elder. But my attachment was not what we call sentimental or romantic; it was just a boy and young woman friend-ship, happy and wholesome. It kept on, regardless of accidents and separa-tion, till she died in 1888, two days after her father. Her mother had been dead eleven years, and also her sister Abbie, who had been known as "May," not more because Abbie thought it a prettier name than because it was a "May" whom Amos Bronson Alcott—the Sage—had married in the begin-ning of things.

The Sage was a lucky man all through his almost ninety years: first in be-coming the husband of Miss May; secondly, in being the father of Louisa, who was later to be known as his "best contribution to literature," and, thirdly, in possessing the unwavering friendship of Ralph Waldo Emerson, who not only extolled and established him intellectually but gave him $500 to help Mrs. Alcott buy the Wayside for him (then known as the Orchard House, because Mr. Alcott took time from Plato to plant apple trees on the hillside at the rear).

Alcott, in spite of his luck, was a total failure from the worldly point of view. He was a tall, bony, mild person, blinking and bleating like a sheep. Emerson strove in vain to teach him how to write his wisdom for publication. The outcome was a few pages of Orphic Wisdom, printed in *The Atlantic*. First copies, uncut, may still be picked up at second-hand shops. It was found more expedient to establish the Conversations: Mr. Alcott to bleat in the centre of the circle and the Circle to give ear round the periphery.

Everybody liked Mr. Alcott. His family adored him, fed him and made clothes for him, and Emerson continued to insist that he was really Plato redivivus. Such persons exist to be hero-worshiped; hero-worshiping being a function of human nature demanding satisfaction, especially in its feminine embodiment. But enough of the dear good old chap, though more might be said; the only harm he did in his ninety years was being the Bore of the Century, and that he never suspected. Meanwhile he begot Louisa; and finally she and he entered the Everlasting Gates hand in hand, and Plato smiled benevolently. Children in heaven still read "Little Women," or sit round Louisa while she tells them stories of that sort. Plato, Emerson and the Sage foregather in the sunparlor hard by, and all is well in the best of all possible Paradises.

Louisa, when I first saw her, was a black-haired, red-cheeked, long-legged hobbledehoy of 28, though not looking or seeming near that age. But there was power in her jaw and control in her black eyes; good nature in her generous mouth, and jollity in her laugh; in short, she was a leader, and, in a place like Concord, she stood out. Honesty, good-will and common sense were in the breath of her nostrils; penetration, too; and humor surpassing the ordinary humor of women—an attitude of comedy in her daily conversation, but poised and inwardly sparkling.

How it could have proceeded from such a source as Amos I know not; he must have bestowed upon his offspring all his own supply and much more; all the girls were jolly creatures and totally un-Platonic. I incline to suspect Mrs. Alcott, a handsome, genial, four-square woman, who had the ideality and faith in God to marry her husband. She was quiet and fascinating, simple as an old shoe, but of perfect breeding. Charles Lamb described a "housekeeper by the wrath of God"; Mrs. Alcott was as good, but with the sunshine and mercy of the Lord. (Four girls and never a boy—but indeed it is impossible to imagine a son of Alcott!) And, oh, such pies, puddings, root beer and pea soup!

Mr. Alcott, as we all know, never ate anything but bread and milk and apples and raw vegetables. I will quote a poem apropos of that. It was composed by a gentleman and friend who dwelt next door, who was seldom stirred to verse save on high occasion, and it happened at a time when the Edward Lear nonsense rhymes had captured us and we were all busy trying to imitate them. The children next door to the Alcotts caught the contagion and applied to the gentleman in question for a contribution. Paper and pencil were produced on the spot, and he wrote:

> There lived a Sage at Appleslump
> Whose dinner never made him plump;
> Give him carrots, potatoes, squash, turnips and peas,
> And a handful of crackers without any cheese,
> And a cup of cold water to wash down all these,
> And he'd prate of the Spirit as long as you'd please,
> This airy Sage of Appleslump—

Appleslump being the New England name of a certain delectable pie-pudding created by Mrs. Alcott, and which sounded more like an allusion to the dilapidated dwelling of that era than to the austere Orchard House of the present. Louisa saw the point and applied it. But neither she nor anybody else ever saw the poem. The most intimate families have secrets from one another.

Louisa was an actress born, and shone in private theatricals, but forbade herself the public stage lest it should interfere with her duties at home, which were many. But at festivals at the Concord Town Hall in aid of the war and other worthy causes she was an able and cordial protagonist, and constructed little dramas which were produced. She was a whole-souled devotee of Charles Dickens, and had by heart such dialogues as that between Sairey Gamp and Betsey Prig; and she and Abbie, or else Ann, the married sister, would dress up a little scene and deliver the play, with applause responsive, of course, to Louisa's genius.

But she had never taken her ability seriously. And though she play-acted for Concord audiences, and also wrote little stories for *The Concord Weekly Monitor*, edited by the Bartlett boys—capital stories they were—and even though she had written a whole serious novel (but anonymously), published by a Boston firm but not adequately advertised and never a best seller, nevertheless she could not be made to believe that she had in her any real literary talent. Yet the prompt and immense success of "Little Women" was waiting just around the corner, and surprised her no less than the book delighted the world—and still delights the great-grandchildren of the children of the 1860s.

The book was not composed *in malice prepense* but was scribbled from day to day for fun, to be read aloud to us and the Emerson children, who lived further west down the road. But our continued applause at last emboldened the author to try it on with a Boston publisher, and her most extravagant dreams of supporting her family were realized. What good times they all had! Visited Europe, too! The blunt and modest and brilliant country girl was taken up by society, dined, wined and complimented—and she with a dry smile at herself and them through it all.

Louisa was modest to the end, and kept her excellent head at its proper poise. She made real money, with which she supported her family and persons she loved, and was no doubt happy. And yet, when I last saw her, a year or two before her death, I felt a sadness in her: the humor of former days was there, but wise rather than joyous. She never married; had she ever been in love? Nobody knows. Yet she was abundantly qualified by nature to be a lover and a mother. Perhaps she may have denied such happiness in her youth because she was needed at home; and when the need was past, the time had passed also. I wish she might have written her own story.

In the midst of her home activities came the Civil War, and in the second year of it Louisa gave all to patriotism and went to the front as a nurse. Her journal of that experience, "Hospital Sketches," was afterward published. Louisa was brought home nearly dead, and she never was well again. After the peace she stood at her home gate while a company of veterans from the front marched with drum and fife, the afternoon sun glinting on their rifle-barrels. At the word of command the dusty and thirsty fellows halted, and were refreshed with gallons of cool lemonade and good plum cake made by Mrs. Alcott and Louisa and the girls, and Louisa spoke a few words with the Captain and the men cheered her as the ranks re-formed to march on into the sunset.

When the last of them had disappeared round the bend of the old highway under the shadow of the elms, Louisa suddenly sank down on the grass beside the rustic fence her father had built long before. Her mother hastened to her; Ann and Abbie stood near her; we boys turned away. But Louisa soon stood up again with a little apologetic laugh and went into the house, leaving us, with a gesture, to the cake and lemonade, which remained in abundance. I had never before seen tears on her face; but she had given her heart to the soldiers and the cause; she had seen them die; she had served them and loved them and now it was all over.

It was then after an interval that she began "Little Women." She was a worthy daughter of New England. But there was sentiment and romance in New England in the '60s, and "Little Women" shows them; the fun bubbles up inadvertently, as happens in real life.

On a frosty April evening, after dusk, as we sat in the library, I heard a light footstep on the porch outside, and a knock on the door. But when I opened the door, no one was there. However, I caught sight of a bit of folded paper, which I picked up and carried within.

My father unfolded it, and after reading it handed it to my mother, who read it aloud to us all. It was the little poem, of about sonnet length, which Louisa had been moved to write on Thoreau, who had died the day before. It is tender and beautiful, and was presently printed in *The Atlantic,* on the instance of my father, who had been much touched by it. But Louisa had been too shy to submit it to him in person, and it had seemed to flutter down like the snowflakes from the evening sky.

I should perhaps confess that there had been a tacit understanding in the two families that Abbie (May) and I were to be romantically attached—though in fact it was one of the interfamily jokes, fostered by Louisa. At all events I assumed airs of proprietorship over Abbie. But it was understood, at the same time, that Abbie was really to wed a semi-mythical English cousin, who was to come over here from his great estates in England and carry her away to the wealth and luxury of Europe. I didn't half credit this yarn, but Louisa would sometimes allude to it with a certain seriousness, and Abbie would smile and not deny.

One afternoon I had a surprise. It was in Autumn. I had been engaged in a strenuous game of hockey with other Sanborn School boys and was coming home disheveled and hungry. As I approached the gate of the Alcott house on my way I descried two figures standing before it in close conversation. One I immediately recognized as Abbie; the other was of masculine aspect. He stood with one arm thrown lightly round Abbie's waist, and she did not seem to shrink from the familiarity. Then I remembered that there had been some talk of the English cousin: could this free mannered person be he? I drew near with a certain indignation: I had never, myself, assumed the liberty of embracing Abbie, and I resented the attitude of this stranger.

He confronted me as I came up; and I saw a slender youth, of less than my height, but undeniably handsome, clad in black, with a soft black hat set jauntily on his head. He had bold black eyes, which measured me with a sort of insolence, rather amused than hostile.

I said nothing. Abbie murmured, "Our cousin, you know," and turned aside. He showed a fine set of white teeth under his small black mustache, and spoke with a slightly foreign accent. "Well, well! So this is our young friend Julian; quite a well-grown boy. I was expecting something a little less immature! But I'm pleased to see you, my child, and when you've had an opportunity to change your attire, I shall be happy to improve our acquaintance!"

This was plain impudence, to be answered with a buffet on the ear: but one must be restrained in the presence of a lady. He had a cane in his left hand, hardly more than a switch, with a silver head; and this he twirled between his fingers, and so near my face as to seem insulting. I knew I could have thrashed the fellow with one hand, and I was feeling bloodthirsty enough for pistols and daggers; but he was a guest and relative of my friends: I must forbear a while! I turned to Abbie: "You haven't told me this person's name."

Hereupon an amazing thing occurred. Abbie, uttering a strange cry, faced about and fled up the pathway toward the house. I made a menacing step toward the cousin, but he sprang actively back, at the same time disengaging the little black mustache from his upper lip and tossing it over my head. He snatched off his soft black hat and with the same movement pushed a hand up through his hair, which broke from its fastenings and cascaded down his back in joyous tumult. Then he turned and pursued Abbie up the path, whooping like a Comanche, but with a feminine consciousness, I fancied, of the pantaloons.

I stood flabbergasted, staring after them, and with a new respect of Louisa's histrionic ability. Her success had been complete, but I was a little astonished at Abbie's cooperation, and did not quite forgive her till after supper, when we all spent a hilarious evening over root beer and raisin cake; Abbie thrumming ballad tunes on the piano.

It seems to me, as I write, that I am telling tales of another race, on another planet. I can find no traces, today, of such people as I was intimate with seventy years ago; and even Concord, when I visited it last, was not the simple village that I had known.

All history is as the voice of one crying in the wilderness, and in an unknown tongue. Day follows day and does not return; neither do the people who lived in them; where they were they no longer are, nor can be forever;

one age keeps its secrets from another, not because it so wills, but inevitably. It is better so; and if my old friend Louisa Alcott, could miraculously come back as she was, she would not be recognized, nor would she recognize, in the present, what the past had been. But I am happy to record these glimpses; what has been gives substance and meaning to what is to be.

"The Woman Who Wrote *Little Women,*" *Ladies' Home Journal* 39 (1922): 25, 120–24. "By One Who Knew Her: Julian Hawthorne's Memories of Old Concord Days When Louisa Alcott Did Not Take Her Talents Seriously," *New York Times Magazine* (27 November 1932): 11, 17.

From *Memories of Concord* (1926)

MARY HOSMER BROWN

Mary Hosmer Brown was the granddaughter of Edmund and Sally Pierce Hosmer of Concord. As a child, Mary had often spent her summer vacations at her grandfather's farm, far away from her home in the West, but when she returned East to attend college, she spent more time visiting the town. Edmund Hosmer (1798–1881) filled his granddaughter's imagination with tales of "Old Concord," as he always called the village. He himself had heard accounts of the famous 1775 Concord fight from eyewitnesses, including his own father, John Hosmer, who had arrived at the North Bridge just in time to witness the death of the first man. Edmund Hosmer had known the Concord authors, Emerson, Thoreau, Alcott, and Hawthorne, and also passed on stories of them to his grandchildren. Mary Hosmer Brown met Alcott herself after the publication of *Little Women,* and her piece is a biographical account of the famous author interspersed with her own recollections and those of other family members. Her portrait, one chapter in a book designed to capture for her own children and grandchildren the memories of those "Old Concord" days, shows the Alcotts as a family filled with high ideals and Louisa May as the providing daughter. Brown's work, like a large part of the recollections of the Alcotts written in the late nineteenth and early twentieth century, helped form the mythic portrait of Louisa May that endured for over half a century: "Duty's faithful child."

Two of the names that have added to Concord's fame are those of A. Bronson and Louisa Alcott. Mr. Alcott was intended for a Plato, but set down on a barren New England hillside, where a living must be made by a profession, a trade, or hard manual labor. To none of these was our impractical philosopher adapted. Incapable of earning enough to pay rent or supply the needs of the family, is it any wonder that he said he had moved twenty-seven times in twenty-nine years? His unusual ideas made him the subject of much ridicule. He wore linen in winter because he disapproved of shearing sheep, and refused to drink milk because cows mourned when their calves were taken away from them. From the same altruistic beliefs he became a vegetarian. Philosophy was meat and drink to him.

Hoping to become a pioneer in reform methods of education, he conducted a school in Masonic Temple, Boston, known as The Tremont Street School. There are two tales which, true or not, embody the practical reasons for its lack of success. One is of the pupil who was obliged to strike his teacher's hand with a ruler instead of receiving the blows himself. The other is of a parent who called at the school one day. "Mr. Alcott," she said, "my boy is playing truant so much I don't see how he can learn anything here." Alcott was astonished, but after thinking a moment replied, "It may be true, since I have been studying so much about his soul that I haven't noticed the absence of his body."

His next experiment was the result of a visit to England, where he met Charles Lane, a man thoroughly in sympathy with Alcott's transcendental ideas. Together after returning to America they bought a worn-out farm of ninety acres in the town of Harvard, Massachusetts. This they named "Fruitlands," a purely ideal name, because, as Louisa said, out of the five very ancient apple trees on the place only one ever bore fruit.

Here their Utopia was started. All labor must be manual, the men with spades replacing plows, oxen, and horses. No living thing was to be killed, not even bugs or weeds, since all life was entitled to its own fulfillment. All products of slave labor, such as coffee, tea, cotton, and wool, were forbidden.

One by one the few people attracted to the plan left, and finally even the Lanes deserted the place. With the collapse of the ideas which had been manna to the soul of the Concord philosopher, the shores of the promised land again receded and Alcott was ill for weeks. Penniless, with winter ahead, Mrs. Alcott was near despair. Finally she said, "I know a woman with a very big heart; I shall go to see her." So she came to Grandmother, who after hearing her story crowded her own large family together and gave up three rooms, and the Alcotts moved in for the next six months, Mrs. Alcott having sold from their meagre stock at Fruitlands whatever furniture she could spare, to provide funds for their immediate use.

Such jolly times as those two sets of children had! Louisa's energy made play even from work. Mr. Alcott had permission to have for his use any wood which he could cut down and bring home from the farm wood-lot. As manual labor was not his forte the wood-box was often empty. For such times Louisa invented a most fascinating game. All would run to the lot and the one who succeeded in riding hobby horse home on the largest branch won the game. She and one of my older aunts used to argue hotly over the respective merits of their younger sisters who were each named Abby. Finally they agreed to amuse themselves by writing sonnets which should embody their admiring sentiments and so the baby Abbys became the subjects of some queer sounding verses, undoubtedly Louisa's first attempts at composing.

On one occasion when I had taken some friends to meet Miss Alcott, after talking to them for a few minutes, she turned to me and said, "When I knew this morning that you were coming, my memory turned back to the winter we lived with your grandmother and a trivial incident came to my mind. I used to go upstairs with your aunts to help them make up the beds. The very first thing they did was to delve down and fish out from somewhere a queer looking bundle. I thought it wouldn't be polite to ask questions, so it was some time before I discovered that those bundles contained a brick or a flatiron." In those days there were no furnaces in farmers' houses and grandmother always insisted that the children must go to bed with warm feet. After supper a long row of bricks and flat-irons adorned the kitchen stove. Each child as it went up stairs must seize one, wrap it up in some convenient cloth, preferably pieces of worn out woolen blankets, and carry it to bed.

Louisa should have been a boy. She could climb a tree like a squirrel and no fences or sheds were too high for her feats of agility. It was doubtless the memory of her own youthful activity that gave her such a ready sympathy with boyish pranks and made her so true a friend to boys and girls in every condition of life..

Mr. Alcott was a vegetarian to whom even milk, cheese, and eggs were taboo, but Louisa loved to go with the children into our cellar and eat pieces of cheese or go to the pantry for her share of slices of brown bread spread with thick cream.

She was very kind to the younger set but when she was tired or wanted to get away she would invent errands to the barn or somewhere. When they returned she and the older girls would be nowhere to be found.

Sunday evenings the Alcotts had simple teas and our children went in with the others. Small baskets were passed around, each basket covered with a red and white checked napkin. On lifting the napkin you might find only two crackers and an apple, for perhaps that week the Alcott purse was slim. There were however good times after supper. Mr. Alcott would read from *Pilgrim's Progress* and the children would choose some scene to act out.

Mr. Alcott made Bunyan so vivid that one day Grandmother missed her youngest boy. He was finally found trudging along the road with an improvised pack on his back.

A woman in Concord said to Aunt Jane, one day, "I can't seem to make *Pilgrim's Progress* interesting to my boy as you do." "Oh," said Aunt Jane, "I learned from Mr. Alcott to be a good skipper."

In the Alcott kitchen a shower bath was set up and its daily use was insisted on. Little Beth was recovering from scarlet fever and Grandmother always thought the treatment was too vigorous for her weakened system, for she went into a decline.

Mrs. Alcott was a remarkable woman, very brave throughout all the many trials of her early married life, and most hospitable as far as her means would allow. The children loved to be with her. One day when she was sewing and they were playing near her, she suddenly looked up and said, "Well, here I've been trying to do something that not one of you will ever be able to do. Guess what it is." They all guessed in vain, until she told them that she had been trying to thread the point of her needle.

During the years when the Alcotts were very poor, Mrs. Alcott with wonderful bravery exalted their poverty by showing the children how to glorify plain living with high thinking.

Many a family has had material wealth and spiritual poverty; the Alcotts taught the world that spiritual wealth might be attained in the midst of material poverty.

In the spring Mrs. Alcott received a small legacy which she decided to use in the purchase of a home. With this and a loan from Emerson The Wayside was bought and Mr. Alcott amused himself by adding a tiny gable in front. Later it was sold to Hawthorne and they moved next door to The Orchard House, where they lived a number of years and where many of the happenings in the first part of *Little Women* occurred.

Over the front door was Louisa's den where she put on her little red cap of thinking. Mr. Alcott made rustic seats and trained vines over them, which the artist daughter, Abby May, later liked to transfer to her canvas.

Their struggles were by no means over when they had settled down in The Orchard House, and many of them are familiar to the readers of Miss Alcott's books. One winter's day there came a severe cold snap and the Alcotts were without wood. Mr. Alcott said, "We will pray that our wants may be supplied." A blinding snowstorm raged all night and in the morning a load of wood was lying by the road near his gate. There was great rejoicing at this speedy answer to prayer and all hands took hold, chopped and lugged into the shed, and the fires blazed merrily away during a storm which made all travel impossible.

At length the sun shone, the roads were dug out, when lo! a man appeared with a wagon seeking the wood which he had dumped there when his horses became exhausted and could drag the load no further. The gift of the Lord was however partly chopped and some of it in ashes. Besides there was no money to pay the man, who furiously demanded his pay and finally threatened to sue. The matter leaked out, probably through the man's anger, and some good friend quietly paid the bill; so the prayer kept them warm for some time.

Mr. Alcott had no conception of the dire straits to which his impractical ways often reduced the family. Mr. Emerson on one occasion gave him twenty-five dollars to expend, as he hoped, on some of the necessities lacking in the house. The money was spent, however, on some expensive stationery, which Alcott brought home with the joy of a child in a new toy. Once when he was starting for Boston, Mrs. Alcott gave him twelve dollars to buy her a shawl much needed for the winter. When he returned he met her with a beaming face and produced from under his arm a long coveted edition of Plato which he had joyfully discovered at a second hand book store. She and the shawl had been utterly forgotten. One can well imagine the length of time it would take for that long-suffering helpmeet to save up the twelve dollars again.

A few things he liked to do with his hands like the rustic seats which at one time so freely adorned the grounds around The Orchard House. Once he made a wind harp which he set up in a tree opposite the side door at Emerson's. It worked best in a gale. Like the harp, Alcott's poetry has passed into forgetfulness and his own personality is seldom spoken of in this generation, yet who can tell how many of those altruistic ideas he sowed so lavishly on bleak mental soil grew somewhere into beauty well worth the while.

Alcott at one time, in the kindness of his heart, planned an outdoor study for Emerson near the latter's house. He called in Thoreau to help adjust it, but Thoreau was disgusted because he could not make Alcott see that buildings must conform to geometry. With Alcott, "curved were the lines of beauty." Some of the shingles were so beautifully curved that they made fine runways for the rain and the building was too damp to be a cheerful study. Mrs. Emerson called it "The Ruin" and it early justified the name.

Like Thoreau, Alcott loved animals, so much so indeed that he refused to eat them or in any way provide for his own comfort out of their suffering. Perhaps he was a forerunner of that saying of Tolstoi's, "The future of the world lies with the Vegetarians."

It is said that in 1867 Mr. Alcott carried with him on the train from Concord a pair of grey squirrels, which he released on Boston Common. He observed that later they had made homes on the Beacon Street side and were rearing families.

In spite of his impractical ways Alcott was a welcome addition in intellectual circles where things of moment were being discussed. Called by Emerson "The Prince of Talkers," little by little he became accepted as an idealist worth listening to. The dream of his life was realized when he founded the "Concord School of Philosophy."

A story which illustrates his power in conversation is as follows. Once finding himself without funds in a city some distance away he decided that he had better get home, so in spite of his penniless condition he boarded a steamer bound for Boston. When the steward demanded his ticket Alcott said that he had neither ticket nor money, but that he would gladly earn his passage. "What can you do?" asked the man. "I can talk," said Alcott. The disgusted steward turned him over to the captain, who finally allowed him to try his skill on the passengers. The result was so successful that the captain invited him to his own table and a free passage was secured.

I have been told that as a young man Alcott was heavy featured, but years of high thinking had softened and refined his features when I knew him. His long white hair and ruddy skin, his dignified but courteous manners, made him a striking personality. He gave out his Orphic sayings from an inner conviction that man may be, if he listens, a vehicle for higher wisdom. He was in his element when presiding at the sessions of the school of philosophy, where so many well known people discussed everything from protoplasm to Plato. He was always ready to answer questions and it wasn't easy to get the best of him. During the summer school period some young acquaintances of mine had a wager as to which of them should ask him what he meant by the following sentence: "When the mind is issing it is thinging things." Finally one of the young men took up the challenge. Mr. Alcott listened sedately and without changing countenance replied, "Young man, if I said such a sentence as that, it must have meant something in the connection with which I said it," and he passed serenely on.

Concord is apt to have sultry weather in summer and the philosophers wending their way through dust and heat came in for more or less ridicule. Even Louisa had her share in the fun when she wrote:

> Philosophers sit in their sylvan hall
> And talk of the duties of man,
> Of chaos and cosmos, Hegel and Kant,
> With the Oversoul well in the van.
>
> All on their hobbies they amble away
> And a terrible dust they make.
> Disciples devout both gaze and adore
> As daily they listen and bake.

Alcott was an unique character. True to his convictions, he went his way without aggressiveness or resentment, finally winning tolerance for his whims and respect for his mentality. Quick to perceive a new idea, he would take some word of Emerson's, ponder it, and retake it to Emerson elaborately clothed in Alcottian language. Emerson would be delighted, often failing to recognize the idea as originally his own.

Emerson thought highly of Alcott, but Carlyle couldn't understand him. Emerson often brought over Carlyle's letters to read to Grandfather. In one of them he said: "A. B. Alcott has been here over night and I have been to take tea with him, but I cannot like him. What business has he to be always living in the future?"

Louisa was born at Germantown, Pennsylvania and went to a Quaker school. When she was very small she saw a colored child sold for debt. She had no use for slavery after that.

Even as a little child Louisa showed her love of independence by running away. When they lived in town, Boston Common was a favorite hiding place. Once the town crier had to be summoned, and as he cried out the description of the child a small voice piped up from the shade of a doorway, "Why, dat's me.". . .

Emerson was Louisa's Goethe to whom she wrote sonnets and whom she once even dared to serenade. Thoreau she loved and walked with. She had a deep sense of fun which helped her over a great many hard places.

Louisa liked literature but was not fond of numbers. When she was in the primary school and became mischievous her teacher could always head her off by calling out suddenly, "Louisa, how many are seven and six? "—a poser which would effectually subdue her for a while.

In order to help out the meagre income of the family, she even took the position of a servant. She was so abominably treated that she had to leave. As Sanborn said, "Louisa was very wonderful in always being willing to try anything, but even she could not stand her treatment as a servant."

At nineteen Miss Alcott was made joyful by having a story published by *Gleason's Pictorial,* for which she received five dollars. A few months later she sent *The Rival Prima Donnas* to the *Boston Saturday Gazette,* and to her great delight it was accepted and a cheque of ten dollars forwarded to her. Still later she dramatized this second story and succeeded in having it taken by a theatrical company, who gave her as payment a pass for forty nights, although for some reason the drama was never actually played.

She herself had natural ability in acting, as those who saw her famous representations from Dickens in her Jarley Wax Works could testify. She had played at amateur theatricals, especially on evenings at home where scenes from *Pilgrim's Progress* were vividly portrayed with childish enthusiasm, much to the approval of Mr. Alcott. At one time she successfully applied for a position on the stage, but unfortunately for her ambition to become an actress, the manager broke his leg and the contract was annulled. Another story was taken by *The Gazette,* and she writes thus of her first glimpses of fame: "One of the memorial moments of my life is that in which, as I trudged to school on a wintry day, my eye fell upon a large yellow poster with these delicious words, '*Bertha,* a new tale by the author of *The Rival Prima Donnas,* will appear in *The Saturday Evening Gazette.*' I was late; it was bitter cold; people jostled me; I was mortally afraid I should be recognized; but there I stood feasting my eyes on the fascinating poster, and saying proudly to myself, in the words of the great Vincent Crummies, 'This, this is fame.'"

Louisa's health was never good after her experiences in the civil war hospitals, which she records in her book, *Hospital Sketches.* In spite of poor health she worked hard to supply ease and comforts for the family. May received a *dol* of three thousand dollars when she married and after her death Louisa educated her child. Her mother's last years were made comfortable at the home in Concord, which she had bought from the Thoreaus with money earned from her writing. Mrs. Alcott grew very large with dropsy, so that she had to be carried upstairs in an arm chair. She would smile with her accustomed bravery and say, "This is the beginning of my ascension." A number of times she would add, "It is beautiful to die."

One day after Louisa's books became popular and poverty was no longer known in the household, a small cousin of mine went in to call. Mrs. Alcott was very busy, but she was too kindly to send the child home, so she said, "Annie, wouldn't you like to sit at Louisa's desk and write a nice long letter to your father?" When that was completed, a letter to mother was suggested as a good idea, and the child was happily amused and always retained a glad memory of a forenoon at Louisa's desk.

One evening we went to a reception at the studio of Daniel French, given on his return from studying in Italy. When the carriage came for us it was occupied by Mr. Alcott and Louisa. The latter immediately became absorbed in chatting with my aunt, which left Mr. Alcott to amuse himself with a young girl like myself. He was as courteous as though I had been a queen:—waited for me while we laid aside our wraps, and escorted me through the rooms in the most charming manner. He certainly won my heart from that day.

Louisa did everything possible for her father at the Louisburg Square house in Boston where he died. I used to go in sometimes at the latter place to help pass away the time for Mr. Alcott when he was grown too feeble to do much for himself. Our chief source of amusement was the checker board, but after a while even that failed, for if I won he wasn't pleased and if he suspected me of letting him win that was even worse.

While the friends were assembled at his funeral in Louisburg Square, word came that Louisa had joined her father in death. Her name will survive for many years through the love of children who delight in the Little Men and Women of her books.

From *Memories of Concord* (Boston: The Four Seas, 1926), pp. 73–87.

"Louisa May Alcott: By the Original 'Goldilocks'" (1936)

MAUDE APPLETON MCDOWELL

Maude A. McDowell was the granddaughter of W[illiam] W. Wheildon, who lived just down the street from Anna Alcott Pratt's Main Street home, which she bought in 1877, a few months before her mother's death. Bronson also stayed there, along with Louisa when she was in Concord. McDowell is the only Alcott "character" besides "Laurie" (Alfred Whitman), "Meg" (Anna Alcott), or "Daisy" (John Pratt) to write recollections of the author. As Louisa once told an aspiring writer: "Materials for the children's tales I find in the lives of the little people about me, for no one can invent anything so droll, pretty or pathetic as the sayings & doings of these small actors, poets & martyrs" (*Selected Letters*, 307).

Since "Little Women" and "Little Men" have appeared on the screen, there has been such a revival of interest in Louisa May Alcott that it may be of interest to my readers to hear some personal reminiscences of her.

I can remember her as far back as when I was a child of four or five for she then lived only a few doors from my grandparents, Mr. and Mrs. W. W. Wheildon on Main Street, Concord. The Alcotts moved there after leaving the "Orchard House." Miss Alcott was a great friend of my two aunts, the Misses Wheildon, and came often to our house where she used to talk to me as I was playing in the garden.

It was a lovely garden with a long row of tall poplars on either side of the beds of old-fashioned flowers. There was a privet bush cut in the shape of a tea-pot—nose, handle and all. This main street, with its overarching elms and fine old houses with their beautiful doorways and fanlights was truly characteristic of New England.

Being fond of children, Miss Alcott had a way of drawing them out and getting at their thoughts which is doubtless why her children's characters are so real. I little knew at that time that she was getting "copy," as it were, out of me for her book, or that I was later to become the original "Goldilocks" of "Little Men" who, you may remember, was the child of "Amy" and "Laurie." Having such golden curls gave Miss Alcott the idea of that name and she made the boys in "Little Men" speak of "Goldilocks" as "part child, part angel and part fairy."

The author even used a story I had told her, putting it word for word into this book. I do not remember telling her this story but I can easily believe that it was "made up" by a very young child for it is too preposterous to have been imagined by a "grown-up."

This is the tale: "Once a lady had a million children and one nice little boy. She went upstairs and said: 'You mustn't go in the yard.' He wented and fell into the pump and was drowned dead. She pumped him up and wrapped him in a newspaper and put him on a shelf to dry for seed."

Miss Alcott was then what one would call "middle-aged" but had all the liveliness, fun and "pep" of the "Jo" we know so well in her books and through Katharine Hepburn's fine acting.

A perfect description of "Jo's" looks and manner as I remember her is found in the following account of "Mother Bhaer" from "Little Men": "She was not handsome but she had a merry sort of face that never seemed to have forgotten certain childish ways and looks, any more than her voice and manner had; and these things, very hard to describe but very plain to see and feel, made her a genial, comfortable person, easy to get on with and generally 'jolly' as the boys would say."

The characters in "Little Women" are almost the exact counterpart of the four Alcott girls: "Meg" was Anna (Mrs. John Pratt); "Jo," Louisa (although Louisa never married and it is well known that she first wrote her story without having "Jo" marry but the publishers insisted that the heroine of the book must marry so it was rewritten and the character of "Professor Bhaer" was created for "Jo's" husband). "Beth," in real life Elizabeth or "Lizzie," was delicate and died young, as in the story, and "Amy" (May) was very like the pretty, young, artistic sister who said her greatest trial in life was her turn-up nose and who actually *did* put a clothespin on it to improve its shape.

"Mr. Lawrence" was the girls' grandfather, Colonel May, and although "Laurie" was partly taken from the Polish boy Louisa met abroad, she told me he was also a combination of all the nice boys she had ever known. "Aunt March" was no one. "Mrs. March," as Louisa says in her Diary: "is all true, only not half good enough." Mr. Alcott never went to the War but Louisa did as nurse. Meg's husband, "John Brooke," died ten years after his marriage; and, instead of "Daisy," "Demi" and little "Josie," as in the book, he left two boys—Freddie and Johnny. I used to play with these lads and my own boy cousins who made much of me.

When Miss Alcott went on the many picnics which my aunts were always getting up, she was the life of our parties and kept us in gales of laughter by her original way of putting things. When I asked her why she wrote "Little Men," she said, "because the roof needed shingling."

Louisa's father must have been a very trying person to live with, being so much in the clouds, and so impractical, but his friends all loved him and his family adored him. He had the most devoted of wives without whom he could never have "carried on."

I have lately heard an amusing story of his absent-mindedness. Someone came to him with the request for the loan of ten dollars to which he replied: "I would gladly give it to you, my friend, if I possessed such a thing—but wait! I believe I have a twenty-dollar gold piece upstairs in my bureau drawer. Would that do just as well?"

Mr. Alcott, as I used to see him, looked very much like his pictures with the tall, silk hat, black clothes and sometimes a long black cape or even a shawl which was then the fashion for men. It always seemed so funny to us children to see our grandfather and Mr. Emerson and Mr. Alcott wearing such a thing.

One of the most precious experiences of my life was when I received the "laying on of hands," as it were, from Mr. Emerson. This is how it happened. My grandparents were celebrating their Golden Wedding with a large reception to which most of the town came, Mr. Emerson among others. And as the occasion was also my birthday, I had felt urged to write a poem, just a sing-song little verse about

> "Oh, the Golden Wedding Day
> On the twenty-eighth of May,"

and ending naively with:

> "Their heads are old and gray,
> But mine is young and gay!"

To my horror I found my grandfather had shown this verse to Mr. Emerson. During the afternoon, when I saw Mr. Emerson coming towards me, I wished the ground would open under me and swallow me up. However, as he came nearer and looked down at me from what seemed to me at least eight feet of height, I saw his benign expression and felt reassured. He laid his hand on my head and said, with a beautiful smile, "Very good, my child."

An amusing incident in connection with Mr. Emerson happened one day when he and Mr. Alcott were dining *en famille* with my grandfather. Their host, the Historian of the Town, and an authority on Revolutionary history, was intimate with these philosophers. My cousins and I had been taken to the School of Philosophy, I suppose so that we might say we had been there, for we surely could not have understood half that was said but we became familiar with the names of Plato, Socrates and Dante and had named our turtles for these "Immortals."

You may imagine how Mr. Emerson and Mr. Alcott were startled when at dinner I leaned across the table and said to my cousin in a stage-whisper which could be heard all over the room: "Oh! Tom, Plato would not eat a thing today but Socrates and Dante have each had a fly and a worm."

Speaking of the School of Philosophy, I remember something that happened there which made a great impression upon me. It was a sultry July day when we children were taken to the simple wooden chapel where the meetings were held. As there were no screens on doors or windows, the flies were plentiful and I shall never forget my Amazement when I saw old Miss Elizabeth Peabody who was sitting on the platform with Alcott, Frank Sanborn, Professor Harris and others, so interested and unconscious that she allowed a fly to crawl *straight across her knee* without brushing it away. Such utter absorption in the talk to which she was listening seemed to me almost superhuman.

In later years, I recall seeing Miss Louisa wheeling her little niece, Lulu, down the street in her baby carriage—and how she adored that child! It was all she had left of her sister, May.

St. Nicholas 64 (November 1936): 29, 45.

"Glimpses of the Real Louisa May Alcott" (1938)

Marion Talbot

> Marion Talbot was the daughter of Emily Fairbanks Talbot, a philanthropist and co-worker with her husband, the homeopathic physician Dr. Israel Tisdale Talbot. Alcott knew the Talbots through their joint efforts at securing women's right to vote. Marion, a graduate of Boston University, had organized a group of women from the university to call upon Alcott in May 1880. Louisa recorded the event: "Thirty girls from Boston University called; told stories, showed pictures, wrote autographs. Pleasant to see so much innocent enthusiasm, even about so poor a thing as a used up old woman. Bright girls! Simple in dress, sensible ideas of life, and love of education. I wish them all good luck" (*Journals*, 225). Talbot's recollections were written to commemorate the fiftieth anniversary of Alcott's death, partly in response to other studies, notably Katherine Anthony's recently published biography *Louisa May Alcott* (1938), that asserted "her life was one long increasing misery."

There are not many living who knew her well or have records of interest regarding her. It is possible that from an assortment which the present writer treasures some selections may add to the picture, real or mythical, of a woman who was great as well as beloved. . . .

When, under the presidency of Mrs. Abby Morton Diaz, the author of *William Henry Letters*, efforts were made to increase the financial resources of the Women's Educational and Industrial Union of Boston, the writer of the sketch arranged a benefit entertainment. She had a vivid memory of playing, as a child of nine years, the role of the Welsh Dwarf in Mrs. Jarley's Wax Works, in which Miss Alcott was the inimitable show woman, and of the delightful home evenings when Miss Alcott joined the young people of the family and their college friends in impromptu charades. Miss Alcott would play the nurse in a hospital scene and gobble up the delicacies intended for the patient, or take any role that came to hand with inimitable humor and skill. So she was asked if she would help in the proposed entertainment. Unfortunately she was feeling the limitations on her strength—"a sad heart and a used-up body," her journal notes—and replied as follows:

Mrs. Pratt and Fred are at your service for Jarley and a farce whenever you want them. . . . I shall be glad to help all I can, but as Mrs. P likes acting and I don't and as both cannot be in town at once, I shall hand this post over to her. Yours for the cause, L. M. A.

The Sunday night suppers when she joined us quite simply were a great treat, especially the talks with the writer's mother, for they had many interests in common. Her stories were unfailing in merriment. Even the tragic experience at Fruitlands had its humorous side. She told how Mr. Lane, the English member of the curious household, would come into the kitchen early in the morning and greet the women as they prepared for breakfast, with such strong language that they would remonstrate. He would then say, "What do the words matter when I mean 'Good morning, it is a nice day!'"

Her devotion to her father and her affection for him were unfailing, and yet with a kind of wistful humor she could tell of episodes in which his personal qualities must have been trying, to say the least. At one time a friend, believing that Mrs. Alcott was not clad warmly enough, gave Mr. Alcott ten dollars with which to buy her a shawl in Boston, whither he was about to go on a business trip. The family eagerly awaited his return with the gift for the mother. He came bearing a load of books which he displayed to the expectant group. "But where is mother's shawl?" was the anxious inquiry. No reaction but patient resignation was possible after long years of experience as he explained that in passing a favorite bookstore he had seen in the window some books he had long wanted, and having the unusual experience of money in his pocket, he bought them. There was a funny side which Louisa fortunately saw and could even share by describing it.

Although we knew that while serving as an army nurse she had been stricken with a terrible illness which nearly cost her her life, we were never aware that it had left indelible marks. A heavy cold or a sprained ankle would lay her up for a time, but it is quite impossible to assent to the opinion that "her life was one of long increasing misery." Nor did her "demonic" or "Cassandra" temperament reveal itself. There was no evidence of "starved and deafened emotions" when she happily and eagerly rejoiced in making plans for little motherless "Lulu" or in bringing comfort and happiness to her father.

Her first story, she told us, was printed when she was sixteen years old, and she received five dollars for it. Thereafter she was paid small sums, which at the time seemed large, for the tales she sent to magazines. Inadvertently she once signed her name "Louisa M. Alcott" instead of "L. M. Alcott." This time the check in payment was for a greatly reduced amount. The publisher said his payment was always less for women. Many times later, when she was famous, he offered to pay her fabulous sums for her stories, but she told us of the delight she took in refusing to write again for his magazine.

New England Quarterly 11 (December 1938): 731–38.

"Miss Clara and Her Friend, Louisa" (1960)

NINA AMES FREY

> As Frey's article clearly illustrates, the people who had known Alcott personally were deceased by the end of the 1930s, and the tales that were left were from secondhand sources. Even the generation of readers who had met the famous author during their own childhood in the 1880s was now almost all vanished. Frey's recollections stretch back probably thirty-odd years to her own youth, when her great-aunt Clara was still alive to tell her stories of growing up in Concord with the Alcott girls. Although she is never identified, Frey's "Aunt Clara" appears to be Clara Gowing, who also published "several slender volumes of poetry." Frey's recollections and those published in Gowing's 1909 volume are strikingly similar in language and content, especially the story of the girls' "postoffice."

For many years while I was a very young girl I spent my summers with my grandmother at her home in Massachusetts. The small town in which she lived was like most New England villages at the turn of the century, ordered and peaceful and somewhat sedate. There were tall pure spires on the Wren churches around the Common in the center of the village and back from the broad thoroughfares, great square houses had shuttered and cool dim parlors where my grandmother and I, visiting of an afternoon, would be treated to raspberry shrub or a thimbleful of dandelion wine.

On Saturday nights during the summer, concerts were held in the high, round bandstand on the Common and under the lovely canopy of the ancient elms we sat elegantly and properly on the thick grass listening to the music of Victor Herbert and John Philip Sousa.

It was a tranquil and halcyon kind of time with no thought of war or bombing and no inkling of what the century was going to produce. If one could go back, if one had a choice, I should like to return to those pleasant unhurried summers with my grandmother and most particularly to my great-aunt Clara.

Miss Clara, as she was respectfully called, lived in the village of Concord quite near us. Frequently during the summer she would arrive for an afternoon's visit dressed in stiff uncompromising black silk, a bonnet "with no nonsense about it" perched on her rigid curls, and a capacious taffeta reticule in her hand.

My grandmother's pale green sitting room with its marble mantle and its stiff Victorian furniture would suddenly come alive and in it I would be tingling with excitement and anticipation.

Miss Clara, who had written several slender volumes of poetry, was vigorous minded, highly literate and had strong, well-considered opinions on every subject. She had lived in Concord during the time of Ralph Waldo Emerson, Henry Thoreau, Nathaniel Hawthorne and William Ellery Channing. She had known them all well, called them by their first names affectionately, and her conversation sparkled with the wit of that inner hallowed circle.

What set her apart in my mind, however, was the fact that she had gone to school and grown up with Louisa May Alcott and had known intimately the entire Alcott family.

As soon as Miss Clara entered the house and before she had taken off her bonnet, she would open the huge reticule and search in it for the striped bag of spicy, wintergreen wafers she had brought for me and the book she had been reading most recently. This would be presented to my grandmother complete with the opinions Miss Clara had formed while reading it. As she sat down she would launch into a vigorous defense of Women's Suffrage and her sentences, informed and articulate, would be laced with the epigrams and satirical witticisms of the time. My grandmother, like most New England women, had decided opinions of her own and the heady scintillating talk would streak across me like summer lightning while the afternoon waned and the shadows lengthened on the soft old colors of the Aubusson rug.

When supper time arrived and my grandmother had gone to oversee the preparation of it I would have Miss Clara's full attention for the first time and be able to produce my own important small questions.

"Were you really Louisa's best friend?" I would ask.

Miss Clara never said any of the silly things with which most grownups felt it necessary to preface their remarks to children in those days. She was never condescending, never arch. She answered me as she would an adult. If there were words I did not comprehend, it was expected that I would look them up in the huge dictionary in the library later and not break into the conversation by asking for a meaning. I was thrown into the discussion to sink or swim as I could. In consequence, as time passed, I swam confidently and with pleasure.

"We were good friends, all of us," Miss Clara would say in her definitive manner, "Anna and Louisa and I, of course, because we were of approximate age, but the younger ones too, Elizabeth and May. Not the first year that they lived in the 'East Quarter' of Concord, however, more's the pity."

The regret in her voice for that lost year never lessened.

"Tell me about it," I would say.

"Mr. Bronson Alcott and his family came to Concord in the Spring of 1845," Miss Clara would begin. "Louisa was then about thirteen years old, a strange and unpredictable creature, full of shyness, and moods, impulsive and loving and fretted always by the restraint of being a young lady, not a boy."

I nodded. "Just like Jo," I thought.

"People were rather agitated by the news that the Alcotts had moved into so quiet and tranquil a community as Concord," Miss Clara went on. "Bronson Alcott was considered a fanatic and it was known that he had actually been arrested for not paying his taxes because he said he could not support a government so false to the law of love."

"He wanted to free the slaves," I would interpolate.

"An Abolitionist," Miss Clara would say precisely, "and of course a Transcendentalist from Harvard. Ralph Emerson was his great friend."

I had looked up the word Transcendentalist before. I had found it vague and elusive in meaning, but it gave me a picture of Mr. Alcott, lofty in ideas and principles and not quite of the world, almost a celestial being. I was not surprised therefore to learn later that Mrs. Alcott regarded him as a man close in character to Christ.

"Was Louisa pretty?" I asked one afternoon.

Miss Clara smiled. "She had the longest legs," she said reminiscently, "and she was very slender. She had thick dark brown hair that was always tumbling down and caused her a great deal of annoyance, grey eyes and such an animated expressive face I cannot recall whether or not she was actually pretty. To me she was beautiful."

"I wish I had known her," I said regretfully.

Miss Clara nodded. "I wanted to meet her and her sisters when they moved into the old house, but our acquaintance did not progress that first year beyond our peering at each other through the fence as I passed by on my way to the village school. The neighbors had not called on the Alcotts at first and we had not been properly introduced, therefore with propriety I could not speak to them. Such a pity. I longed to know them and be a part of their gayety. They had such jolly times."

"Didn't the girls go to school?" I asked.

"Not at first," Miss Clara said. "Mr. Bronson Alcott had very unusual ideas for those times about schooling. He believed that love and gentle kindness should be a part of learning. He taught by discussion and conversation. Correction was aimed at the mind not the body because he believed that the mind had made the error in the first place and thus should be corrected. Constant uniform kindness was more successful than corporal punishment, he maintained."

"But they did go to the village school with you," I said, "finally, the second winter in Concord."

"They did indeed," Miss Clara nodded. "Anna and Louisa finally prevailed upon their father to let them go to the district public school, something they had never done before. Mr. Alcott had taught them at home in his own peculiar manner. He did not believe in text books and in the school he had opened in Boston before they moved to Concord, for instance, they had never been taught grammar yet they spoke beautifully grammatical English. They read French and German and Mr. Alcott had taught them other subjects by his method of 'conversation.' He read to them from the works of Plato and Aristotle, from Carlyle and Bulwer and constantly from the Bible. He felt that learning should be made intensely interesting and that a serene spirit and a desire for spiritual knowledge could be best instilled in the child by intellectual discussion. At first his school in Boston prospered but later people began to be concerned about Mr. Alcott's advanced theories and when he admitted a little negro girl into the classes, other parents withdrew their children and the school had to be discontinued for lack or money."

Miss Clara paused.

Supper was almost ready in the kitchen and today's visit was nearly over.

"I should like to hear again about the postoffice," I begged.

"Oh yes," Miss Clara said, "Well now, where were we?"

"The first year of school in Concord," I prompted.

"We all became such good friends that year," Miss Clara went on. "When summer came and we could not be together every day, Louisa originated the plan of having a postoffice. So on a hillside midway between our two homes a hollow stump was cleared out and a box installed to receive our letters. We visited it almost daily and felt cruelly abused if we did not receive something. Those letters were very unlike the usual writing of the day which began in formal style such as 'I now take my pen in hand—.' No, Louisa's letters especially were refreshing, witty and warm-hearted and earnest, indignant at wrongs, sympathetic, full of energy and shy daring, much as was Louisa herself."

"And you kept them?"

"Some of them," Miss Clara said. "I'll bring them with me the next time I come to visit. There was one, however, I do recall. It was on the occasion of my birthday and in the postoffice box was a beautifully arranged bouquet of wild forest flowers. Tied to it by a ribbon was this verse,

> 'Clara my dear, your birthday is here
> Before I had time to prepare,
> Yet take these flowers, fresh from Nature's bower
> All bright and fair.'"

After supper when I was excused and had said my good nights to my grandmother and to Miss Clara I would go upstairs to the small room that was mine each summer, hearing in the distance the rumble of talk, the laughter and the rhythm of sound that pervaded the house when Miss Clara was in it. I would undress slowly, turn the gas-lighted globe to its fullest and take a thick well-worn book from a shelf.

Lying back in happy anticipation against the fat pillows of the great brass bed I would open to a page that was forever new to me, forever loved.

I might have thought of the thousands of small girls who like me had felt the magic of this book, who had been projected into its problems, its gentle humor, its warm friendliness and its timeless enchantment.

The chances are however that I felt only the familiar rapture of reading a well-loved, well-remembered opening line.

"'Christmas won't be Christmas without any presents,' grumbled Jo, lying on the rug."

Yankee 24 (December 1960): 60–63, 90.

Index